GUY DE MAUPASSANT

GUY DE MAUPASSANT

GUY DE MAUPASSANT

by

STANLEY JACKSON

DUCKWORTH

3 Henrietta Street, London, W.C. 2

First published in 1938

95302

Made *and* printed *in* Great Britain
By The Camelot Press Limited
London *and* Southampton

To
SIDNEY AND EVE

FOREWORD

THIS book first took root in a London public library. I had come in search of Mr. Somerset Maugham's latest novel, only to find myself forestalled by at least two hundred eager ratepayers. By a logical association of thought and geography my hand strayed further along the shelf labelled "MAU." To my astonishment and chagrin, Maupassant seemed to be completely unrepresented. I decided to tax the librarian with the deficiency.

"No call for his work," he announced, with a hint of disapproval.

I gasped. It seemed impossible that a public library in the heart of London should be without Maupassant's novels and short stories.

There was a whispered consultation behind official palms and the Head Librarian at last emerged. He was both intelligent and conciliatory.

"Maupassant will be in the 'Foreign' section," he explained smoothly.

To his credit, I recall his genuine surprise that not one volume of Maupassant stood on the shelves devoted to French Literature. Balzac, Dumas and Anatole France leaned heavily upon each other, but there was no attempt to separate Loti from the bulkiness of Zola.

I was conducted to the catalogues. Yes, it was unmistakable. Several titles were devoted to the name of the great French writer.

"But surely all these books are not in use?" I exclaimed.

The librarian's voice sank to a confidential whisper.

"We can always get them if they're asked for," he

assured me. " They keep them at the Central branch. Nobody reads him, you know."

" That's not surprising when you omit to keep him in stock," I put in dryly. " Supply creates demand in these cases."

He shrugged and withdrew, leaving me oppressed by a sense of having connived at a literary felony.

This experience was repeated at various times and places. Often I was directed to an anthology of short stories where Maupassant was represented (usually by " The Necklace "). There was nothing remotely approaching a complete edition of his works in any public library. I was soon grounded in the conviction that Maupassant was widely regarded as a writer of naughty or pornographic literature.

For many years I had read and admired his work. I now began to re-read him in a spirit of marginal inquisitiveness. My interest in his personality awakened, I tried to look beyond the sundry petty amours which have clung to his name. Finally, filled with some urge to impart my conclusions, I began to sift my data. This book is the result.

All biography is a kind of intellectual self-indulgence on the part of the author. I have attempted to acquire discipline over my feelings before setting pen to paper, but cannot lay claim to a violently didactic purpose. If this book succeeds in interesting new readers in Maupassant's work, or enlarges the pleasure of those who already know his writings, I shall have accomplished far more than I ever dared hope. The result will be none the less gratifying.

For useful information of Maupassant's medical history I am indebted to several doctors whose anonymity I am reluctantly compelled to respect. I must, however, express my gratitude to the Secretary and Librarian of the Royal Society of Medicine for giving me access to a valuable dossier.

Through the courtesy of the French publishers, Albin

Michel and Louis Conard, I am enabled to include numerous letters which have not previously been available to
English or American readers.   Finally, I must thank
Messrs. Hachette for their energetic assistance in procuring
for me little-known but invaluable works.

CONTENTS

PART ONE

CHAPTER I

ROOTS

FOUR children once played at Literature in the house of a French surgeon. They enacted plays, composed and recited verses, and were in turn actors, audience and critics. Little Gustave Flaubert, hardly ten years old, wrote many of the pieces, but the leading spirit of this youthful coterie was Alfred le Poittevin who was five years older than Gustave and never appeared in that billiard-room in Rouen without his sister, Laure. Gustave's sister, Caroline, made up the quartette without lending more than a sympathetic interest to the proceedings.

Dr. Flaubert was then Resident Head Surgeon at the Rouen Hospital and, with his family, occupied a wing of that building. It was not a cheerful environment for the children who could actually see the operating table from the windows of their playroom. But the impression went deeper than the pervasive odour of ether. These children were all glutted with sensibility and the hospital at once fascinated and repelled them. Under the leadership of the bookish Alfred le Poittevin, they gave themselves up to intellectual antics, mouthing speeches which they hardly understood but which brought sweet-sad tears to their eyes. Caroline and Laure would cut and trim old costumes while the boys recited long sensuous passages from the more sentimental poets. It was all very innocent and youthful, but that play-acting was to have a profound effect on those who took part, and more indirectly upon the career of Guy de Maupassant.

Wandering through the gloomy corridors of the hospital,

Alfred le Poittevin came to know the problems of life and
death far too early. His morbidness did not evaporate,
and quickly infected Gustave Flaubert and Laure. Dr.
Flaubert smiled indulgently and refused to see an unhealthy
melancholia in the pale sad faces of the children. He had
taken precautions to see that they were not brought into
contact with his patients, but he did not know that they had
already picked up the germ of pessimism.

This early friendship increased with the years. Alfred,
a passionate lover of beauty, developed into a poet but
stifled in a routine job. Plodding through his petty muni-
cipal tasks, he wrote feverish lyrics at night in a desperate
attempt to escape his drudgery. He died of heart disease
in 1848, at the early age of thirty-two, leaving behind
a few emotional pieces which librarians guard but never
read.

This unfortunate young man ruled his companions from
the grave. The author of *Madame Bovary* never forgot him,
and fifteen years after his friend's death, wrote : " What
journeys we made into the blue ! How I loved him ! I
believe I have never loved anyone (man or woman) like
him. . . . How often in the weariness of my work at the
theatre in Paris, during an interval, or alone at Croisset by
my fireside in the long winter evenings, have I seen and
heard him again. I can never forget our endless conversa-
tions, our studies, our dreams and lofty aspirations. I have
preserved a great respect for the past : we were very
wonderful and I did not want to fail."[1]

Alfred's influence was even more marked upon his sister.
A fanatical scholar, he had imbued her with his own passion
for Literature and his profound contempt for bourgeois
values. Like Flaubert, whose lifelong friend she remained,
Laure le Poittevin stayed faithful to the ideals of the past.
In an age of fluttered muslins and demure debauchery, she

[1] *Correspondance*, Flaubert, Book III, p. 273.

read Shakespeare in the original and scandalised Rouen by smoking and riding like a man. But a pretty young woman of good family is not long left to her verses. In the spring of 1846, a dashing cavalier, named Gustave de Maupassant, asked her hand in marriage.

Laure le Poittevin did not hesitate. She had a natural dignity which sometimes dovetailed into snobbishness, and the young nobleman, " living on his revenues," attracted her. Gustave possessed a certain voluptuous charm which made him a ready favourite with the ladies. Besides, he had a pretty talent in painting and could discuss Art with all the fluent emphasis of a dilettante. Gustave de Maupassant and his sister, Louise, had painted water-colours since their early childhood and the house was always open to fashionable artists.

Laure le Poittevin was completely charmed by the young man. She sprang from the rich Norman middle-class and, in spite of her brother, preserved a feminine taste for the aristocracy. Gustave de Maupassant listened gravely to this beautiful but earnest young woman and found himself attracted by sheer force of contrast. Like all the members of his class, he was blasé and dandified, living for amusement and little else. For years he had picked up his women on the boulevards and spent most of his time bragging of conquests or gambling. These young gallants were ready to fight a duel on the smallest point of honour, but thought nothing of stealing a man's wife or bilking some unfortunate tailor. When the pace became too hot or the palate too weary, they could always rely on a wealthy marriage.

Nothing attracts a profligate so much as innocence, and Gustave found his little blue-stocking charming after the pavement beauties. She had looks, dignity and a solid purse, and he could at least be certain that his friends had not anticipated him. And virginity was a decided novelty in the life of a fast young boulevardier.

Saints love cads, and Laure le Poittevin married in the

age-old hope of reforming a libertine. He was very hand-some. His black curly hair made the perfect setting for the beautiful Creole eyes which he had inherited from an aunt. Those large, sleepy eyes, full of inscrutable meaning, gave to his remarks a depth which they did not often possess. Apart from his charm he had another claim to Laure's consideration, for her beloved Alfred had married Louise de Maupassant, the young man's sister.

The Maupassants had established themselves in Nor-mandy in the middle of the eighteenth century. The family had sprung from the middle-class, but in 1752, Jean-Baptiste Maupassant was given a patent of nobility by the Emperor of Austria, by virtue of which he was en-titled to the rank of Marquis. Guy's father did not use the title, and Maupassant always laughed when his valet spoke of " M. le Marquis." Edmond de Goncourt once said that the only book ever found on Maupassant's drawing-room table was the French *Debrett*. We shall see how far the gibe was justified, but it is well to remember that Con-court's malice pursued him to the end. Several of Mau-passant's early stories appeared under a *nom de plume*, but this was rather due to literary diffidence than pride of name.

Part of the family wealth was the fruit of an erratic marriage. Louis de Maupassant, who was at the Court of Louis XVIII, married a wealthy Creole in Mauritius and provided generously for his family. His brother, Jules, was Guy de Maupassant's grandfather – an impulsive man who had made a runaway marriage with a tax-collector's daughter. A kindly, easy-going personality, he was later to figure in his grandson's novel, *Une Vie*, as the Baron Perthuis des Vauds. By occupation an agent for the Gov-ernment tobacco factories, he was irresistibly attracted by speculative concerns which showed huge paper profits. This attraction was later to devour his son's dowry and limit Guy's education. The writer's only link with

Literature on his father's side appears to have been a distant ancestor who wrote a Life of Anne of Austria !

Guy de Maupassant was born on August 5th, 1850, the year that Balzac died. There is some doubt as to his exact birthplace. The official view, emphatically asserted by his mother, is that he was born at the Château de Miromesnil, which the Maupassants rented for a short period. They had lived for some time at Fécamp, but Madame de Maupassant sought a more aristocratic cradle for her first-born than " the town of tradesmen and fish-salters." Situated a few miles from Dieppe, the château was a romantic old place, wind-lashed and gable-roofed. The deep boom of the waves could be heard distinctly and, sometimes, a whiff of tar came on the wind.

Much French ink has been spilt on this question. It is certain that Madame de Maupassant hastily summoned a local midwife to Miromesnil on August 5th, 1850. This woman appeared, but was soon sent packing by madame who thought her coarse and vulgar. A country doctor, M. Guiton, arrived and satisfactorily attended her. The baby had a head as round as an apple and his father's beautiful eyes.

The birth was duly registered, but the official document has not convinced the theorists and hair-splitters. Headed by M. Georges Normandy, they claim that Maupassant was born in Fécamp and transported to the château by a socially self-conscious mother. M. Normandy refuses to accept the validity of the birth certificate as final and points out that the registration of births in the provinces was notoriously unreliable. This cannot be denied. The position is still further obscured by the death certificate :

" Seventh of July, 1893, at 9 a.m. Henri-René-Albert-Guy de Maupassant, aged 43, man of letters, *born at Sotteville near Yvetot* (Seine-Inférieure). . . ."

Wherever the writer was born it is certain that he had Norman cider in his veins. It is equally certain that after a few months the Maupassants moved to more modest quarters in the village of Etretat. Madame de Maupassant complained that she had been most irritated by the noise, but her departure from the beautiful château was probably dictated by ways and means. Gustave had been given 4,000 francs a year by his father, while his wife had a slightly larger income. They could live in moderate comfort, but it was impossible to maintain a château.

Gustave's income limited him to the less expensive vices. He buzzed from flower to flower, many of which bloomed below stairs. A profligate, at once unprincipled and romantic, he understood women without appreciating them. He could not, however, hope to conceal his shoddiness of intellect from his studious wife. After a time, he gave up the attempt : she chilled and depressed him.

Guy de Maupassant soon heard the rustle of forbidden petticoats. His father was so industrious in these matters that his art did not always conceal itself. At the age of nine, Guy had already begun to guess the truth :

" I was first in composition," he wrote to his mother, "and as a reward, Madame de X—— took me to the Circus with Papa. She seems to reward him also, but I don't know with what."[1]

As the lad grew older, his father's manœuvres no longer deceived him. On one occasion he had been invited to a children's party by a lady who then stood high in M. de Maupassant's favour. As madame would not go, Gustave came forward eagerly, but Guy dawdled so long over dressing that his father became angry and threatened not to take him.

" Ah ! " murmured Guy, " I don't mind. You are the more anxious to go there."

[1] Cited by Ed. Maynial, *La Vie et l'Œuvre de Guy de Maupassant*, p. 24.

" Come along," shouted his father, " lace your shoes."

" No," replied the boy coolly, " you come and tie them for me."

Gustave obeyed and hurried his son away to the party. The writer's father was later to supply the model for Julien de Lamare, the inconstant husband in *Une Vie*. Like many men who exploit their charm, Gustave and Julien were both extremely alive to petty finance. After his marriage M. de Maupassant had slowly shed his charm and elegance. He became slovenly in his habits and seemed to take pleasure in humiliating his wife. He would suddenly develop a panic of economy and cut down the little luxuries which made her life tolerable. They had soon given up their games of bezique, and Gustave spent most of his time out of the house. The unhappy woman could have forgiven much, but there was a pettiness about her husband's romances which made her more contemptuous than angry.

Julien's affair with a maid the night after he came home from the honeymoon may well have been based on one of Gustave's romances. A curious fact deserves a word in this connection. Soon after the memorial to Maupassant was put up in the Jardins Solférino, a journalist stumbled upon an amazing story. He noticed that one of the keepers, a man called Lecuyer, bore a remarkable resemblance to the statue. They chatted together and he discovered that Lecuyer was a native of Miromesnil and the son of a labourer who worked there. His mother had definitely given breast to the writer. Had Maupassant survived, the men would have been of an age. . . .

Disgusted with Gustave, Madame de Maupassant turned more and more to her son. As Guy grew into boyhood, she idolised him and, hot on the trail of a memory, saw in him a resurrection of her beloved Alfred. To her delight he seemed to inherit, both physically and spiritually, from his uncle. Alfred had taught her to understand Shakespeare :

she now passed on the precious heritage to her son. Under
her adoring eyes, the lad read and recited passionately.
Soon his brain began to swirl with golden images. *A
Midsummer Night's Dream*, in particular, seemed to touch
all the fleeting impulses of his heart. Crouching by the
sea, he listened to his mother's impassioned recitation
and repeated lines which he barely understood.

Laure de Maupassant was a writer's " dream mother,"
and Guy served his apprenticeship to Life under one who
had abandoned heart and head to him. She directed his
work and play, watching his every movement with almost
animal apprehension. Sensing that books alone would not
evoke the poetry that she divined in her son, Madame de
Maupassant encouraged him to direct his fugitive imagination to facts and to study Nature at first hand. Years later,
the blind old woman would protest that she had educated
him herself because she wished to foster the poetry in
him. It is far more likely that Gustave's infidelities had
made her savagely and selfishly maternal. The lad was,
however, fortunate in his home. " Les Verguies " was a
pretty white house surrounded by a delightful garden; and
a balcony, overhung with creeper, jutted from the " dear
place " as Maupassant always referred to it.

It was here that Guy spent his happy childhood. He was
an active lad, swimming, wrestling and boating, the moment
he escaped from his books. An excellent memory gave him
hours of leisure which would not otherwise have been his,
and Madame de Maupassant used to recall that he had
memorised his catechism by glancing through it once or
twice.

As a boy, Guy was certainly not a snob. He had a
genuine love for the local fishermen and peasants and
delighted in their simple pleasures. He loved to fish by
moonlight or prowl among the caves along the coast. With
his two dogs at his feet, he would row for hours, his mind

absorbed with plans for shooting or fishing. An anecdote related by his mother, shows how careful he was not to wound his humble companions. One day he had arranged a picnic with Charles, a fisherman's son, and another lad of his own class. The latter's mother received Guy effusively but scarcely noticed his companion.

" Charles," she observed coldly, " will, naturally, carry the provisions."

The urchin reddened, but Guy at once protested against the injustice.

" No, madame," he said, picking up the basket, " we shall take turns, and I am first ! "

The sea excited his intelligence and hardened his body, nothing delighting him more than to go out with a Fécamp pilot, particularly if the sea were rough. When he was out in a storm, Madame de Maupassant would sit for hours with the fishermen's wives praying that the boats would come in. " I feel that I have in my veins the blood of the sea-rovers," he once said. " I have no greater joy than on a spring morning to sail my boat into unknown ports."[1] That spirit of adventure was to send him later from one boudoir to another.

For the present, however, he gave himself up gladly to the delicate authority of a mother who denied him nothing and romped gaily by his side. Sometimes she would complain of headaches and tell the boy to join his companions. In later years he remembered his mother's ailments, and psychologists would add another name to the list of hereditary sufferers. For Guy de Maupassant had inherited something more than a taste for Literature from his devoted mother. And none suspected, he least of all, that he already carried the seeds of neurosis and melancholia.

These were golden days, and the writer never forgot the

[1] Cited by R. H. Sherard, p. 76, *The Life, Work and Evil Fate of Guy de Maupassant* (Werner Laurie). An excellent introduction to the subject.

gentle winding valleys fleecy with gorse blossoms, and the brown fishing-nets hanging out to dry. Far below, the grey, cold sea beat at the rocks, but in the valleys all was fertile and peaceful. The air smelt of crushed apples, and there was nothing so pleasant as to stop by a tavern for a hunk of brown bread and a raw onion.

Sometimes, he would go out with the men and fish for mackerel by moonlight off the harbour of Etretat. Most enjoyable of all were the " bals champêtres " under the apple-trees. Madame de Maupassant would excuse herself and watch the rustic revels from a window, but nothing could restrain the boy. The peasants danced and guffawed to the strains of a couple of wheezy fiddles and a clarionet, while the less active did justice to the barrels of cider, the sausage and cheese. At night huge torches were lit, and the boy would not run home until the last torch was out and the last barrel empty. For days afterwards he would talk of nothing else, repeating every joke and scrap of gossip to his delighted parent.

He was high-spirited, but there were times when a sadness lay over the house and it was not easy to keep the truth from him. Gustave had at last given up all attempt to preserve appearances and his infidelities were now public property. When Guy was six, Madame de Maupassant gave birth to another son, Hervé, but this did nothing to reconcile the couple. Throughout his childhood, Guy was aware of all the miseries of an unhappy marriage, a subject to which he returned again and again in his novels and short stories. The novel, *Une Vie*, rightly regarded as Maupassant's most autobiographical work, shows how clearly the boy realised his mother's suffering. Here is all the agony of disillusion, all the heartbreak of a neglected wife. And in another story, *Garçon, un Bock*, a character attributes his moral downfall to having seen his father beat the mother whom he had idealised.

The wronged woman figures in many of Maupassant's situations, and critics have not hesitated to read autobiography into the most brutal episodes. In the absence of direct evidence, it is well to ignore these footnotes and state the facts. When Guy was thirteen, Madame de Maupassant decided to separate from her husband who was by no means unwilling. He agreed to settle 1,600 francs per annum towards the education of his sons and went off gladly. Even after the separation, however, he spent holidays with his family, though he never again shared an apartment with his wife. All his life, Guy continued to correspond with his father and was always ready to defend his misconduct whenever the subject was discussed. This attitude, it will be noted, was entirely consistent with the writer's tolerance in all matters of sex and religion. He could forgive, but never respect, his father, and Gustave always complained bitterly that Laure had turned the boy against him.

With the departure of her husband, Madame de Maupassant seemed to find a new happiness. Filled with nervous energy and rejoicing in her new freedom, she sometimes surprised her neighbours who considered her " eccentric." In the early hours of the morning she would often be observed, pacing back and forth, reciting verses which had pleased Guy.

She had indeed become a fanatical mother, casting about her an air of imperious mastery like a pregnant woman who knows that she is giving life to the world. Deceived in her hopes, abused and humiliated, she now had but one thought, her children. Hervé was a sickly child who had inherited her tape-worm, and it is safe to surmise that Gustave had not welcomed the new arrival. One need perhaps look no further than this passage from *Une Vie* :

" Julien, whose habitual routine had been interfered with and his overweening importance diminished by the arrival of this noisy and all-powerful tyrant, unconsciously jealous of this mite of a man who had usurped his place in the house, kept on saying angrily and impatiently :

" ' How wearisome she is with her brat ! ' ' "

Madame de Maupassant, for her part, devoted herself passionately to Guy's education, and the younger child was never to occupy the same place in her heart. Guy was sharp and observant and his mother marvelled as he grew daily more like her beloved Alfred. He was more robust, more dare-devil, perhaps, but there were little resemblances which touched her heart and made her dream of the past. Like his uncle, Guy could memorise verse and recite with remarkable facility, and both shared a taste for the supernatural. Yet here the resemblance ended. There was nothing of the æsthete in this sunburned, thick-set lad who scrambled over the rocks and bribed fishermen to take him out at nights. Sometimes Madame de Maupassant would protest at his fluent use of the local patois and regret his inability to learn English or any other foreign language. But she did not know that he was already educating himself to observe intelligently those about him. And it was this very lack of book knowledge, this talent for sober observation which was to give his work its real value.

But the dream years soon slipped by. Soon after Gustave's departure, Madame de Maupassant suddenly packed Guy off to the famous seminary at Yvetot, which was nearer than the Rouen Lycée. Apart from a few lessons in Latin and arithmetic from the Vicar of Etretat, she had been his only tutor. But family affairs called her more insistently, for Hervé was sickly and she was now without the help of her husband. Everything had conspired suddenly to remove her son from her loving care. She had of late grown somewhat fearful of arresting his studies through her own selfishness : Gustave's allowance of 1,600 francs now decided her.

Yvetot irritated and depressed the boy. Accustomed to

a healthy outdoor life, the " wild colt " lay tethered between cold walls. The joyous *camaraderie* of Etretat was suddenly replaced by the austere discipline of the seminary. Here, religion stamped itself on his mind as a succession of bleak fripperies. Accustomed to a life without any form of restraint, he was shocked to discover that he was expected to bend his knee to the dull gods of tradition and authority. He saw about him the gawky sons of rich squires who regarded Latin as a social asset, and an ecclesiastical training as an easy escape from conscription. And he began to mope, and long more and more for the vigorous peasant lads and the rugged old pilot of Fécamp.

For a while things seemed to be going smoothly. His ready fists had earned him the respect of his fellow-pupils, and his first-year report speaks of his " good character " and excellent progress. But he was chafing for liberty, and soon began to feign illnesses which alarmed his teachers and gave him holidays in Etretat. On his arrival, his mother would scold him half-heartedly and send him back to the seminary.

Apart from these bogus ailments, he lightened the dreary hours by playing practical jokes on both boys and masters. At home he had been a ringleader, and it was easy to lord it over the refined young gentlemen at the seminary. Some took fright at his bold exploits, but he was always ready to convince the wary ones with his fists. One night, we learn, he led a party of his friends to the cellar, where they addressed themselves liberally to the Father Superior's stock of wine and provisions. Soon afterwards, he amused his classmates by mimicking a professor of theology who had that day lectured on the torments of hell. The boys tittered uneasily, their amusement tinged with the fear of blasphemy. To their secret delight, Guy was discovered and severely reprimanded.

This prank branded him as suspect. In spite of his early emotion at Communion, he had steadily advanced towards a

shallow agnosticism. His teachers were uncouth and
tyrannical; religion was ridiculous. It was at Yvetot that
Guy de Maupassant first came to detest the rank and file of
the Church. Here, at this clerical recruiting station, he
studied at first hand all the weaknesses which he was to
expose so ruthlessly.

The principal's displeasure decided him. He would
court expulsion by attacking the mealy-mouthed professors!
Like Shelley, he took up his pen and was driven out. He
dedicated several sentimental verses to a newly married
cousin, and took no pains to conceal them. The principal
pounced and read. The eroticism and sentiment might
have been overlooked, but not the attack upon ritual:

> *Oh ! do not imagine*
> *That in the lonely cloister*
> *Where we are buried*
> *We aspire to nothing more*
> *Than the cassock and surplice !*

This verse could not be dismissed as an insolent aside. It
was repeated three times! Principal and pupil were alike
overjoyed at this opportunity to part company.

The young scholar was sent home to his mother, who
listened gratefully to his excuses. She saw in this accident
something that pleased her mightily. Like his uncle, Guy
was already suffering for his Art and learning to despise the
narrow-minded bourgeoisie! It was a good sign, and she
could not find it in her heart to scold him. She lied beautifully to Flaubert in her account of the expulsion, but the boy
himself succeeded in pleasing the man who was to pilot
him through the years of revolt and suffering.

" I can't tell you how much pleasure your son's visit has
given us," wrote Flaubert's mother to Madame de Maupassant. " He is a delightful lad, and you have cause to
be proud of him. Your old friend, Gustave, is charmed

with him and asks me to congratulate you on having such a child. Why didn't you come with him ? "

The boy remained at home for some time after his expulsion from the seminary. Madame de Maupassant was too indulgent a mother to allow him to plunge headlong into the next stage of his scholastic career. Soon he was swimming again, joking with the fishermen and roaming the countryside at the head of his urchin band.

During this period Guy figured in an adventure which the local peasantry long remembered. Swinburne was staying with another eccentric Englishman at Etretat, and the most extraordinary rumours were current. They were supposed to be terrible drunkards and addicted to eating human flesh. The poet seemed to derive his inspiration from nibbling a skeleton hand which still bore traces of human blood !

One day Swinburne found himself in difficulties while bathing at Etretat, and it was young Maupassant who first reached his side and assisted him to the beach. The lad was invited to luncheon by the grateful poet, and described his impressions some years later. He says that they were served with roast monkey, but those who knew Maupassant took this dish with a liberal pinch of salt. It is certain, however, that the boy saw and never forgot that skeleton hand. Amused by his fascinated horror, Swinburne afterwards presented him with this grisly relic.

A few months after his return from Yvetot, the boy became aware of a sweet malaise within him. The son of a cynical Don Juan and a broad-minded mother, he had no illusions as to the mysterious message. To the young Frenchman of that time, chastity was almost an avowal of cowardice. Madame de Maupassant refused to check her broad-shouldered son, and the " beautiful E——" soon removed the reproach and converted him to a new pleasure.[1]

At the age of sixteen Guy de Maupassant had acquired a

[1] A. Lumbroso, *Souvenirs sur Maupassant*, p. 303.

mistress and a facility for verse. Neither of these accomplishments was in any way remarkable: he was typical of his time. What impressed most about him, however, was his great strength and pugnacity. Young and bulging with health, he was never happy unless he was pitting his muscles against some burly fisherman or farm-hand. He was, in his own words, a " glutton of life," insatiably fond of all physical pleasures. While poor little Hervé limped painfully about the garden, his more robust brother was wrestling and fighting with all his peasant-boy companions.

But madame's conscience would not allow this vacation to go on indefinitely. Guy was sent to the Lycée in Rouen, where he began to apply himself at once to verse-making. Happier than in the seminary, he was nevertheless far from contented. He loved the cliffs and meadows of Normandy, and suffocated in his stuffy little room in Rouen. Madame de Maupassant did her best, however, to lessen the gap between them. She recommended him to Louis Bouilhet, a well-known poet and playwright, and a childhood playmate of Alfred le Poittevin and Flaubert. Out of affection for his friends, Bouilhet willingly agreed to act as the boy's guardian and literary tutor.

Maupassant soon began to work with a will. Discovering that poetry appeased his restlessness, he began to pour out lyrics and madrigals, which were submitted to Bouilhet every Sunday. Many of these pieces were sickly little affairs of nostalgia and twilight, artificial and precise in form. The pre-occupation with sex was clearly marked. One of the poems was an " Epistle addressed to Madame X——, who found me wild," and another was entitled, " Last evening spent with my mistress."

Maupassant's attitude towards women was never lyrical. His first essay in love had been conducted on a businesslike basis. The " beautiful E——'s " successors appear to have been selected from the Maison Telliers of Rouen.

Calf-love had no place in the life of this young scholar, who began eagerly to hunt all the enchantments of disenchantment. To a born countryman, the gloomy lodgings were torture.

Outwardly, Guy seemed a normal, intelligent student. On one occasion he recited two hundred Alexandrines which he had composed for a St. Charlemagne dinner at his school. Apart from this feat, he does not seem to have distinguished himself, and never gained a higher place at school than fourth. Bouilhet offered good advice, warning the youth that conscientious work was essential to real artistic success — " A hundred verses, perhaps fewer, suffice to make the reputation of an artist, if they are faultless and contain a man's essential talent and originality."

Guy continued to write poetry, but he was already finding another gateway to Literature. A brilliant mimic, he never failed to organise theatricals during his vacations at the villa, " Les Verguies." He not only composed but acted in innumerable charades, and reminded his mother of her own childhood dramas. Guy's talent for dramatics led naturally to practical jokes. One day he disguised himself as a girl, powdered his shadowy moustache, and presented himself to a frumpish English spinster as " Mlle Renée de Valmont." The Englishwoman soon began an intimate conversation with the young " lady " whose shy bearing had impressed her favourably.

" You have travelled a good deal, I understand ? " said the lady.

" Yes," admitted her visitor. " I have just come from Nouméa " (a French convict settlement).

The Englishwoman looked a little surprised, but attempted to be tactful.

" A young girl travelling all that way alone ! " she murmured in protest.

" But, you see, I have two maids," whispered Maupassant,

Cм

demurely straightening his dress. Then, with a far-away expression, " I have also a dragoon and a cuirassier who look after me ! "

The Englishwoman was so shocked that everyone began to laugh, and " Mlle de Valmont " picked up her skirts and showed a very muscular pair of calves. It took much apologising from Madame de Maupassant before the lady could be coaxed into forgiveness. She was destined to appear again in the rôle of " Miss Harriet," one of Maupassant's most sympathetic studies.

Another of his regular practices was to mislead the more gullible tourists. Some old boats which had been hauled up the cliffs at Etretat once attracted the curiosity of a sightseer. Guy explained gravely : " The waves are so mighty that they sweep over the cliffs and leave the wreckage ! "

At the Lycée he shared in the lucky dip of a classical education, but it was during the vacations that he was being unconsciously educated. Chatting with an old seaman on the cliffs, dancing at some village fair, drinking his cider on the steps of an inn — these were the happiest days of his life, and they were to serve him later in one book after another.

At last schooldays were over. On July 27, 1869, Maupassant took his degree of *bachelier-ès-lettres*. The one word of comment, " Passable," adequately summarises his academic career. A few days earlier, he heard of Bouilhet's death. " Had he lived," Madame de Maupassant used to say, " he would have made my son a poet." It was reserved for a greater man to show Maupassant his vocation.

Guy left the Lycée with the conventional equipment of an educated young man. He was comfortably agnostic, self-confident and possessed vague literary ambitions. Like half the human race, he was destined for the Law. Apart from his dislike of priests, which he displayed so pitilessly in all his books, he appeared to have no prejudices. After taking his degree he went back to Etretat and seemed in no hurry to start pettifogging.

The Law is a respectable occupation, but it could not excite a high-spirited and athletic young man. There was, moreover, the question of funds. Guy's grandfather had invested all his savings in a stupid agricultural scheme and was forced to withdraw his son's allowance. Gustave was reluctantly obliged to work as clerk with a stockbroker and could no longer make the payments agreed upon under the settlement. Saddled with a sickly child, poor Madame de Maupassant found it difficult to give Guy enough to live on in Paris.

The young man was well content to let matters remain as they were. There was much to amuse him in Etretat. The peasants were jovial and fond of pleasure, while the pretty farm girls were free with their favours. The whole country-side was his playground. Later, in all his books, he would express his animal love of Nature.

" With me," he wrote in *Mont Oriol*, " it seems as if I were open to every impression, and everything flows in and pervades me, making me weep or gnash my teeth. When I look at that hill facing us, that great green fold, that nation of trees scaling the mountain, I feel all the forest in my eyes; it penetrates, pervades me, flows in my blood. It seems as if I devoured it and it filled my being – I become myself a forest."

When the war against Prussia broke out in 1870, Maupassant showed no great eagerness to slaughter the " Boches." A great egoist and an unbeliever on principle, he loathed war and had inherited the family opposition to the Bonapartists.

He enlisted with a shrug, joined the non-combatant section of the Army, and saw more uniforms than guns. His department moved from Rouen to Havre, and Guy supervised the stores while his fellow-countrymen queued up for death. But, although he witnessed little fighting, he had seen enough to reinforce his pacifism and to leave him for ever with a passionate hatred of militarism.

The young man's principles were certainly not dictated by an excessive fondness for his own skin. He was tough, a good shot and a complete stranger to physical fear. But his state of mind had changed, and he was no longer the carefree " Monsieur Guy " whom the fishermen greeted like a brother. To outward appearance, he was still gay and easy-going, still the " glutton of life," but the verse-making had already left its mark upon him. Some of these pieces were full of a free-thinking pessimism, partly felt, partly imagined. Already he had tasted Schopenhauer, whose bitter philosophy he would never discard. And the war, with all its petty routine, its weary sneaking forward or backward, its shrill patriotism, disgusted him. To the young man this sniping, digging and taking cover had none of the glory of high endeavour. With the French Army in retreat, waiting for an ignoble peace, the whole business became tiresome and stupid, a nightmare of men dragging themselves through the slush. And it was this side of war, the cruelty and demoralisation, which remained in his mind.

His letters to his mother were, however, brief and matter-of-fact.

" I escaped with our retreating Army," he says in one message. " I was nearly captured. I had passed from the van to the rearguard carrying a message from the commissary of stores to the General. I did fifteen leagues on foot. After marching or running all night, I slept on a stone floor in an icy cellar. Without my good legs I would certainly have been caught. I am very well, however."

Soon afterwards he adds to this letter :

" I will write another few words to-day, dear mother, because for the next day or two communications will be interrupted between Paris and the rest of France. The Prussians are pushing on. There is, of course, no doubt as to how the war will end; the Prussians are beaten, and they know it, and their only hope is to take Paris by surprise. But we are ready for them."

Brave words, but the Prussians still advanced, and the young soldier retreated with the others. In November 1871 he was bought out of the Army, or rather replaced by another man who was willing to shoulder his bayonet for a few hundred francs.

Maupassant's part in the war had not been a glorious one, but the experience was of the greatest significance in his literary development. He was still unaware of any acute social purpose, but the war had deepened his pessimism and contributed to his fuller vision of life. In his early youth he had stored his unconscious mind with the peasants and scenes of his beloved Normandy. Those were happy days when the heart was young and the mind received beautiful images without discrimination. Now that he was in his twenties and already anxious for the future, he began to interpret what he saw about him.

The war had depressed and irritated him, and he was not as apathetic as his fellow soldiers supposed. They saw a sturdy young man, rather short but well built, with a straight nose, thick fair moustache and wavy chestnut hair. There was nothing in his manner to suggest the quality of his mind or his social position. To the sharp little Parisians strutting in their red breeches and discussing plans of campaign, the young provincial looked a rough country bumpkin. He was strong, and never shirked a fight or a long march, but he kept to himself and had little to say. There was, however, much to interest a pair of good ears and a mind that had already slipped from maternal apron-strings. His companions would have been astonished and angered at what was passing through his head as they retreated before the Prussians.

War was hateful, and he could find no love in his heart for the arrogant Hussars or the peasants who stabbed a Prussian in the back. Stories of civilian heroism floated down the line, but young Maupassant knew these peasants and discounted much of what he heard. He could see the bourgeois population trembling for its commerce and more agitated by the loss of money than hatred of the invader.

Maupassant's pacifism gave him a detachment and a sense of proportion which show up strongly in many of his war tales. More important than his pacifist sentiments were the characters and scenes which stamped themselves on his mind while he handed out stores to the grumbling soldiers. Small talk and scraps of gossip, as miscellaneous as the straggling French Army itself, filed past him in shadowy formation, to take shape later as Walter Schnaffs, Mademoiselle Fifi and a host of others.

One yarn soon went round the Army. A fat prostitute of Rouen had refused her favours to the Prussian commandant. The Army chuckled and Maupassant picked up the details later from his uncle, Charles Cord'homme, a staunch democrat who never forgot the Prussian invasion. It seems that this harlot, Mlle Adrienne Legay, was a rosy-cheeked lass, "fat as lard," and much in demand among the burgesses of Rouen. Like everyone else, Mlle Legay found trade conditions difficult after the outbreak of war, and was forced to travel to Havre, where her protector, a wealthy cotton merchant, had been drafted. It was on one of these journeys that the Prussian had demanded her collaboration.

Maupassant was amused by this story, but Mlle Legay and her Prussian seemed the figures of an idle hour. Ten years later the plump young woman would again squeeze her bulk into the coach at Rouen. And sitting opposite her would be a gentleman who bore a distinct, if unflattering, resemblance to M. Charles Cord'homme.

CHAPTER II

" OUI, MONSIEUR "

A FEW weeks after leaving the Army, Maupassant found himself in need of a regular salary. A legal training was utterly beyond the family purse, but Madame de Maupassant hoped that her son would be able to fit in time for jurisprudence after his salaried work was over. Her motherly faith and pride made beautiful plans, and she was quite certain in her own mind that the young man would also find the leisure to write poetry ! Gustave Flaubert, the famous author, had promised to keep an eye on him although he had suffered too much himself to encourage anyone to adopt a literary career. Four years of hard nerve-racking toil had gone to the making of *Madame Bovary*, and the result had been a police court prosecution for obscenity and the applause of the enlightened few. Illness, lack of recognition and the unhappy love-affair with Louise Colet had embittered Flaubert, but nothing could rob him of his passion for Literature. No genuine artist can turn his back on a fellow-writer who needs help, and Madame de Maupassant's plea was reinforced by all the sentimental bonds with the past.

Flaubert gladly accepted the commission to supervise Guy's literary education but he refused to commit himself. " We must encourage your son in his taste for verse," he wrote to Madame de Maupassant, " because it is a noble passion, because Literature consoles one for so much, and, besides, he may have some talent. So far he has done nothing on which I can predict his future as a poet. Anyhow, who can decide a man's future ? "

Madame de Maupassant, like so many proud mothers who live in the country, could already see her son taking Paris by storm. She had confidently advised Guy to apply to the Minister of Marine for employment, and her husband promised to pull a few strings. The young man made his application, which was promptly returned with the familiar phrase, " No Vacancy." But Gustave knew Government offices too well to be discouraged, and quickly buttonholed one or two influential friends. The applicant was told to write another letter, which his father arranged to place in the Minister's hands. This letter, which was sent from " Les Verguies," has been preserved, and reads as follows:

" MONSIEUR LE MINISTRE,

" I have the honour to solicit from Your Excellency a favour which would be of great value to me, that of being attached to the Ministry of Marine. I was admitted Bachelor of Letters on July 27, 1869.

" When the war broke out against Prussia, I was beginning my Law studies. Called to the colours as a soldier of the 1870 class, I passed at Vincennes the necessary examinations for admission to the Intendance Militaire.[1] I was next sent to the second division at Rouen and remained with the divisional stores department until September 1871, when I was replaced.

" The favour which I ask of Your Excellency will be all the more valuable to me as it will allow me to continue my legal studies in Paris, so rudely interrupted by the war – that will not, of course, prevent me from fulfilling my duties with zeal and accuracy.

" I have the honour to be Your Excellency's most humble and obedient servant,

"GUY DE MAUPASSANT."[2]

---

[1] Stores Department.
[2] Cited by Dumesnil, *Guy de Maupassant*, p. 81.

More wire-pulling followed and a place was at last found for the young man. He was given the position of fourth-class clerk at a commencing salary of 125 francs a month.[1] It was a poor post, but Madame de Maupassant had hopes that Guy would not long remain an inferior clerk.

The burly young Norman soon found himself longing for the free-and-easy home where good sport and plenty of food were so automatic. He was now expected to work from 8 a.m. until 6 p.m. in a fusty little office lined with green cardboard dispatch-boxes. Every day the same trivial duties, the same old jokes, and the same faces about him. He had come to Paris dreaming of wealth and beauty, and now, for ten hours a day, he was condemned to issue forms and stationery to clerks in the other departments.

Guy de Maupassant never forgot those wretched days in the big Government office. Around him were men who had left their youth and hopes in a few forgotten ledgers. They were all fussy and cramped, eager to take offence, men grown old with nothing to show for a lifetime of mechanical service. Their only comfort was to bully a subordinate or disparage those above them. To Maupassant, accustomed to a hearty and vigorous life, the prospect was terrifying, but he could not give up a situation so dearly won and in such evident demand.

To his fellow-clerks this ruddy-faced Norman was something of a puzzle. He seemed disinclined to make friends in the office and adopted a rather supercilious manner. Sometimes they thought he despised them, but that was probably his poetic licence. Everybody in the department knew that he wrote verses on the office stationery whenever he had a free moment. Nobody ever published this stuff, of course, and the clerks would cough behind their hands when he approached, and raise ironical eyebrows.

The drudgery was wretched, the clerks stupid and

[1] Less than 25s. a week.

irritating, yet Maupassant seems to have commended himself to his superiors. He was always carefully dressed and respectful, and carried himself like a gentleman. And there was something gratifying in the deference of a young man of good birth who knew his place ! The bureaucrats nodded benevolently and reported most favourably on the new clerk.

" M. de Maupassant has been in our offices for nearly a year: he is a very intelligent and very efficient young man who has had an excellent education. We are very satisfied with him."

A good-natured Admiral added his testimony to the clerk's progress:

" I have heard the most favourable reports on this young man who has made himself known for his intelligence, his zeal and his perfect bearing."

These worthy gentlemen would have been surprised and somewhat shocked at the private life of their model clerk ! He was living in a tiny room at 2 Rue de Moncey – a cubby-hole with one window looking over an alley. The wallpaper was scratched and dirty, the carpet worn and the whole place reeked of the lower middle-class. This was not the poverty of the miserable artist or the beggar, which can be pictur-esque in its ugliness, but the utter threadbare shabbiness of those who wear white collars and cannot afford tobacco. On the table was usually a pile of foolscap or a washing-bill; in the corner a rusty bed. No different this room from a thousand others in Paris or any other big town, yet one queer object on the mantelpiece attracted the attention of visitors. It was the skeleton hand which the English poet, Swinburne, had given his rescuer.[1] Maupassant was very fond of this grisly souvenir, and would have used it as a bell-handle had not his friends dissuaded him.

[1] Later, when he became famous, Maupassant wrote an introduction for the French prose version of Swinburne's *Poems and Ballads*.

Friends ? They were men who had become known to him through a common love of rowing, for this was the young clerk's secret vice. Here was his escape from the drudgery of the office, to feel his skiff knifing the water and his muscles flexing with the effort. Every morning he would get up at dawn, wash his boat and row furiously until it was time to jump into the train and rush to his desk. These were feverish minutes, and he had to effect as quick a change as any vaudeville artist. From the brawny oarsman, with his arms bared to the shoulder and his chest covered with a striped jersey, he had to transform himself into a solemn and correctly dressed young bureaucrat. Puffing furiously at his pipe in the last precious minutes of liberty, he would reluctantly pack away the old straw boater and assume his tall hat. The metamorphosis was complete, and for the next ten hours M. de Maupassant would greet fussy little men with a respectful "Bonjour, monsieur," and hand out foolscap for other clerks to cover.

The nights were long. Paris dazzled and hurt him whenever he walked the boulevards. The streets rattled with gay hansoms, beautiful carriages, victorias. There were attractive women in hooped skirts with tight waists and pretty hats balanced on pyramids of curls. Outside the large cafés sat the comfortable middle-class with its wife. You could see them in the glare of the street lamps – shining bald heads and nicely striped trousers, and big paunches and soft white hands ! And they were all drinking something, or smoking, and on very good terms with the waiter.

Those walks were heavy with unrest. Often he was tortured by the thought of a cooling bock, when surrender would have meant no lunch on the morrow. He had brought a countryman's appetite to Paris, and it was not easy to last out from supper until bedtime. Ten hours of hard drudgery, and nothing at the end but some bread and sausage and a small bock on the boulevard. His

salary was too small, he repeated to himself savagely, and the
end of the month always presented him with the same
miserable option – to sacrifice lunch or dinner.[1]   The
thought of facing a long, cheerless evening without his
dinner was often too much, and he would force himself to
take luncheon for granted.

Paris was not Normandy, and the little grisettes had no
use for a cavalier who could not pay for a good dinner or
two seats at the Vaudeville Theatre.   How far-off were the
days when he could take some well-built peasant lass and
spend a carefree hour in a barn !   Here, in Paris, the girls
of the working classes were only too eager to earn a few
francs on the boulevard.   As for the handsome women in
their pleats and flounces and bows, what could a poor clerk
offer them ?

At times this urge for physical love became unbearable,
and he would find it hard to go back unappeased to his
cheerless little room.   In the brothels it was light and warm,
but such delights are expensive and the young man was too
fond of his stomach to forfeit a dozen meals for a few
minutes of mechanical passion.   Occasionally, like the hero
of *Bel-Ami*, " he gleaned a few crumbs of love here and
there," but he was always hoping for a mistress, a real
woman who would be his alone.   But these were pipe
dreams, and he would find himself drawn to the low-class
bars and dance-halls where women peddled their bodies for
bread.   One could not always afford the price of a few
minutes' pleasure, but it was still satisfying to be in that
atmosphere of flesh and rub shoulders with women.

Sometimes a flash of lechery would drive him into the
arms of a woman whose face and voice he would have
forgotten before he reached home.   More often than not, he
would sit outside a café near the little ladies with their lap-
dogs on leashes, and dream of budding young flesh.   And,

---

[1] Cf. the opening passages of his novel *Bel-Ami*.

while the women talked about the comparative merits of their clients, he began to observe small intimate details and became familiar with their lives.

The prostitutes could not place him at first. He was handsome in a ruddy masculine way and wore good clothes. His hair was carefully brushed and his moustache turned up at the ends. A young officer, you might have said, yet he seemed to have no money and was not at all particular in his women. After a while, he was accepted as a very muscular young man who could not always pay for what he needed so badly.

Guy de Maupassant never lost his taste for the haunts of low-class women, but within a few months of his arrival in Paris he had found a new gaiety, less sordid and infinitely more amusing. Rowing had become his passion, his escape from drudgery, his outlet for the bull-like vitality of his body. Nothing satisfied him now so much as to row twenty or thirty miles down the river accompanied by a friend who could laugh and joke with him. " How simple, how good, how difficult to live like that between the office in Paris and the river at Argenteuil ! For ten years my great, my only, my absorbing passion was the Seine. Ah ! the beautiful, calm, changing and stinking river, full of dreams and filth ! I think I loved you so much because you gave me a sense of life."[1]

The young clerk soon found himself in congenial company. The four " scamps," as he called them, were Robert Pinchon, who was nicknamed " La Tôque," a languid young man who always refused to row; a journalist who was called " Petit Bleu"; " Mr. One-Eye," a hearty young oarsman who sported a monocle; and " Tomahawk," a big fellow with a wild look. Maupassant completed the gang, and was baptised " Joseph Prunier," the name under which he published his first short story.

[1] The opening lines to his story *Mouche*. Cf. *Yvette* and *La Femme de Paul*.

They were a gay crowd, all poor and determined to squeeze
the last morsel of fun out of their leisure. The week-ends
were devoted to rowing and drabbing, and neither rain nor
snow would keep these young men from their rendezvous
on the river. Their boat had been bought with a common
fund, and aptly named *La Feuille à l'Envers*.[1] It was a large
yawl, rather heavy but solid and comfortable, and they
" laughed as they would never again laugh." Maupassant
was looked upon as the leader of this happy band, and every
oarsman on the river knew of the young clerk who had
rowed three of his friends from Paris to Rouen.

On the river, Maupassant seemed to shed all his
pessimism and dissatisfaction. Muscular, stockily built,
with the round florid face of a countryman, he was still
" the glutton of life," hard-drinking and eating like four
men, particularly at the beginning of the month ! He
was again the practical joker, and none of his friends ever
forgot the tricks he used to play on the unfortunate
bourgeoisie.

One evening they were returning to Paris on a train
crowded with tradesmen and other respectable folk. The
newspapers were then full of sensational accounts of
Anarchist plots, and Maupassant could not resist the
opportunity to hoax his fellow-passengers. To their
astonishment, he kept glancing mysteriously at his friends
and seemed greatly concerned for a small package on his lap.
It was only an alarm clock, but the ticking acquired a new
significance when Maupassant leaned forward and began to
drop stage whispers about dynamite and infernal machines !
His friends played up admirably and were soon engaged in a
most heated discussion, strongly flavoured with subversive
theories. Maupassant was particularly emphatic, and his
pseudo-Russian accent did not reassure the respectable people
in the carriage. But the joke succeeded only too well, and

[1] *The Wrong Side of the Figleaf.*

the "Anarchists" were arrested in Paris and thoroughly cross-examined by a zealous police-inspector !

All the week he was forced to be polite to everyone, condemned to play the part of the respectable young clerk, but in the week-ends he reversed the rôle. He would meet his friends at the arranged spot and shout his welcome like a madman. Hearty back-slapping was natural, but Maupassant would make the most obscene remarks, particularly if a dignified bourgeois was in the neighbourhood ! Nothing gave him more pleasure than to shout obscenities within a few feet of a smug little picnic party. And as he rowed, he would tickle his companions with his experiences in the *bistros* of Montmartre.

The headquarters of this party was a disreputable tavern at Argenteuil where they usually spent the night. It was a happy-go-lucky place which soon attracted other oarsmen and a few harlots. Some of these women were only too eager to spend a day or two by the river after the noise and strain of Paris, and Maupassant's party was always most eager to entertain them. The writer was later to draw upon some of these experiences in his stories, and it is not difficult to reconstruct the life which the crew of *La Feuille à l'Envers* led on the river-bank.

Life was a dull, dreary routine for five days a week; here all was friendly and gay. The food and beds were rough, but fresh air and laughter remained on tap. The five young men occupied a rough dormitory in the pothouse at Argenteuil, and often they shared the favours of a young woman who was not over-particular. Sometimes they would throw poker-dice for the privilege of making first advances to a riverside beauty, but the winner was usually charitable and none of his friends suffered except in the order of precedence. A young woman would attach herself to a man for a day or a month, according to his means, and there was always the opportunity of effecting exchanges.

During the week they would resume their respectable occupations, counting the hours until Saturday came round again. They were long hours for Maupassant, who could find little love for these narrow-shouldered bureaucrats, so sly and primed with small-talk. Later he was to vent his feelings in more than one tale,[1] but he was too much the prudent Norman to betray his feelings in an office where personal favouritism might rob a man of promotion and even lose him his desk. He was still polite and attentive to those who counted, and only his fellow-clerks could feel his contempt. How well he concealed the rough week-end side of his life was obvious from the attitude of the other civil servants. His superiors suspected nothing and spoke well of him, while " the galley-slaves " were ready to dismiss him as a silly poetaster who covered the office notepaper with verses and gave himself airs.

Sometimes, but not often enough, the other four oarsmen would come to his dreary lodging and plan excursions for the following week-end. Maupassant at once threw off his depression and told stories that kept them roaring with laughter. An excellent mimic, he could hit off the other clerks to a nicety, framing a cruel caricature in half a dozen sentences. When funds allowed, they went out on the boulevards for dinner, and it was Maupassant who led his companions to the restaurant and chose the best and cheapest *table d'hôte*. He had memorised every menu-card on the boulevard !

Saturday and Sunday were for rowing, but there were always delicious details to be settled in advance. Was it to be Argenteuil or Chatou or Bezons ? Fresh air was the first need, but the young men were all connoisseurs of scenery and did not decide in a hurry. Fishing was pleasant on a quiet summer evening, but sometimes the weather made rowing unpleasant and Maupassant had to find other forms

[1] Cf. *L'Héritage*, *Les Dimanches d'un Bourgeois de Paris*, etc.

of exercise. He loved walking, and one day persuaded a young painter to accompany him on " a little excursion." Rain was in the air and the others had wisely decided to stay under cover, but nothing could restrain Maupassant. It was Sunday, and in a few hours he would be back in the office stamping documents or checking the notepaper issued by his department ! The unfortunate painter soon began to lag, but Maupassant seemed tireless and quite indifferent to a drenching rain.

" We walked from five in the morning," he wrote to his mother. " We did 15 leagues, or, if you prefer it, 60 kilometres, about 70 thousand paces. Our feet were like jelly ! "

Nothing could take the place of his beloved Normandy, but here was the fresh air he needed so much, and forgetfulness in violent exercise. Besides, he was a trained observer of Nature and could enjoy the country with the careful palate of a gourmet. When he felt too despondent to share a jaunt with his friends he would install himself in some lonely inn. Here he would perhaps spend a night when the office doors had closed, writing verses and short pieces of prose, while the sun sank splendidly into the river.

His mother alone understood his loneliness, and it was to her he turned when Paris saddened and depressed him.

" You see that I don't put off writing to you, but, to tell the truth, I could wait no longer," he writes on September 24, 1873. " I feel so lost, so isolated and so *demoralised* that I must beg you to send me some bright letters. I'm afraid of the coming winter, I feel so alone, and the long lonely evenings are sometimes terrible. When I'm alone at my table with my sad lamp burning in front of me, I often have such moments of dejection that I don't know where to turn. Last winter when I had the same feeling I often told myself that you were also going through the

Dm

sadness of those long, cold evenings in December and January. . . .

" To cheer myself up a bit, I've just written something on the lines of the *Contes du Lundi*. I'm sending it on to you, but I don't think very much of it, as I dashed it off in a quarter of an hour. Please let me have it back as I might be able to make something of it. Many of the phrases are not quite right but I'll correct them when the time comes. . . .

" Adieu, my dear mother. I kiss you a thousand and one times, likewise Hervé.   " Your son,
            " GUY DE MAUPASSANT."[1]

When summer comes round again he is a new man.

" The good weather has come at last. I hope you will now be able to let the house. It's terribly warm to-day, and the last Parisians are surely running away. As for me, I row and bathe, bathe and row. The rats and frogs are so used to seeing the lantern on my boat at all hours of the night that they come out and say good evening. I handle my big boat like another would handle a yawl and my boatmen friends at Bougival ($2\frac{1}{2}$ leagues from Bezons) are terribly surprised when I appear about midnight and ask for a glass of rum. I'm still working at my sketches of rowing life, which I've mentioned to you, and I think I might be able to do a little book, fairly amusing and realistic, by selecting the best of the anecdotes I know, and amplifying and polishing them, etc.   " Your son,
            " GUY DE MAUPASSANT."

Nothing he wrote at this time foreshadowed the master-pieces to come. He had chaos within, a passion for physical life which surged from a clogging melancholia, part

[1] This letter is cited by M. Pol Neveux in his celebrated edition of *Boule de Suif* (Louis Conard). Unless otherwise stated, all the writer's letters to his mother are taken from this edition.

acquired, part hereditary. He was still far too interested in his own personality, too involved in petty irritations, to transmute experience into Art. His pessimism urged him towards self-expression but his first attempts were little more than a relaxation from the monotony of office life. He was still the emphatic enjoyer of life, conscious of nothing more literary than a facility for verse and the raconteur's urge to share his experiences.

These early attempts were known to his friends, who listened sympathetically to the first drafts without being aware that they were in the presence of genius. There was certainly nothing in Maupassant's sketches to suggest his *métier*, and his hearty companions merely proved their good nature by lending a polite ear. " Petit Bleu " was perhaps the most attentive, but he would never have given Maupassant credit for more than a lively eye for an amusing scene. Himself a journalist, he good-naturedly assisted Maupassant to publish his first short story in a provincial collection.

Robert Pinchon alias " La Tôque," was Maupassant's closest friend at this time. Four years older than Guy, he was also a Norman by birth and outlook. His father was a professor whose literary tastes he had inherited, and Maupassant had made the young man's acquaintance at the house of his cousin, Louis, the son of Alfred le Poittevin. The two lads had quickly discovered a common interest in the theatre, and Robert was frequently invited to take part in the amateur theatricals at " Les Verguies." After the war they had renewed acquaintance in Paris, where Pinchon took up sculpture which he soon deserted for play-writing.

" La Tôque " was not as passionate an oarsman as his more robust friend, but both were interested in Literature. Pinchon was quickly off the mark. A charming and personable young man, he soon interested Ballande, the director of the Third French Theatre. Within a year or two of his arrival in Paris, he had written a full-length play on Molière which Ballande put on at the Théâtre Italien.

Meanwhile, Maupassant went his own way and seemed quite indifferent to the desire for a startling literary success.

" I am in no hurry," he would say. " I'm learning my job ! "

That was a sound and sensible outlook, surprising in a high-spirited young man who could see no escape from his prison at the Admiralty. These were his words, but the advice had come from the man who was to shape his literary career from the very beginning.

Maupassant's long apprenticeship to Gustave Flaubert is undoubtedly unique in Literature. Here is an association so close and affectionate that for many years it was rumoured that the two were father and son ! That was silly gossip, but Flaubert's interest arose more from early friendship with the Le Poittevins than any real perception of the young man's quality. The unique nature of this apprenticeship lies in the fact that a young writer put himself unreservedly into the hands of an established author without losing his own individuality.

Maupassant owed much to the author of *Madame Bovary*, and he was always eager to acknowledge the debt.

" I worked for seven years with Flaubert without writing a line (understand by that, without writing for the public, without thinking of publication)," he says in his famous preface to *Pierre et Jean*. " During those seven years he gave me literary principles which I could not have acquired after forty years of experience."

The friendship which was to prove so fruitful opened very quietly. Flaubert was already tired and embittered, ignored by the public and a prey to nervous disease. He was a literary force when Maupassant approached him, but already knew what it meant to be respectfully neglected.

His work marked the transition between Balzac's realism and Zola, but, although no literary history could overlook him, he had been steadily passed over for men like Octave Feuillet and Edmond About. His dearest friends were dead — Alfred le Poittevin, Bouilhet, Louise Colet, George Sand — and nothing remained but to polish his phrases until the pen dropped from his hand. He had known the indignity of a police-court dock, the bitterness of failure as a dramatist and the loss of his fortune through the ruin of a relative. Too proud to accept the tiny librarianship which his friends had tried to procure him, he was left with little more than his artistic integrity and the appreciation of a handful of men who loved and understood beautiful French prose.

Guy de Maupassant could not have been more fortunate in his choice of mentor. Flaubert worshipped *style*, not literary tricks, and had declared war on clichés. In his own work he was painfully scrupulous over perfection of phrase and rhythm, and could forgive every literary fault except slovenly writing. So scrupulous had he become that he often wrote sentences on a blackboard to see how they looked ! His respect for clarity and architecture in his prose was only equalled by an exacting attention to detail, and he was said to have consulted a hundred and seven agricultural works before writing a certain chapter. Small wonder that he did not hail the muscular young clerk as a heaven-sent poet and urge him to fly into print !

Maupassant, who had first met Flaubert at Bouilhet's house, might have been pardoned for not finding himself attracted by the novelist. Genius does not always suffer fools gladly, and Flaubert could be both violent and ironical when Literature was being discussed. " He had the gestures of a Don Quixote and the voice of an Army trumpeter," says Alphonse Daudet, and few could quarrel with that description. Although nearly fifty when Maupassant came to know him, he still looked like a guardsman, with his big square shoulders and enormous moustache. He had the head of a Viking, and one did not easily forget his broad forehead or those sharp satirical eyes.

Flaubert soon learned to like the young man who amused him so much with his anecdotes of the river and office life. They were fellow-Normans, and Flaubert enjoyed the melancholy pleasure of recalling his own early youth with its hopes and dreams. But the poet had a more direct claim on the older man.

" Your son reminds me so much of poor Alfred," he wrote to Madame de Maupassant. " I am sometimes almost frightened by the resemblance, particularly when his head is bent and he is reciting his verses ! "

Nothing pleased Guy's mother more than her old friend's kindly interest. Reluctant at first to give up part of his precious holiday, Maupassant had soon formed the habit of calling on Flaubert every Sunday morning. The novelist was then living in a small apartment in the Rue Murillo – a couple of shabby narrow rooms overlooking the Parc Monceau. To this flat Maupassant hurried each week, bearing the verses which he had scribbled on office stationery, or afterwards in his cheerless room. And Flaubert would correct these verses like a schoolmaster, reshaping phrases, hacking, expunging, substituting with the passionate intensity of an outraged craftsman. Maupassant never lost his temper, rarely argued, and watched gravely as the older man ripped his blue pencil through a purple passage. The poem would be analysed and discussed before the clerk was allowed to take it home again for a more thorough treatment. The following Sunday, Maupassant would be back with his lyric, ready for the master's final dictum. Flaubert might still grumble, but sometimes the young man left the Rue Murillo feeling that his critic was not altogether displeased.

Often he was asked to stay for luncheon, and in the afternoon Zola, Cézanne and Goncourt would come in for the violent arguments which Flaubert always provided. Maupassant used to say very little in those days, preferring to listen attentively to what was being discussed. He had come to love this burly master, and nothing gratified him so much as the respect which the others showed Flaubert.

The author of *Madame Bovary* had begun this literary mentorship out of affection for Laure de Maupassant, but soon he found himself looking forward with pleasure to the young man's visits. Maupassant had a round, healthy Norman's face, a splendid appetite and a laugh that often brought echoes from the good Gustave. Besides, he was a lusty, powerful fellow who could brag endlessly of his affairs with women and always bring out the funny side. Here was all the full-blooded vigour of a true Norman, and Flaubert warmed to him from the first. After all his trouble and disappointment, it was something to be tutor to this young man who was so obviously grateful and sincere.

" You cannot believe how charming, intelligent, what a good boy, how sensible and witty . . . I find him," he writes to Madame de Maupassant.

Nothing could persuade Guy to give up his rowing, but Flaubert's Sunday mornings soon became a habit, and he felt that the week was without significance when the older man could not see him.

" Dear Sir and Friend," he writes in one letter. " Our discussions each week have become a habit and a necessity with me, and I cannot resist the desire to chat a little by letter. I do not ask you to reply to me, of course: I know that you have other things to do. Pardon me for saying so, but when I am talking with you, I often seem to hear the uncle I never knew, but of whom you and my mother have so often spoken. . . ."

Flaubert was touched and gratified by the young man's devotion, but his tutorship did not relax in severity. Maupassant had always felt the urge to write verse and the

novelist did not discourage him. He insisted on balance
of phrase and rhythm, although still unconvinced of the
clerk's seriousness of purpose. Only when Maupassant
proved his capacity to absorb criticism did Flaubert begin
to see in him something more than a dilettante and versifier.

There was as yet no question of a literary career, and
Flaubert would have been the last person to advise the clerk
to leave his desk on the strength of a few verses. Soon the
young man was bringing sketches, pieces of prose, and
Flaubert at last glimpsed a little promise in these trivial
anecdotes. Now began the real work of guiding Maupassant towards a prose style.

Flaubert first taught his pupil how to observe accurately.

"When you pass a grocer sitting in his doorway," he
would say, "or a porter smoking his pipe, or a cab rank,
show me that grocer and that porter, their pose, their whole
physical appearance and moral nature, in such a way that
I could not confuse them with any other grocer or porter,
and – by a single word – make me see in what way one
cab-horse differs from fifty others before or behind it."

The young man took these words to heart and began to
see the significance of accurate detail in any work of art.
Flaubert urged him to be objective, but he was careful not
to be too discouraging.

"If one has originality," he used to say, "one must
bring it out as soon as possible. If not, one must acquire
it." And the young man would be told to describe some
scene in a hundred lines. Every Sunday came the usual
explosive outbursts from the novelist, but even Flaubert
had to admit the young man's persistency. He had set out
to train Maupassant's vision and there was so much to
learn ! No young writer likes discipline: he sees himself
hemmed in by established names and often decides upon
shock tactics. Sensationalism and sex are at hand, and most
prentice quills do not hesitate. All technical trades demand

a long training, but few young artists are prepared to wear swaddling-clothes.

Guy de Maupassant was exposed to the same temptation to dive headlong into print. He had written verse since his schooldays, and men like Bouilhet and Flaubert had praised some of his poems. The bookstalls were littered with names which he could not respect, while crowds hurried to the theatres to see Sardou's mechanical pieces or the boudoir nonsense of Dumas *fils*. Sometimes, sitting in his room, he would be dazzled by the vision of his own name on the playbills, with all Paris flocking to applaud ! His friend, Robert Pinchon, had put on a piece, so it could not be as difficult as people imagined !

That frowsy room in the Rue de Moncey was made to house such dreams. There was no fire and the furniture consisted of a great shabby bed, a wardrobe and a dressing-table. Money would have meant an end to all this dirt and shabbiness: above all, an escape from the drudgery of the Ministry of Marine. Sometimes he was so poor that a small train-fare was completely beyond his means. It is on record that he once declined an invitation to a literary lunch in Rouen where Flaubert was then living.

" If you have not the money to pay for your ticket," wrote the author of *Madame Bovary*, " I have a splendid double louis at your command."

After a year at the Ministry, his salary had been increased by the equivalent of ten shillings a month !

Flaubert had too great a respect for his Art to be influenced by his pupil's need of a few easy francs. Zola, Daudet and the others who came to the Rue Murillo or to his cottage at Croisset knew that Maupassant was his pupil. In a sense, therefore, the quality of the young man's output was of the greatest personal interest to Flaubert.

The slow training went on, and the older man had still not given the signal for publication.

"Remember that no two grains of sand, no two flies, no
two hands or noses, are absolutely alike," he told Maupassant. "Go out and use your eyes, and then come back
with a few phrases in which you have distinguished these
things clearly and accurately." Another day: "Go for a
walk, young man, and tell me in a hundred lines — *no more* —
just what you saw."

General principles are not enough, and Flaubert helped
his disciple to gain the clinical experience without which
all tuition is valueless. "Talent is a long patience," he
used to say before setting the young man some apparently
trivial exercise. But soon these tasks became more practical,
and Maupassant knew the great pleasure of assisting the
master in his own work. Nothing was allowed to interfere
with rowing but he could always find time to do some errand
for his beloved tutor. Sometimes it was to a theatrical
producer or an agent that he hurried, and before long the
sturdy figure of "Gustave's pupil" was known to most of
literary Paris.

Of more use to Maupassant was the research work which
Flaubert set him in connection with his great satire, *Bouvard
and Pécuchet*. It was a colossal task, but Flaubert was
characteristically determined to achieve perfect accuracy of
detail. His young pupil was sent out to study catalogues and
authorities, engaged to write notes and urged to make
himself useful. Knowing Guy's enthusiasm for Nature,
Flaubert also asked him to do a detailed description of the
Norman coast which was to be the setting for one of his
scenes. Nothing delighted the young clerk more than this
task, and he wrote out a very full sketch of the landscape
between Antifer and Etretat. Flaubert was grateful but
did not forget to note that it was too complicated. "I
wanted something simpler," he grumbled.

Simplicity and patience — these two words the giant in his
shabby dressing-gown never tired of repeating. At times

he was a little afraid that the young man did not show enough self-discipline. A clerk condemned to a sedentary life should exercise his body when ever possible, but was he not overdoing this rowing? Rumours also reached Flaubert that Guy was addicted to women and rarely spent an evening in his room.

" I think our young man is a bit of a shirker and not too keen on work," he writes to Madame de Maupassant.[1] " I should like to see him start on a full-length book, however bad. What he has shown me is as good as what is being printed by the Parnassians. . . . In time he will gain originality, an individual manner of seeing and feeling (for that is everything); anyhow, what is success, after all? The real thing in this world is to keep one's soul on a lofty plane, far above the bourgeois and democratic mind. The cultivation of Art gives one pride, of which one can never have too much. That is my code. . . ."

Flaubert's anxiety to see his protégé do a full-length work came from a real insight into the young man's mind. Without hopes of a masterpiece, he was nevertheless aware of Maupassant's restlessness and imagined that a sustained piece of work might cure him. The beginner needs discipline, and there was something disquieting in Guy's pessimism. He had shown himself a good pupil, yet the benefit of his lessons might well be lost in despair and self-distrust.

" I did not write to you, my dear master, because my morale has completely gone. For three weeks I have tried to work in the evenings without being able to write a single page. Nothing, nothing. Then I gradually sank into the depths of sadness and depression. . . . My job is destroying me bit by bit. After seven hours of office work, I am no longer able to shed the sorrows that weigh me down. I tried to write some articles for *Le Gaulois* in order to make a

[1] *Correspondance*, Flaubert, IV (February 1873).

few sous. It was impossible. I cannot do a line and feel like weeping over my notepaper. Besides, everything about me is going wrong. My mother, who went back to Etretat a couple of months ago, is no better. Her heart is still troubling her and she has had some bad fainting attacks. She is so weak that she can no longer write to me and I only hear from her about once a fortnight when she dictates a word to the gardener. . . . How is it that Zola has not been decorated as M. Bardoux promised ? The affair has caused quite a fuss because all the papers had already announced the award. I ought to go and spend a Sunday with him, I'm so anxious to hear what he has to say about it. I'm sure he's very annoyed. Why did he want it, anyway ?

" I met Turgenev a few days before he left for Russia. He was sad and upset. He has had heart trouble and the doctor diagnosed an affection of the left ventricle. Has everybody got weak hearts ?

" I salute you with all my heart, dear master, and beg you to write me a few words between bits of *Bouvard et Pécuchet*.

"GUY DE MAUPASSANT."

Flaubert knew too much about the " artistic temperament " to leave his pupil in the slough of self-pity. All his letters have a gusty, back-slapping quality, but one famous note from Croisset completely hits off the relationship between the two men. It is also a valuable index to the young clerk's state of mind, so often obscured by the ruddy face and Rabelaisian laughter.

" You complain that women are monotonous," Flaubert writes. " There is a very simple remedy, and that is, avoid them. You say events have no variety — that is a realist's complaint, and, besides, what do you know about it ? You must look at things more closely. Have you ever believed in the existence of things ? Isn't everything illusion ? . . . Now, my dear friend, you seem to be very put out, and your boredom upsets me, because you could use your time more pleasantly. You must work harder, young man, you *must*. I have begun to suspect that you are rather lazy. Too many tarts, too much boating, too much exercise. Civilised man does not need as much locomotion as the medical gentlemen imagine. You were born to write verses: do it ! You live in a hell, I know it, and pity you from the bottom of my heart. But from five in the evening until ten in the morning all your time can be given up to the Muse, who is still the best wench. So come along, my good fellow, lift up your nose ! What is the good of burrowing into your sorrow ? You've got to square up to yourself like a strong man; that's the way to become one. My word, a little more pride ! The other lad [Alfred le Poittevin] had more guts.

" You need principles ! Easily said, of course, but the trouble is to know what principles. For an artist there is only one: to sacrifice everything for Art. Life must be regarded as a means, nothing more. . . ."[1]

Flaubert was right in steering the young poet clear of self-pity, but he, like everyone else, could not know what Maupassant was suffering. He had left the home he loved, and saw himself fading into one of the shabby hacks who surrounded him in the Ministry. Money was the only way out – a big success which would shut the guffawing mouths of the other clerks and give him the things he had so often seen in dreams. Beautiful women, good food, the company of his friends, a house on the river, perhaps a boat of his own, even a yacht ! And when his head ached he would curse the office which cramped his muscles and shut out the fresh air.

After five years in Paris he was still a checking clerk in the stores department, but his salary had been increased – to 1,800 francs a year ![2] No chance of becoming rich there, he knew, unless he married the Minister's daughter. But

[1] *Correspondance*, Flaubert, IV, p. 302.   [2] About 30*s*. a week.

marriage made him smile; he could scarcely keep himself on the salary, and Ministers do not embrace humble clerks, except in the story-books. Besides, it was so much more amusing to spend one's leisure with the others on the river taking a woman who would demand no more than a meal or a few francs.

His pen still seemed the only lever with which to raise himself from the rut, but there was as yet little to show for the many long evenings spent in his fireless bed-sitting-room. He had covered sheets of paper with verses, sketches, fragments of plays; yet Flaubert still declined to advise publication. Poor Madame de Maupassant, ailing and worried by her son's unhappiness, wrote anxiously to her old friend:

" Should not Guy leave the Ministry and devote himself to writing ? "

But Flaubert could not be stampeded.

" Not yet ! " he replied. " Let us not ruin him."

Students of Maupassant's short but meteoric career as a writer have sometimes considered Flaubert unduly severe in his discipline. One cannot deny that the older man's attitude was coloured by his own disappointments, but there was solid common sense behind his advice. Maupassant had written very little prose, and the work he brought to the Rue Murillo did not justify any hopes in a literary career. He showed a certain facility, but many other young men in offices wrote verse without surrendering a monthly salary on the strength of an editorial compliment.

Some of these studies of rowing life were not bad, but much more was needed to make a writer. This young man's prose was still mediocre although there was a rough sensuality about his lyrics which interested Flaubert. He was still very young and amateurish, this pupil of his, and sometimes Flaubert smiled into his huge moustache as he noted a line with more than an echo of Bouilhet or Alfred de Musset.

Nothing is so stimulating as another man's success, particularly to the young artist, and Maupassant was soon hot on the heels of his friend, Robert Pinchon. There is something peculiarly inviting in a theatrical coup, and most authors have at one time or another attempted to take the stage by storm. Flaubert and Zola – practised novelists – had flirted and failed, but it is the prerogative of youth to ignore the experience of others, and Maupassant began to dream of a quick success which would solve all his problems. The author of *Madame Bovary* tried hard not to discourage the eager young playwright, but Maupassant instinctively addressed himself to the man who could already claim some success in the theatre. Pinchon, for his part, was eager to write another play, and enthusiastically welcomed the idea of collaboration.

This play, which was completed in 1875, did not enjoy a sensational success. *La Maison Turque à la feuille de rose* was nothing more than a bawdy farce, much of the action taking place in a brothel. The "plot" centred round a young married couple who enter the establishment in the mistaken belief that it is an hotel.

This crude piece was first performed in the studio of an artist, Maurice Leloir, all the parts being played by amateurs. Maupassant himself took the rôle of one of the prostitutes; Pinchon assumed half a dozen parts, including that of a lecherous hunchback; while " Petit-Bleu " played the innocent young bride. Leloir, genial host, designed the costumes and painted the whole of the scenery. All the invitations were written out on the stationery of the respectable Ministry of Marine !

The curtain went up in front of an audience far more distinguished than the play deserved. Flaubert had duly buttonholed Turgenev, and the two men were gasping with exhaustion and merriment when they finally reached the studio on the fifth floor. The gigantic Norman had taken off his overcoat on the first floor, his frock-coat on the second and his waistcoat on the third. He arrived in the " theatre " carrying the garments over his arm and attired only in his flannel underwear. They took their places beside Zola, rather pale and serious-looking with his eye-glasses and black beard. Edmond de Goncourt soon joined them. He stooped a little, sat down carefully and ran a meditative finger through his beautiful imperial. He looked somewhat out of place, more like the stage diplomat than a militant man of letters. Céard, Huysmans and others came in and, as the lights went down, two actresses appeared in masks, taking their seats with elaborate unconcern.

Before the play was half finished one of the ladies had swept out in great indignation, confessing herself disgusted. Turgenev clapped politely but Flaubert sat back and roared, congratulating the authors on having greatly " refreshed " him. Two years later the piece was performed in another studio, but no attempt seems to have been made to gain a larger public.

Flaubert had been " refreshed " but not impressed by the vulgar farce. He was not unsympathetic, however, when his pupil showed him another piece – this time a play in verse – called *La Répétition*.[1] It had already been refused by a manager, and Flaubert was most careful not to wound the sensitive young playwright.

" Very amusing, very nice, charming," he observed. " The part of René would make the reputation of an actor, and it is full of good bits, such as the line on page 53. I won't mention all the others because I'm rather busy. Send a copy of the volume to Princess Mathilde, with your card attached to the title-page. I should very much like to see it performed in her drawing-room ! "[2]

[1] This piece was first staged at Rouen on May 6, 1904. It ran for four performances.
[2] Cited by Dumesnil, p. 98.

Poor Maupassant was still in his room at 2 Rue de Moncey, still dreaming that the *very next* piece would make his name. Only Pinchon, himself losing his faith in play-writing, knew how Maupassant suffered by his failure.

" The managers are certainly not worth the trouble we take for them ! " wrote the saddened young clerk. " Yes, they find our plays charming, but they don't put them on. As far as I'm concerned, I'd rather they thought them bad and staged them. I need only tell you that Raymond Deslandes thinks my *Répétition* too subtle for the Vaudeville."[1]

Still desperately sure of himself and encouraged by polite but evasive managers, Maupassant applied himself to the " full-length " work which Flaubert had so often urged him to attempt. This time he sat down and wrote a three-act historical drama in verse, *La Comtesse de Béthune*. The older man hoped to cure his pupil of a tendency towards dilettantism, and, to his surprise, Maupassant attacked the work with extraordinary energy. Poverty, misery at the office and the craving for a sensational success on the stage were the motive forces behind this new industry; but the important thing was that the young man had to concentrate on a large-scale work. The good Flaubert had sustained heavy reverses on his own account in the theatre, but he was sincere, if rather pessimistic, in his hope that Maupassant would be more fortunate. And in his New Year greetings he could think of no better wish than " a good dramatic subject which will be well written and make 100,000 francs ! "

The winter of 1875 found Flaubert dependent for shelter on his niece, but his welcome to Maupassant was characteristically kind.

" Dear old chap," he wrote, " it is arranged that you lunch with me every Sunday this winter." Maupassant, who had come to depend on these friendly, if severe, lectures, accepted gratefully and went over to the little flat in the Faubourg Saint-Honoré, where the master received him with bluff good-humour. The young clerk was too self-centred at this time to understand how much Flaubert suffered under all this bulky joviality. Later, when his own feet were more firmly planted on the road to success, he came to realise that the older man had spared him many a querulous complaint. Flaubert's poverty and disappointment he was aware of, and nothing gave him more pleasure than to see his host broaden into a fit of laughter as he told some ribald tale of sex or perversion. But during this apprenticeship these two men, the seasoned author and the fledgling, always tried to conceal from each other the heartache which both felt so acutely.

Maupassant's new play went the way of the others. It had given him so much trouble, so many nerve-racked nights, that he almost prayed for a failure — anything, in fact, but the sickly bog of faint praise into which it had drifted.

" I've lost nearly the whole of the winter in revising the play which didn't please me," he confided to the faithful Pinchon. " I swear never to do any more for the stage ! "

Flaubert had encouraged him with more sympathy than hope, and the playwright himself seemed to have lost all confidence in the piece.

" I will show it to you when you get back," he announced limply. "I have also done the plan for a novel which I shall begin as soon as this play is finished."

At last the play was completed and Pinchon undertook to show it to Ballande, who had produced his own play three or four years before. While Maupassant kicked his heels at the Ministry of Marine, the kindly director was seeking a way to spare his feelings.

" This play is nice, very nice," he told Pinchon, " but I'm afraid it's too expensive to put on." Time-honoured plea of apathetic managers ! Pinchon did his best but Ballande could offer only one suggestion. " Couldn't your friend put up the money to defray the expenses of the production ? " Poor Maupassant, living on a miserable pittance and staking a winter's evenings on a play, was now exposed to the supreme indignity of being invited to pay for his own play ! Pinchon quickly explained that this was not the work of a rich dilettante anxious to impress his friends.

" Well," murmured Ballande, " if M. de Maupassant will give me a play that I can put on without expense, I'll do it at once."

And with that the young playwright had to be content. Not so Maupassant, who gulped down the crumbs of comfort and vowed that he would write a simple comedy with only two characters and no more scenery than a couple of easy chairs and a fireplace !

Failure in one medium usually tempts an artist to hunt success in another. Maupassant had never ceased writing verse and now addressed himself more industriously to his Muse. Flaubert was encouraging but could not be blamed for refusing to see a great poet in the young man. Verse yields notoriously poor dividends, and there was very small reason to hope that his pupil would prove the gilded exception. But he did not deny that the later verses were an improvement on the first attempts.

Maupassant had at last escaped from the young poet's world of twilight and impotent inquiry. Again and again he showed a vigour, an actuality of description, so often denied the poetaster. But his lines lacked the fierce necessity, the idealism, and, above all, the sheer music of great verse. He no longer trailed his pencil through the day-dreams of his youth, but he was still too self-conscious to be poetically effective. His realities were not spiritual enough, and when he tried to describe something he had not seen or felt his fingers become thumbs. If his burden of music was slight, one could make the same criticism of his subject-matter. His song rarely soared higher than a woman's waist.

At last came the luxury of print – the first thrill of recognition which can never be repeated. He was twenty-six now, with little to show for a long training, but these few lines of published verse seemed to compensate for all his disappointment. The poem entitled " Au Bord de l'Eau " appeared under the pseudonym of " Guy de Valmont," its publication as much due to Flaubert's patronage as to any intrinsic merit. Flaubert professed a great admiration for the verses and read them out to those of his guests who were likely to be useful to the young man. He went so far as to recommend Catulle Mendès to publish them in his review *La République des Lettres*. Mendès had been a little sceptical, but could not offend Flaubert who was one of his pet contributors. The piece was duly sandwiched between a fragment from Poe and a Flaubert fantasy, but Maupassant had tasted printer's ink. Nothing is so heady, and the young man soon called on the editor, eager to press home his advantage !

" There was nothing romantic in his appearance," says a member of the editorial staff at that time.[1] " A round florid face, like a fresh-water sailor, frank looks and easy manners. . . . His talk was largely of the literary principles which Flaubert had instilled in him, and the various likes and dislikes, more enthusiastic than profound, which constituted his literary creed. He had an inexhaustible fund of low stories and made some violent attacks upon the staff at the Ministry of Marine. Of this last subject, he never wearied. . . . One liked him for his pleasant manners and good temper."

But Mendès was not as impressed as Gustave Flaubert.

[1] Henri Roujon, cited by Dumesnil, p. 107.

He, like most of his readers, dismissed the new contributor as a dilettante and amateur. Maupassant himself seemed unconscious of any editorial tepidness. Like all beginners, he needed only a little encouragement to send him headlong into golden visions. The difficulty was subjects.

" Try to find me a few ideas for stories," he writes to his mother. " During the day, at the Ministry, I could find time to do a little work on them. My plays take up all my evenings, and I could try and get some things into some journal or other."

Maupassant was at this time thinking about a series of short tales and sketches, but plots seemed very few and far between.

" I've got half a dozen subjects that seem all right," he tells Madame de Maupassant. " My word, this is no fun ! "

Flaubert continued to keep a benevolent eye on his disciple. Although one of Maupassant's short stories, " La Main Ecorchée," had appeared over the signature " Joseph Prunier " in a provincial collection, there was nothing as yet to point to a distinguished career in Literature. Flaubert had an artist's contempt for journalism, but he was psychologist enough to know that Maupassant would profit enormously by seeing his work in print. He had served a long and patient apprenticeship, yet there was always the danger of his becoming disheartened and losing the urge to sit down at his table in the evenings. " Writing for the papers " might bring in very little money, but the underpaid clerk would surely react to the psychological impetus.

Flaubert smiled to himself as he saw the young foal sniff wistfully at the footlights before galloping off to the duller but more nourishing pastures of journalism. From the year 1876 onwards, Maupassant began to contribute to the newspapers, with Flaubert in benevolent attendance. The correspondence which passed between the two men is filled with evidence of the valuable part which Flaubert now assumed.

" Only yesterday," he writes,[1] " I spoke up for you to Raoul-Duval. . . . I asked him to give you a trial at doing two or three book reviews. He has agreed. As soon as Parliament is open I will give you a letter of introduction to him. That's settled. Madame Lapierre has seconded me very warmly in that recommendation. Always women, little pig ! "[2]

The last reference is to the wife of Charles Lapierre, the editor of the *Nouvelliste de Rouen*, who seemed to have taken a liking to the young man. He was good company and Madame Lapierre used to welcome him at Rouen whenever he could find the time and the railway fare. Another kind friend was Madame Brainne, widow of a well-known journalist and something of a power in social and Press circles. These two ladies were sisters, both remarkable for their beauty and good-nature. They were great favourites with Gustave Flaubert, whom they treated with profound affection and respect.

The young clerk was soon welcomed at the widow's house in Paris. He seemed quite tenderly disposed towards Madame Brainne, but each visit also brought him nearer to the editor of the *Nouvelliste de Rouen*. Later, in *Bel-Ami*, he was to draw cruel but authentic sketches of the women who helped his hero to stage a journalistic début.

Flaubert had no illusions about writing for the Press, and his advice to the young man was both shrewd and cynical. While he is lifting back-door latches he urges his pupil to chase everyone who might be useful. The *Nouvelliste de Rouen* supports the politician Raoul-Duval, and Flaubert realises that Maupassant cannot do better than worry this man into assisting him. In the autumn of 1876,

[1] Letter of October 25, 1876.
[2] " Toujours les femmes, petit cochon," are Flaubert's actual words.

Raoul-Duval had founded a journal called *La Nation*, and Flaubert is confident that he can find Maupassant a place on the new paper. He pulls strings on all sides and puts forward his pupil as dramatic critic and book reviewer. But Maupassant is unknown and must force himself under the nose of the politician.

"Now that the session has begun," writes Flaubert, "Raoul-Duval should be in Paris. . . . Go to his house early in the morning, between eight and nine, and you will have a good chance of finding him in. If they shut the door in your face, say you come from me."

Not content with this friendly advice, he also mentions subjects to tickle editorial palates.

"If you suggested some ideas to him [Raoul-Duval] you would save him the trouble of thinking up something, and the whole business might go more quickly. Nobody has yet done a history of modern criticism. It's a rich subject. Take, for example, Planche, Janin, Théo, etc., and analyse their ideas, their poetics. You can also explore the question of 'Art for Art's Sake' or even the fantastic element in Art. Nobody has yet done a study on the enormous work of George Sand. A good parallel might be drawn with the work of Dumas — the novel of adventure and the novel of ideas. Finally, my boy, if you get into *La Nation*, I want you to begin with something startling."

Maupassant at once hurried to the all-powerful Raoul-Duval. He had invented some excuse for being late at his desk, but it seemed worth while to risk the displeasure of his superiors. The politician smiled like a politician, read Flaubert's glowing recommendation and seemed cordial.

"Quite right, we haven't yet engaged a book reviewer," he told Maupassant. "Do me an article on a new book: I'll get it in. You can do another in about a fortnight and I'll see that it's printed. Then I'll get you on to the staff as literary critic."

The young clerk flew back to the Ministry and that day sat down to a desk stacked with beautiful dreams. A small but steady income, a growing reputation, perhaps fame. . . . And such delicious luxuries as *table d'hôte* dinners on the boulevard two or three times a week, a little apartment and a plump mistress who would look after him. So often he had longed to go home and visit his mother, only to be defeated by the railway fare! His articles would pay for all that and he might even be able to help his brother, Hervé, who had just become a non-commissioned officer in a cavalry regiment and had very little money to spare.

These glorious mirages quickly faded, leaving him still more depressed. He had scraped together a few francs and bought Balzac's *Letters* which had just been published in book form. Night after night he spent in his dreary bed-room, poring over the correspondence and making notes. It was his great opportunity and he could not afford to be apathetic. Flaubert had shown him how to approach the work of research, but he lacked the scholarly mind and found it difficult to concentrate.

At last the article was finished and sent off to Raoul-Duval. While Maupassant impatiently awaited its appearance, he was shocked to learn that another competitor had entered the field. It was a M. Filon, formerly tutor to the Prince Imperial, and *La Nation* had begun to publish his articles on literary subjects.

Maupassant could no longer control his impatience and again called on the politician. The latter was still friendly and smooth, but there was something evasive in his manner when the young man taxed him with his promise. It was now obvious that Filon had already been adopted as literary critic, and Maupassant had to be satisfied with another assurance that a place would be found for him on the staff.

The article on Balzac duly appeared in *La Nation*, and

Maupassant at once dashed off a review of Richepin's *Les Morts Bizarres*. This was turned down by the editor but so politely that the clerk decided to try again. This time he wrote a study of the French poets of the sixteenth century, which *La Nation* accepted but seemed in no hurry to print.

Irritated by the delay he wrote a bitter report to Flaubert.

"I did a third article which Raoul-Duval seemed to like. He asked permission to cut down several phrases because in journalism *you need short sentences*. He told me the article would appear very shortly. I'm still waiting ! ! !

"He asked me to do some dramatic reviews. I chose *L'Ami Fritz*, which is certainly the best thing that's been put on this year. That's the view of Daudet, Zola and Turgenev, and, what's more, it's my own. To-day I learn that M. Raoul-Duval thought the piece idiotic and very poor, and tells everyone to stay away. Is that his view or that of the Bonapartist clique ? I don't know, but my article did not please him, although my praise of the piece was couched most moderately.

"Well, I see with my own eyes, I judge according to my own views, and I refuse to say that black is white, because that happens to be someone else's opinion. I'm thinking of doing another trial article for *La Nation*, after which I'll give up. Not only have I spent twenty-five francs on books and theatre tickets — an expense which I would not otherwise have incurred — but I've lost a month's work, which is far more important. This continued indecision worries me, these irregular articles disturb me, and I'm still in the dark. M. Raoul-Duval is still undecided, and, in his fear of the editorial opposition to a newcomer, he may keep me waiting all through the spring, asking me for trial articles which lead to nothing and are not paid for. . . .

"M. Turgenev told me yesterday that you might not be back before the end of February, and that saddens me. I have a great need to chat with you; my brain is full of things to tell you. I'm suffering from too much spiritual self-denial, which is just as bad as protracted chastity. . . .

" Come back quickly, dear master. I salute and await you with filial affection.

" Yours,

"GUY DE MAUPASSANT."

Flaubert grieved for the luckless young man and advised him to take a strong line.

" This is what I'd do in your place," he writes on January 8, 1877. " I would go to Duval and tell him what you've told me. Make him see that you cannot afford to go on wasting your time. But perhaps you would rather wait until I get back on the 3rd of February. We shall greet each other on Sunday three weeks. What a lot of things we shall have to talk about ! "

The article appeared a few days later, and Flaubert immediately wrote to congratulate his pupil. The study was excellent, he thought, although the author had not quite done justice to Ronsard.

Maupassant continued to write poems and articles with little success. He had found it difficult enough to place his articles, and, when Flaubert quarrelled with Catulle Mendès, he flatly refused to take sides. Mendès had printed a most offensive article on Renan, which greatly annoyed Flaubert. No man was ever more loyal to his friends, particularly when they were unjustly attacked, and Flaubert at once decided to sever all relations with Mendès. Always impulsive, he told the unfortunate editor to cancel his name from the list of subscribers and vowed that he would never again contribute to the paper. Maupassant was urged to follow suit, but he was far too practical and knew Flaubert too well to regard the breach as irreparable. Instead of turning his back on Mendès, he contributed an article on

Flaubert which was accepted by *La République des Lettres*.[1]

That article deserves more than a passing word. Its appearance in the circumstances proved that Maupassant was not Flaubert's boot-licker. He loved the author of *Madame Bovary* like a son, but would not sacrifice his independence as an artist. Opportunism may have played some part in his decision, yet one cannot help admiring his courage in refusing to be involved in Flaubert's quarrel.

The article itself gave Flaubert enormous pleasure. He was miserably poor and had suffered much, but it was surely something to see this generous tribute from his pupil's pen.

" You have treated me with the tenderness of a son," he wrote. " My niece is enthusiastic about your work. She thinks it is the best thing that has yet appeared on her uncle. I think so too, but dare not say so."

While Maupassant was thrusting his articles into the hands of anyone who might help to place them, he had not given up his old Bohemian ways. The strain and disappointments of the literary life had indeed made him keener to enjoy the crude pleasures of the river. He became terrified at the thought of losing his muscles and becoming pigeon-chested like the other clerks in his department. He had to work at his articles and verses because they might open the doors of his prison, but every possible minute was spent on the river. To snatch an hour or two in his boat became almost a necessity in the evenings. When the weather was bad and there was no money for a woman, he would go down to his little shed by the Seine and paint his boat. Sometimes passers-by would stop in amazement as they saw a young man dive off a tempting bridge in mid-winter. No, it was not a suicide, for he would soon come up and shout some obscene remark at the spectators !

Nor did his literary activity in any way interfere with the

[1] Flaubert, consummately inconsistent, at once suggested that Maupassant should write to thank Mendès for using the article !

usual week-ending on the river.   He was still the same high-spirited whoremonger.   Only Robert Pinchon, among his friends, knew that there was often a crackle of hysteria in his roaring laughter.   Nobody else suspected that Maupassant already suffered from headaches which drilled him with pain. Those who saw his ruddy face and noted the powerful shoulders would never have guessed that he occasionally threw down his pen and waited until the darkness had swept from his eyes.   But when the gay young bachelors had set off for Paris in their yawl, one of the bargees at Argenteuil would sometimes detect the sickly fragrance of ether where M. de Maupassant had hung up his clothes.

There was nothing wrong with him, he reassured himself, as he carried his skiff, too impatient to wait for the lock-keeper.   His right shoulder was already a little hollowed from carrying that boat, but he could not waste a second of his valuable leisure.   Only when he was cutting through the water, with the wind thrashing his cheeks, did he feel free again.

There were few oarsmen on the Seine with his physical strength and endurance.   His friends accepted his long stretches of rowing as commonplace, but an athlete would have been astounded and horrified by this young clerk's utter lack of discipline.   He often sandwiched a long day's clerical work between two hard spells on the river, morning and evening, and still found the energy to write an article or poem !   And after a vigorous swim in the river, when it was so cold that the beggars huddled gratefully in their rags, he would wander about the boulevards, eager for the vicious caresses of a *poule* !

Occasionally he became very anxious about his health. These headaches were painful, yet his muscles were still enormous and he could row as well as ever.   He cursed his misfortune in having to slave in an unhealthy office, and attributed all his misfortunes to lack of fresh air.   His eye trouble was due to overstrain, he told himself, but there was no way out. The Ministry meant bread, and something might yet come of his articles and verse.

He was not finding it easy to place his work. Ballande still waited for the play which would cost nothing to put on, and the editors were showing no great eagerness to welcome his work in spite of Flaubert's warm recommendation. The author of *Madame Bovary* refused, however, to be disheartened by this lack of recognition. He was more perturbed by the symptoms of which his pupil continually complained. " Always women, little pig," he had once said in jest, but now his counsel took a more serious note.

" I urge you to moderate your life in the interests of Literature," he wrote. " Be careful ! Everything depends on the end in view. A man who sets up as an artist has no right to live like others."

Sane advice, but Maupassant could not, or would not, give up his violent pleasures. It was in any case too late, although no one, least of all the victim, suspected that he already carried his own death warrant.

In 1877 he applied to the Minister for leave of absence.

" M. de Maupassant, third-class clerk at the central office, requires leave to take the waters at Louèche," reports the Health Officer.

Leave is granted for two months' absence with pay, and Maupassant goes off to Switzerland in search of health. As the train screeches delightedly, he smiles to think of the dust that will rise upon his hated desk. He spits out of the window, spits as only a man can who has just escaped two months of nicely regulated deference and routine. He sits for hours trying to study the scenery, bemused by a feeling that there is something bogus and illicit in this sense of release.

His optimism has halted by instinct, checked by something very like fear.

CHAPTER III

A PROSECUTION

MAUPASSANT'S tragedy is a drama of undetected disease. His blood was infected with syphilis, a germ which does not at first affect the physical appearance of its victim. Poor Maupassant came back from Switzerland little improved in condition and pathetically unaware of the real cause of his headaches. Thirty years were to pass before Wassermann made his famous tests of the blood serum, but long before then the great writer would be in his grave.

When the headaches left him, Maupassant at once resumed his old life. Rowing, whoring, verse-making – he seemed indefatigable. In appearance he was still the powerful young Norman whose round and rosy face gave the lie to all his complaints about ill-health. He took ether and spent most of his spare cash on drugs, but many young artists are hypochondriacs and it was easy for others to pooh-pooh his grumblings. Everyone knows that head-aches are usually due to eye trouble. " I must be overdoing things," he told himself. " Too much reading in that damned office. I must try not to write at night."

But his head still ached and he became irritable and depressed. The reports of his superiors were no longer polite. " An intelligent clerk who might be useful one day," wrote his chief, " but he is slack, not energetic, and I'm afraid his tastes and talents distract him from his office work." That was a fair criticism, although the young clerk's slackness was only partly due to his literary activities. He could no longer hide his contempt for his fellow-clerks, and now shed all pretence of civility.

With Flaubert spending so much of his time at Croisset, Maupassant felt utterly isolated. During the summer months he laughed and joked on the river with his friends, but winter meant peaked faces and gloom. He could still row on the Seine, but there was no laughter, no flirtation, none of that languid joy that sunshine and warmth always brought to his limbs.

" I imagine that you are feeling very lonely, my dear mother, and the coming winter frightens me on your account," he writes in the autumn. " December terrifies me also; it is the black month, the deep, sinister month, the midnight of the year. They've already given us lamps at the office, and in a month we shall be lighting the fire. I'm looking forward so terribly to the day when we can put them out."

He could discuss the weather or his work with Madame de Maupassant, but shrank from adding to her worries by telling her of his real unhappiness. Only Flaubert, among his friends, could understand what he was suffering at his miserable desk. Writing from Paris on July 5, 1878, Maupassant says[1]: " My office wears me out. I can't work, my mind is barren, worn out by the arithmetic which I have to do from morn till night. Sometimes I see so clearly the uselessness of everything, the evil of creation, the emptiness of the future (whatever it may turn out to be), that I feel a melancholy apathy for everything and I just want to stay put, quietly in a corner, without hopes or worries.

" I live quite alone because other people bore me, and I bore myself because I can't work. My ideas are dull and commonplace and my spirit is so crushed that I cannot even express them. I make fewer mistakes in my arithmetic, which shows how stupid I've become.

" From time to time I spend an hour or so with Madame

[1] Pol Neveux, *Boule de Suif, Correspondance*, p. 106. A mine of interesting information on Maupassant as letter-writer.

Brainne, who is the best woman in the world and whom I admire with all my heart. I tell her many stories which she thinks rather indecent. She considers me too unsentimental and relates her dreams while I talk about realities. I meet other beautiful ladies at her house and whisper lewdities to them — I fall into discredit because I won't kneel before them. . . .

"Every evening I say to myself, like Saint Anthony, 'Another day, another day gone.' They are long days, long and sad, between an idiotic colleague and a chief who —— me. I don't talk to the former and never reply to the latter. Both rather despise me and consider me unintelligent, and that consoles me."

Madame de Maupassant, still clinging to her literary ambitions, imagined that Guy's pessimism was entirely due to the life of the office. A letter which she wrote to Flaubert at this time points directly to that state of mind.

"Since you call Guy your adopted son, you will forgive me, my dear Gustave, if I instinctively address myself to you when I think of the boy. The tenderness which you have shown him has been so gentle that I can't help hoping that you assume quasi-paternal duties. I know you are acquainted with the facts ; and the poor clerk at the Ministry has already told you of his unhappiness. You have proved yourself wonderful as ever, you have consoled him, and he hopes that he will soon be able to leave his prison and bid farewell to the boss who guards the door."

Flaubert good-naturedly took the hint and began to pull more wires on behalf of his pupil. Unlike Madame de Maupassant, he could not honestly recommend the young clerk to give up his work for a literary career, but he was prepared to assist him to find a better place. Chance favoured Maupassant. Later that year, Agénor Bardoux, an old friend of Flaubert's, was appointed Minister of Public Instruction. Something of a poet himself, the

Minister was flattered by Flaubert's friendship and listened politely to what the author of *Madame Bovary* had to say. Would the Minister transfer M. de Maupassant from the Admiralty to his own office ?

Bardoux hedged and scratched a cautious ear while Flaubert read " Au Bord de l'Eau " to him. He did not wish to displease his friend but was not over-anxious to add another poet to his department. Things dragged and the application was almost lost to view under a pyramid of red tape. Months passed and still nothing had happened. Meanwhile the young clerk was finding himself exposed to the pettiest backbiting in his own office. Restrictions had tightened up and he was now sat under the watchful eye of a man who spread dizzy columns of figures before him. No longer any time for day-dreaming and writing verses, only an occasional glance at the door, as if he expected Flaubert to come rushing in with the news of his reprieve !

Forced to exclude his literary work from office hours, Maupassant would hurry back to his room as soon as he had swallowed his dinner at some modest restaurant. Drugs cost money, and each little jar of syrup drained the savings he had set aside for a summer holiday. But he was still hoping for a literary success which would solve all his problems. We do not know what he had in mind at this time but he was certainly sketching a plan for some novel.

" I'm working at the moment on my story," he wrote to his mother. " It's awfully difficult, especially to put everything in its proper place. In four or five months I shall be well on the way."

This idea seems to have been shelved, like so many others that occupied him while he was desperately searching for plots. One or two stories had appeared in illustrated weeklies,[1] but he seemed to be more successful with his verse. His

---

[1] " Le Donneur d'eau bénite " was published by the *Moniteur Universel* under the name of G. de Valmont.

FM

poem, " La Dernière Escapade," had been accepted by the *République des Lettres* after being turned down by the conservative *Revue des Deux Mondes*. It had been reprinted within a short time by *Le Gaulois*, a compliment which was not lost upon the poet.

Flaubert himself seemed pleased with this piece of work, and did what he could to push his pupil into circles where a young man's name might be remembered. He was often invited to read his poems in drawing-rooms by ladies who prided themselves on their literary taste. This was the recognised method of making a poet known, but Maupassant gained little more than raw material for later novels from these polite *séances*.

Far more welcome was the news that Bardoux had at last agreed to find him a place in his department. It was torture to wait so many months, but Flaubert would not fail. In the autumn Maupassant had rushed off to Etretat, where his mother was suffering from her old nervous trouble. Flaubert had also come to see her, but she could talk of nothing but her son and urged her old friend to continue his efforts to have Guy transferred.

The two men had taken the opportunity to explore the coast, as Flaubert was still looking for the right setting for *Bouvard et Pécuchet*. Maupassant seemed a new man as he pointed out the features of this landscape which he knew and loved so well. Eager to help his master, he drew elaborate sketches and planned walking-tours which might be of service to the novelist.

Back in Paris, he was again despondent and irritable. The clerks seemed even meaner and his duties more trivial. Then, one afternoon, he approached the head of his department and opened the dialogue which he had so often rehearsed in his mind.

" I am going over to the Ministry of Public Instruction, monsieur," he calmly announced.

" But you can't do that," spluttered the outraged official. " I won't allow it ! The whole thing must go through the regular channels."

The clerk smiled ironically. " You have nothing to say, monsieur. This matter is over our heads. It is a question of Ministers now ! " With that parting shot Maupassant threw down his pen and sauntered from the office. The rest of the story has been told by Henri Roujon, who had been on the staff of *La République des Lettres* and was now working in the Ministry of Instruction. Maupassant rushed into his office with a beaming face.

" I've left the Admiralty ! I'm in with you now ! " he shouted. " Fun, isn't it ? "

" We began by dancing round a desk dedicated for the occasion into an altar to friendship," says Roujon. " Then we toasted Bardoux, protector of Literature. I think Maupassant finished up with a spate of insults – a last farewell to his old chiefs in the Admiralty."

All seemed to go well. Maupassant enjoyed the companionship of men of culture, and congratulated himself daily on his release from the Ministry of Marine.

" Now you will be left alone more," writes Flaubert. " You will start working again." Having tasted a little liberty, however, Maupassant could not be content with anything short of complete independence. He at once complains of lack of money.

" When I was at the Admiralty," he grumbles to Flaubert, " I had a railway pass and only paid a quarter of the usual fare. I could get to Rouen and back for nine francs. To-day, a second-class ticket costs me thirty-six francs and, for a man who spends hardly four francs a day, that's quite an item. Anyhow, I shall see how my finances stand at the end of the month, and I do hope I shall be able to spend a day with you."

Apart from his small salary, Maupassant seems to have

had little cause for complaint. He had been appointed
private secretary to Xavier Charmes, a genial young man
who was himself a lover of Literature. The two men were
spiritually in sympathy, but Maupassant could not have
shared an office with an angel !

" My dear master," he grouses to the long-suffering
Flaubert, " I shall always be a victim of Ministers. For
eight days now I have wanted to write to you without finding
half an hour to do so. I am on splendid terms with Charmes,
my chief: we are almost on an equal footing. He has given
me a nice desk. But I belong to him; he unloads half his
work on me; I'm walking about and writing from morning
till night; I'm an object tied to an electric bell. To cut a
long story short, I shall be no more free than in the Admiralty. We are on pleasant terms here, that is the only
advantage; and the work is much less dull. Charmes has
promised to find me time to do my own work. Yes, indeed !
I'm useful to him, and he takes advantage of it. It's always
the same."

That was a most ill-natured view of things, but one
cannot overlook Maupassant's state of mind. He was
twenty-nine with nothing more than a salary of £5 10s.
a month to show for his seven years in the galleys. He had
tasted printer's ink and heard the sweet applause of a
drawing-room audience. Only the need of his miserable
little pittance separated him from the leisure to write. The
Ministry of Public Instruction had dangled before him as
an easy means of earning a salary and working at his verse.
To his embittered mind, it was not so very different. The
fittings were glossy but an office is always an office ! He
was back in the cage again.

Maupassant's illness seemed to make him suspicious and
unfriendly; only his affection for Flaubert survived. His
mentor was at this time in great financial distress, having
lost all his savings in an attempt to save a relative from

bankruptcy. Wires were pulled strenuously and M. Ferry, who had succeeded Bardoux as Minister of Public Instruction, finally offered a pension to the unfortunate novelist. But such matters move slowly, and it was Maupassant who kept his master informed of developments and encouraged him to be hopeful. No son could have taken a more personal interest in the affair than did this young clerk.

" I told you they would offer you 5,000 francs, and they will," he assured Flaubert. " But you know how long they take over the slightest thing. And this is quite a big thing, because they are completely changing the pension system and putting it on a more equitable basis."

Flaubert's pension claimed his affectionate interest, but he could muster no enthusiasm for his other tasks. Xavier Charmes, his kindly superior, tried hard to find him congenial work, but Maupassant refused to exert himself. Asked to draw up reports on a variety of subjects, he begged to be excused.

" It's the fault of my work at the Admiralty," he explained. " As soon as there is the trace of officialdom in what I have to write, the official style cramps me and I simply can't get out." He therefore declined to do anything even remotely connected with Literature, and asked permission to handle only routine matters like registration checking !

This curious attitude was perhaps dictated by his instinctive fear of becoming too interested in his bureaucratic duties. He had seen men of talent lulled into acquiescence by the hope of promotion, and may well have been on his guard against a similar fate. Liberty implies responsibility, and he had before him the example of men so taken up with their duties that they closed their ledgers reluctantly and seemed apathetic until the doors of the Ministry re-opened the next morning !

There seemed little danger of such a fate in his case. M. Charmes shrugged his elegant shoulders and continued to show every kindness to this curious young man. Soon Maupassant was again finding it possible to write verse during office hours. He had his own room – a damp ground-floor office – where he could unveil his Muse behind a thick screen of registers. According to official reports, he used to stay away from the Ministry two or three days a week. Bad health was the excuse if not always the true reason. He suffered from painful headaches – his letters to Flaubert and his mother are filled with symptoms – but he had not altogether lost his schoolboyish love of malingering. Nor did his ailments appear to have interfered with his pursuit of women or his boating excursions. One may, perhaps, be forgiven for suggesting that M. Xavier Charmes would have found him at his work in his apartment when he failed to appear at his desk.

He was now living at 19, Rue Clauzel where he occupied two small rooms and a kitchen. He seemed to leave his ill-humour at the Ministry, and was very popular with his neighbours. He was the only male tenant in the house ! Old friends – Pinchon, " Petit-Bleu " and the others – still called on him, but new faces had already made their appearance. Like calls to like, and Maupassant had gradually become part of a circle of young men who dreamed mightily but had as yet produced little.

Maupassant had almost literally drifted into this clique which was so dramatically to change his destiny. His verse had made him known to Catulle Mendès who sometimes asked him to dine in the Rue de Bruxelles. Here he made the acquaintance of J.-K. Huysmans who, like himself, had entered the civil service after a short period in the Army. He was, however, a most successful bureaucrat and stood high in official favour. Only two years older than Maupassant, Joris-Karl Huysmans was much further advanced as a writer. Although his first book, *Le Drageoir à épices*, had sold only four copies one or two critics had been kind.

When Maupassant first met Huysmans, the latter had just brought out his novel, *Marthe, histoire d'une fille*, which had to be smuggled in from Belgium because of the French censor. The respectable civil servant was soon in trouble with the authorities, but men like the Goncourts and Zola were sympathetic and he refused to be discouraged. Maupassant liked this slim young intellectual with his silky fringe of beard. Huysmans, sickly and neurotic, always discussed his symptoms with Maupassant, who enjoyed this kind of talk and never hesitated to cross-examine doctors on the most delicate subjects.

Through Huysmans he came across Henry Céard, a tall, soldierly-looking man who favoured a monocle and a toothbrush moustache. A year younger than Maupassant, he had studied medicine before taking up a post in the Ministry of War. Although a pessimist and something of an æsthete, Céard had the knack of friendship and seemed to know everybody. He had met Zola, his friend and literary idol, under rather amusing conditions. One Sunday afternoon he had just come from a Manet exhibition of pictures refused by the Salon, when he decided to call on Zola, whom he had long worshipped from a respectful distance. With beating heart the young man rang the bell and sent up his card. Unfortunately, his card bore the word " Bercy," his country address, and Zola at once concluded that his visitor was a wine merchant ! He was nevertheless too polite to turn away the salesman and agreed to see him. The mistake soon evaporated as Céard explained that he wished to congratulate Zola on his Rougon-Macquart novels. The worthy Emile was touched: he was still the neglected author who had not yet forgotten his own early struggles. He would always remember the time when he had worked at

the docks for sixty francs a day, before finding a berth as a
book-packer with Messrs. Hachette. Yes, it was pleasant
to sip the nectar of a young man's flattery and feel that his
writing inspired somebody, if not the book-buying public !

" Your friends will be welcome," he assured Céard, who
went off joyfully and soon returned with Huysmans on his
arm !

Through Céard, Maupassant had come across another
young writer, Léon Hennique. The son of a General, he
allowed himself a monocle and a goatee beard, but there was
nothing of the dilettante in his work. Like the others, he
felt at war with tradition and was prepared to tilt his pen at
all who denied freedom to the artist.

Hennique had first met a young poet named Paul Alexis
at the offices of *La République des Lettres*. Alexis, like
Maupassant, was still making a painful début with his
verse, but his name was already known to Paris through
a daring hoax. Eager to find a publisher for his poems,
he had come from the provinces a year or two before
Maupassant. It was not easy, but a friend, Marius Roux, soon
thought of a scheme to persuade the reluctant publishers. It
was very simple: he suddenly put forward a number of
poems which he declared to be the unpublished work of
Baudelaire. Suspecting nothing, a grateful publisher
snapped up Alexis's poems and printed a liberal edition.
The hoax was soon exploded by the indignant editor of
Baudelaire's work, but Paul Alexis was launched as a poet.

Huysmans introduced Alexis to his friends Hennique
and Henry Céard. The following week Maupassant made
his appearance. Henceforth they were a solid little band of
young writers, sworn enemies of established names and all
opposed to the pretty-pretty school of romantic writers.
They were young and enthusiastic, reeking with Schopenhauer and utterly dissatisfied with established literary
standards. Sheer rhetoric and phrase-mongering they

professed to despise, and all talked rather vaguely of
" Realism." " The novel must renew its contacts with
Life," they shouted. " Nothing must be hidden. Man
should be studied in a documentary, scientific way. Plot,
imagination, and that kind of thing don't really matter.
Observation and absolute accuracy count above all else."

Youth and a common background of unpublished
masterpieces were enough to mould these five young men
into a firm clique. Every week they met for dinner at a
restaurant in Montmartre. The food was bad, but they
expected rather too much for two francs a head. Here they
spent hours, shouting and arguing, spilling their likes and
dislikes with all the prodigality of youth. Maupassant –
who was better known to them as " Guy de Valmont," his
pseudonym – had very little to contribute to all this talk of
style and æsthetics. He was a healthy oarsman who had
written one or two good poems and bragged about his
women. The others did not pay him too much attention.
He was Flaubert's " pet " and therefore deserved some
respect, particularly as they all admired *Madame Bovary*.

Sometimes his voice would rise above the others, but only
to emphasise some jest. No one looked less like a man of
letters than this red-faced Norman who had once cut a
gadfly's sting from his hand with a pocket-knife. Yet he
was good company, with his cruel imitations of civil servants.
He seemed to have a genius for hitting off the weaknesses
of those about him. No one was spared. Paul Alexis was
a favourite butt because writing was such a mental agony to
him, and Maupassant never ceased from chaffing the poet.

" He is doing a Flaubert ! " he used to observe slyly,
and the unfortunate Alexis would hurriedly rouse himself
from a reverie !

When it was a question of a dinner, Maupassant was
consulted first, out of respect for his enormous appetite.
And he was always changing the rendezvous in the

hope that he would succeed in finding a cosy little restaurant where they could eat satisfactorily for two francs each ! It was not easy. The little café in the Rue Coustou soon lost their patronage through some putrescent kidneys, and they wandered off to a noisy place, half dairy, half restaurant, where the windows rattled all the time.

Not infrequently they adjourned to Maupassant's apartment, but they were always certain of meeting again " *chez* Flaubert " in the Rue Murillo every Sunday afternoon. Here they could see and hear the author of *Madame Bovary*, whom nothing seemed to conquer. Tall and square, with his long moustache lapsing over his mouth, he would dominate the room, physically and spiritually. Freedom for the artist, he yelled; we don't need schools or groups ! Having aired all the accumulated prejudices of the previous week, he would sink back and watch the others. Maupassant was always there: he looked so strong and healthy that it was difficult to believe he ever suffered from a headache. There he sat, square-shouldered and calm, with a faint smile on his face. Close behind, attentive but eager to burst into the conversation, were Céard, Huysmans and the others. " Naturalists," they call themselves, and Flaubert shudders like a wet terrier. He cannot stomach these silly affectations. As if an artist needs a label !

Flaubert cannot rid himself of the feeling that Emile Zola is seducing these young writers. They listen tensely as Zola talks in his high-pitched voice. " A Colossus with dirty feet," muses Flaubert, " but a Colossus for all that." Zola's eyes glint behind the lenses. His face is pale but he is excited. " Analysis, not synthesis," he repeats. " They will laugh at first but they'll finish by imitating us. A new century of Literature has begun." The author of *Madame Bovary* smiles into his enormous moustache. He sees something ironical in his position of patron of the new Naturalist School.

He respected the desire for documentation, to be sure, but at heart he was a romantic. Style and accuracy of detail were essential to him, but his so-called " Realism " was merely the road to a romantic goal, not the goal itself. Yet, as he listened to Zola, he was almost convinced. " Observation and experience," the shrill voice repeats. " We must fight for our principles. Shall we allow magistrates to set themselves up as arbiters of literary taste ? " The young men shout their defiance, and even Flaubert joins in. He can never forget the storm over the publication of *Madame Bovary*.

With Zola well launched, one scarcely notices that Turgenev has come in. He lounges in his arm-chair with his arms limp and his long legs outstretched. He is very much at home among these Frenchmen, this gentle Russian giant whose flowing beard and silvery hair give him the appearance of a genial professor. He has " the air of an Eternal Father or a River God from Ovid," says Maupassant,[1] who greatly enjoyed the Russian's subtle tales of the supernatural. There was a lazy charm in his conversation, a hesitancy, which sometimes deceived those who were not qualified to receive his judgments.

He carefully sets aside his tall hat, and Flaubert gives him a bright smile of welcome. The Russian smiles back understandingly – he still has Flaubert's last letter in his pocket.

" To my mind," Flaubert had said, " Realism should only be a springboard. Our friends have persuaded themselves that it is everything ! That materialism makes me see red, and every Monday I get irritated when I read Zola's articles. After the Realists, we have the Naturalists and the Impressionists. What a procession ! A set of humbugs who want to persuade us and themselves that they've discovered the Mediterranean." Maupassant bows

[1] In the story " La Peur."

politely to the great Turgenev and asks himself whether it would not be a good idea to follow up his article on Flaubert with one on the Russian novelist. The latter is very polite and gracious to Flaubert's pet, but the young clerk is not yet aware that Turgenev thinks little of his possibilities as a poet.

Taine, the famous historian, peeps in timidly, bringing with him the musty smell of old documents. He goes out very little, but would not willingly miss one of M. Flaubert's Sunday afternoons. Like Flaubert, he recognises Zola's power, but is suspicious of the new Naturalism. Zola smiles benevolently on the famous philosopher who had complimented him on his *Thérèse Raquin*. Later, when Taine took fright at Zola's noisy literary campaign, he learned that the good Emile did not mince words. " He crept into history like an uneasy rat," was his stinging comment on the man to whom he now bowed so politely.

It was an atmosphere of exasperation and highly seasoned polemics. Behind all the noisy proclamations, private ambitions were shuttered and many judgments reserved. Only the young men, eager to shed their last drop of ink in the cause of Liberty, listened eagerly and made ready to storm the shadows.

But it was at Zola's flat in the Rue St. Georges that they felt most at home. There was something warm and friendly about these Thursday evenings with Emile. He was now thirty-seven and had already done *Thérèse Raquin* and the Rougon novels. A force in Literature, as even his enemies admitted, but his books had to be asked for at the stalls. He had not yet forgotten the days when he had no coal in his grate and his coat dangled from a pawnbroker's hook.

Maupassant always enjoyed these evenings " *chez* Zola." This was not the absurd Bohemia of Murger. All these young men were working for a living and laughed at the idea of black hats and long hair. Even Murger had admitted that it was possible to be a poet and still have warm feet and three square meals a day !

Zola worked harder than a bricklayer without parading himself as a professional man of letters. He alone, among this little company, was a full-time author, and the others admired and envied him. Apart from being their senior in years and experience, he was also a married man with a comfortable if unpretentious flat. And Maupassant, like the other young cynics, found it remarkably restful to be welcomed in this house, although a wife and her mother-in-law were in constant attendance !

While they argue and plot, Madame Zola brews the tea. Maupassant relaxes in that atmosphere but contributes very little to the discussion. It is Paul Alexis, among the young warriors, who gives Zola his cues and regards him with the shining eyes of a disciple. The others listen respectfully and Maupassant finds himself speculating on the black-bearded novelist who sits astride his chair like a schoolboy. Zola is a hard worker who sits down to his desk at nine every morning and burrows for hours in books on biology and medicine. He studies all kinds of technical works and masters details of trades which may be useful in his novels about working men. On his desk are piles of notes, probably the material for his next book, *L'Assommoir*.

A painter called Cézanne comes in, and the atmosphere is at once charged with violence. He is a great friend of Zola's, this bald, sunburned artist who argues with every-body in a Southern accent. One can't help looking at that ugly but interesting face – hooked nose, spiky beard and beady aggressive eyes. He is living in a studio in the Rue Beautreillis and spends most of his time in the Louvre. The Salon has indignantly rejected all he produces, but he goes on painting his own vision of colour and design. People call him a madman, but Zola has known him since they were

schoolboys. He respects Cézanne without understanding
his work. A very eccentric chap, says Maupassant to
himself, as he runs a critical eye over the red waistcoat
and checked trousers. Cézanne sucks loudly at his pipe and
suddenly flings his dirty cap into a far corner. It lies there
all the evening in the shadow of the only picture in the
room – a Manet portrait of Zola.

Emile is lucky, thinks Maupassant enviously. His wife
and mother look after him and he has friends and the ear
of one or two publishers. But most of all he envies him
his leisure to write. Zola is not well off – far from it – but
he has two or three novels to his name and can now afford
to work at Literature alone.

While he tries to shake off his growing depression,
Cézanne's voice rumbles out of the tobacco haze. He is
always grousing at something, that painter, but he can be
witty, particularly when he is tilting at some established
name. He is philosophical, even a little pathetic about his
own failure, but nothing can shake his judgment. Every
time Zola opens his mouth, Cézanne stands beside him
ready to pick up a phrase, turn it inside out and fling it
back. The young men listen, half-amused, to this extraordinary debate in which each protagonist pours his judgments into a phrase, scarcely waiting for the other to
retaliate.[1]

Claude Monet's name comes up and someone mentions
that the painter is still fighting a losing battle with the
bailiffs. That is the signal for Cézanne to wrench a newspaper from his pocket and attack some stupid critic. And
while Cézanne growls his disgust, snapping at timid
interruptions, Emile Zola exchanges a look with his wife.
That glance means that something must be done about

[1] M. Barbusse shows the remarkable relationship between Zola and
Cézanne in his *Life of Zola* (Dent). It is particularly valuable on the
background of Naturalism.

Monet.   Can they spare fifty francs for the unfortunate
painter ?

Suddenly Zola's novel, *L'Assommoir*, burst upon Paris.
It was crude, gross but powerful, a mighty study of drunk-
enness which could not be ignored.   Zola submitted the
novel to the editors of *Le Bien Public*, who agreed to publish
it in serial form.   Eight thousand francs for the author and
a ready-made public !   It was a fine prospect, but prudish
minds were waiting to be shocked just around the corner !
Soon the unfortunate editors of *Le Bien Public* were sub-
merged with complaints from outraged readers.   Subscrip-
tions were withdrawn and Zola was asked to take his novel
elsewhere.

" Let me finish the other instalments in my paper,"
suggested Catulle Mendès, and Zola gladly agreed to
publish in *La République des Lettres*.

But it was an uphill battle, and the printer of Mendès's
journal suddenly received a visit from the authorities.   A
solemn hint was dropped and taken, and the printer refused
to go on with the work.   Publication was interrupted for a
week before the next instalment reappeared.

This free advertisement did the author more good than
harm.   When *L'Assommoir* appeared in book form there
was already an eager public, and the bookstalls were
besieged.   Everyone discussed Zola, particularly those
who professed to be shocked, and thousands of copies were
sold.[1]   It was Zola's first substantial success.   He now
counted as a literary force, an author who was *read*, but it
proved to him that the battle had only just begun.

From all sides came outbursts of abuse.   Zola was accused
of being a scavenger and a vulgar sensationalist.   He had
discredited the French working man, and many people
discovered a sudden affection for the proletariat.   For once

[1] Within four years 100,000 copies had been printed.

the critics linked hands with the lay reader and danced round the author, screaming " Pig ! " His writing was " putrid," his treatment of the subject exaggerated. But underneath all the abuse was the charge of " bad taste." Even people who liked and respected him shook their heads uneasily.

Gustave Flaubert could not muster much enthusiasm for the novel. Like Anatole France he thought the book " powerful but not lovable," and wrote to Turgenev of his misgivings concerning this new and so-called " Naturalism." The author of *Madame Bovary* disliked the novel on æsthetic grounds, and hated the very sound of the word " Naturalist," but those who shrieked against *L'Assommoir* were threatening the writer's freedom of expression.

" To my great friend, Gustave Flaubert, in hatred of ' taste,' " Zola had written on the fly-leaf of *L'Assommoir*. And Flaubert realised that he was slowly being enrolled in a cause which he had resisted from the first.

Maupassant and the other young men had no such misgiving. They saw in these attacks upon Zola a chance to prove their loyalty and devotion. For many months they had groused and ranted against public opinion, which lapped up romantic nonsense and persecuted those who looked life in the face. Emile Zola had struck the first blow: it was for them to rally to his banner and march forward. Neither Maupassant nor any of the others had a very clear idea where they were to march, but they were intoxicated with words and had waited so long for a Cause ! Here was a perfect opportunity to cock a public snoot at the bourgeoisie.

Huysmans sat down to write a highly eulogistic appreciation of *L'Assommoir* for a Belgian paper, but Zola's youthful bodyguard decided to mark their devotion rather more personally. And it was " the sturdy fellow " Maupassant, to use Zola's phrase, who suggested that they should entertain the author of *L'Assommoir*. But that dinner in the Rue Condorcet was not a success. The food was bad and the atmosphere so suffocating that the young men at once decided to make amends.

Maupassant was very taken with the idea of "compensating" Zola and guaranteed to bring Flaubert. The suggestion was applauded, and someone put forward the name of Edmond de Goncourt. Here was a most eligible candidate for the third place as guest of honour at this Naturalist banquet. He and his brother Jules could in fact lay claim to a very powerful influence on the new "School." These two gentlemen of letters had aimed at "Realism" in their work and an individual style in which to express themselves. The artist must have "style," they had insisted, but after that he must cherish a very real respect for documentation.

A passion for style had led the Goncourts into an artistic alliance with Flaubert, but there was nothing in common between their impressionistic and rather precious touches and the sonorous cadences of *Madame Bovary*. It was their pessimistic Realism and hatred of literary hypocrisy that really placed them in the vanguard of the New Realism. After the death of his brother, Edmond de Goncourt had become even more attached to Zola. They wrote each other warm letters of appreciation and seemed to be linked in eternal brotherhood.

When Maupassant suggested the dinner, nothing had yet come between the three guests of honour. Goncourt and Zola were still congratulating each other, and the former was eager to take his place on the Naturalist side of the barricade. Besides, the young men seemed to have invested him with an honorary presidency. It was all very flattering and he had so little to lose. His books were not selling and this was an excellent opportunity to align himself with a group which might have some influence. Flaubert's presence was, after all, a guarantee that these young writers

GM

" counted." Reasoning smoothly and choosing his phrases
like a diplomat who has salved his own conscience, Goncourt
announced himself pleased to attend the dinner.

The arrangements were left to Maupassant, who seemed
to have a knack for catering and entertainment. He at once
suggested the Restaurant Trapp, near the station in the
Rue St. Lazare, where he had once dined. The others
agreed, and, on the evening of April 16, 1877, the famous
dinner took place. The five young men – Céard, Alexis,
Hennique, Huysmans and Maupassant – had been joined
by Octave Mirbeau, a young journalist on *Le Gaulois* who
soon afterwards left the group. The three guests of honour
were, of course, Flaubert, Edmond de Goncourt and Zola,
but it was to the last-named that the incense really floated.

The menu and small talk at that dinner are of no importance, but the meeting itself was destined to play an active
part in Maupassant's career. Until that evening they had
been united in artistic and personal sympathy, aware of a
common impulse to defend *L'Assommoir* against the attacks
of a blind rabble. But this dinner at Trapp's gave these
young writers a sense of solidarity which had previously been
felt but not acknowledged. It marked, in fact, the public
launching of the Naturalist School. Henceforth, they could
regard themselves as a Committee of Defence with a fixed
literary *credo* and something approaching a programme.[1]

Maupassant did not seem to realise that the movement
fairly bulged with cross-purposes. He was far too primed with
hero-worship of Zola and Flaubert to be aware of any violent
cleavage between the views of the two men. Still locked in
his official prison and piling up manuscripts which he could
not place, poor Maupassant could see nothing but harmony
in this literary group. His very presence at this public
dinner made him feel " a literary man," and the atmosphere
of violence completed his pleasure. For the first time in his

[1] For a fuller account, see Barbusse : *Zola*, ch. vi.

literary life, he felt himself free of the amateur's gooseflesh. He was no longer Flaubert's nursling, and had enlisted with a group of men he respected. If he was wrong, he was erring with the mighty; a comforting thought to a beginner ! Besides, was he not marching shoulder to shoulder with Gustave Flaubert himself ?

While the traffic rattled the windows of the little restaurant, the author of *Madame Bovary* was laying down the law. He was soon knee-deep in fallen corpses. He pleaded violently for the freedom of the artist and did not hesitate to register his dislike of any " systems " or " schools of literary thought." Naturalism as a system was most distasteful to him. Zola listened politely and tried to pacify the Grand Old Man. Flaubert might dislike labels but he was nevertheless one of the founders of the School, if only for his respect for literary form. Whatever his private misgivings, poor Flaubert was now one of the honorary patrons of the movement !

Goncourt, as usual, spoke carefully and seemed a trifle *distrait*. Not so Zola, who was as violent, if not so personal, as Flaubert had been. The latter's conception of the aloof artist did not make a great appeal to Zola, but he could afford to overlook it. What seemed most important – and very gratifying – was that he was no longer living in the wilderness. His novel *L'Assommoir* was pouring from the presses and he seemed to have formed his own Defence Corps. It was all a little confusing, and nobody seemed quite certain where they were heading.[1]

The young men had really affiliated themselves to the author of *L'Assommoir*, although – with the exception of Alexis, Zola's personal disciple – they would not have admitted it. They had all reached a common stage of literary development, but had it not been for the attacks on Zola's novel they might well have remained unorganised.

[1] See Barbusse, p. 122, for an amusing sidelight on the Flaubert–Zola axis.

As it was, Maupassant soon found himself calling again at the flat in the Rue St. Georges.

These arrogant nurslings were, at first, a little disappointed at their failure to achieve notoriety. How discouraging to have a Cause of which the world remained unaware ! *L'Assommoir* had been published and reviled, but the attacks soon fizzled out. It really began to look as if the Naturalists would have to wait until Emile brought out another book ! Their only hope of advertising their aims was to goad the critics into a display of violence. And it was Paul Alexis who decided to achieve this publicity by attacking the new " Group " under cover of a pseudonym !

" There were half a dozen of them at Trapp's and there's still half a dozen," he wrote in a gossipy sheet called *Les Cloches de Paris*. " It's enough to make a cat laugh. We must smash them up because they threaten to spoil everything ! Ah, if they should happen to have pups ! " And Alexis attacked all the young writers, himself included, with the exception of Huysmans, who had " a bit of talent."

The critics allowed themselves a mental smile and nothing more. Zola was the " name," the big fish, and it was not worth hurling their javelins at the sprats who swam in attendance. To their great delight, however, one of the journalists on *Le Gaulois* devoted a page or two to poking fun at the group. He seemed to regard the young warriors as rich dilettantes whose tongues were busier than their quills.

" It is all very nice to meet and chat by the fireside. But, the devil take it, gentlemen, produce more if you want to become better known. Otherwise one might say that you do your fiction like a tapestry – *en famille*."

Zola was pardonably surprised at this article. So much seemed to be known about their private lives that one could have sworn that a member of the group had supplied the information ! But the article is particularly interesting because it omits all mention of Maupassant and Mirbeau.

Each of the others is discussed, and the conclusion is obvious. Mirbeau had never been more than a temporary member, and Maupassant had not really done enough to be of any account. He was still the uncertain dramatist with little more to his credit than a bawdy farce and one or two poems. "Au Bord de l'Eau" had first earned him the respect of the other young Naturalists. The poem was simple and vigorous – very much in the new tradition – but it was his status as Flaubert's disciple which had really won him his place in the coterie.

Echoes of his association with a disreputable group reached the Ministry, but Maupassant no longer seemed aware of his surroundings. He was still wretched, and the drudgery had become automatic.

"How I pity you for having no time to work," writes Flaubert in December 1878. "As if a good verse were not a hundred thousand times more *useful* to the instruction of the public than all the solemn small talk which keeps you busy!"

Meanwhile, Maupassant wrote and Flaubert continued to correct. One of his poems, "Désirs," did not at all appeal to his mentor, who laid a heavy hand upon it. Flaubert urged the young man not to publish the poem and Maupassant seems to have taken that advice. He did not submit the work to any of the periodicals, although the verses subsequently appeared in his collection *Des Vers*. By that time, however, the poem already carried the marks of Flaubert's hearty blue-pencilling.

Verses, stories, articles, poured from his pen, but he had little success apart from an occasional appearance in the newspapers and weeklies. At last, however, he finished writing *L'Histoire du Vieux Temps*, the play which the worthy Ballande had promised to put on "if it cost nothing to produce." This time there was no excuse, for Maupassant had made good his vow to write a play for "two characters and a fireplace."

The piece was duly rehearsed and produced on February 19, 1879 – a very proud but anxious day for the young author. It was not a triumphant success, but there was applause at the end and the piece finally found its way into the repertory of the Comédie Française.

Maupassant could not wait to read all the critics, and reported at once to Flaubert.

" My play succeeded even better than I dared to hope," he says. "Lapommeraye, Banville, Claretie were charming; *Le Petit Journal* very good, *Le Gaulois* quite pleasant, Daudet false. He has said: ' M. de Maupassant has brought back to the stage, without knowing it, the yellow roses of Alphonse Karr. Nobody has forgotten the subject, here it is again.' . . . Zola has said nothing. I hope he's waiting for next Monday. His crowd is a bit aloof, as I'm not ' naturalistic ' enough; none of them came up to shake hands after the show. Zola and his wife applauded warmly and congratulated me. Some other papers have written in praise of the piece but I haven't got hold of them yet . . ."[1]

The playwright could not hope for any real financial return, but his name was becoming known. Only one thing marred his pleasure – Flaubert had been prevented from attending through a fractured leg.

" My dear Master," wrote Maupassant, " *Le Figaro* has just announced that you have broken your leg. I am in an agony of anxiety. I've written to Pouchet [Flaubert's doctor], who should be at Croisset on Sunday. Your accident has laid you up, but if you could still manage to write me a line, please do so.

" I will do my best to try and get away one Sunday and come and see you, chat with you, bring you the news and atmosphere of Paris, and a little cheer in your sadness. Truly, this is the last straw. Does heaven, like Governments, hate Literature ? How wretched you must feel in

[1] Pol Neveux, p. 119.

bed, unable to work. When the heavy hand of Fate falls on somebody, it crushes him in every way.

" Your misfortune not only saddens, but disgusts me, because I can see the cowardliness of Destiny which strikes at your body, being unable to conquer your spirit. Could you not be brought here where at least we could see you ? . . .

" I found it impossible to go and see Madame Commanville [Flaubert's niece]: I am sorry and ashamed of not having done so. But I get to my office at nine o'clock and never leave before half past six at the earliest, which doesn't give a minute to spare. Naturally, I haven't been able to see Turgenev either."

" How angry I am to give up my seat to another," Flaubert writes in reply.

Apart from illness, the unhappy novelist was facing another financial crisis. Turgenev, Taine and Princess Mathilde pulled wires in the hope of finding him a sinecure, but his pride or their tactlessness made it difficult. But, with all these worries, it was his pupil's welfare which gave him most anxiety.

" How annoying not to be able to meet," he writes from Croisset. " I've so much to say and ask ! It will be good if I can get to Paris towards the end of April. We must resign ourselves, I suppose. How is your poor Mamma ? Where are you publishing *L'Histoire du Vieux Temps*? When I get back to Paris we must get Madame Pasca to play it at Princess Mathilde's. I undertake to put that through. Your old pal sends his tenderest regards."[1]

It seemed to Maupassant that his luck had changed. His eyes troubled him, but no doubt that would pass. He was still rowing and swimming like a professional, and – at twenty-nine – he could lay claim to a splendid physical appearance. Nobody could have guessed that he spent

[1] February 27, 1879. Unfortunately for Maupassant, the plan was shelved through Madame Pasca's illness.

hours at a desk, least of all that he carried a deadly bacillus in his blood. At the Ministry he was still earning a pittance, but there were compensations. His half-hearted attempts at efficiency were now taken for granted in his department. Indeed, there seemed to be no need to exert himself overmuch when so little satisfied his tolerant superiors. And, irony of ironies, this unwilling bureaucrat received the violet rosette of an Officer of the Academy towards the end of that year ! He wore it only once – at a Ministerial reception.

Like Flaubert, Maupassant despised official honours. Zola, on the other hand, nursed a sentimental patriotism and would have been delighted at this time with the Cross of the Legion of Honour. M. Bardoux, Flaubert's old friend, had promised his support in 1878, but the author of *L'Assommoir* waited ten years before he was nominated Chevalier.

In other directions Emile Zola was finding it not unprofitable to have shocked the bourgeois reading public. He was vilified and accused of being a pornographer, but the sales of *L'Assommoir* softened the blow. In the summer of 1878 he bought a charming little house on the Seine which was to change Maupassant's whole literary career. Nine thousand francs Zola had paid for it, and the young men could not suppress their keenness to see and share the new retreat. It sounded charming, this village of Médan, not far from Poissy. The " Naturalists " were eager to see Emile installed, and assisted with good advice, but it was to Maupassant that the new tenant first turned. Zola wanted a boat, and he could think of no better agent than this hearty young Norman who knew every inch of the river. Maupassant duly purchased the boat on his behalf and rowed it over from Bezons.

" What are you going to call it ? " he asked Zola, a trifle wistfully.

" I shall give her the name of my new heroine, Nana."

Zola went back into the house and took up the threads of his novel. He felt happy, perhaps for the first time in his life. His publisher had become almost affectionate, and the prospect of completing *Nana* in the country was delightful.

" I have at this moment," he wrote to Flaubert, " that little quiver in my pen which always tells me that a good book is about to be delivered ! "

Maupassant could not boast of a similar feeling. In the train back to Paris he finds himself envying, without grudging, Zola's good fortune. The little flat in the Rue Clauzel seemed so lonely and cramped after Zola's pleasant house on the Seine. Too tired and dispirited to work that evening, he walks up and down the floor, debating whether to call on one of his neighbours ! But he is still at heart something of a snob, and cannot bring himself to parade his loneliness before his social inferiors. Not even his literary friends know that he is a pessimist. He laughs too often and too heartily, and it is so much easier to commit his misery to paper.

A woman's shrill voice pierces the ceiling. He picks up his hat and decides to drink a bock on the boulevard. Perhaps Alexis or Huysmans might stroll in for news of Zola. He shakes himself impatiently, forcing himself not to think enviously of Médan. In a few hours he will be back at his desk at the Ministry, already piled high with arrears of work. A fine drizzle is pattering on the windows: it will be melancholy on the boulevard to-night. He throws down his hat and walks over to the mirror. Sometimes, when his headaches come on, he spends hours in front of his glass staring at his eyes. But there is no pain in his face now, only a hard discontented look. It slides off as he grins at his reflection. The round, rosy cheeks and the heavy black moustache say that he is a fool to worry over his health. Nobody would take him for thirty, he tells himself, as he carefully twists the ends of his moustache. The woman's voice is joined by a man's gruff laughter. The discontented look returns to Maupassant's face and he goes back to the window. The postman comes up the stairs, hesitates, knocks. . . . It is Flaubert's letter — he has not written for over a week.

" I've heard so much nonsense about your illness that it would please me enormously and ease my mind if you would go and be examined by my doctor, Fortin." A sudden wave of affection sweeps over Maupassant, leaving him more sentimental but lonelier than before. Flaubert is really worried about his pupil's headaches. Only last month he wrote a grumbling note: " Your eye annoys me, and I would like to get to the bottom of the whole business." Maupassant reads the letter again and decides to see an oculist. It is an unhappy thought, and he can imagine how his boating companions will laugh when he meets them on Sunday wearing a pair of eyeglasses. He shrugs away the intended visit to the oculist, claps on his hat and runs down the stairs.

" Bonsoir, monsieur," murmurs the concierge philosophically. " Il fait lourd ce soir. Je crois. . . ." But Maupassant is in no mood to spend the rest of the evening on the draughty landing. He hurries down the street, suddenly aware that he is hungry, although he had dined scarcely two hours before. Roast partridge and quails, green peas and *foie gras* with crisp lettuce float mistily from a menu outside a restaurant. He hurries in fussily, as if looking for someone. Waiters trip delicately by, balancing trays and exchanging harassed whispers. The music floats from an inner room, skirts rustle, and the women all wear the pink wooden look of tired dolls. But their dresses are bulging with pink delicate flesh, all done up with bows and little silken things like boxes of bon-bons. He waves aside a glossy head waiter and strolls out into the fresh air.

For two or three francs he can eat a good plateful of *bouillabaisse* and share of bottle of white wine with a woman he knows. An unpleasant reminder of dirty linen creeps from a corner of his mind, and for a brief instant he dreams of a beautiful boudoir, all scented and perfumed. Then he jostles through the crowd and hurries up the hill into Montmartre. . . .

A month or two later Maupassant came to realise how much his place at the Ministry meant to him. In his own mind he had come to regard the post as secure, if underpaid. He still dreamed of the day when he would be able to give up his desk and devote himself to writing, but never had he seriously considered the possibility of losing his position. Towards the end of 1879 he received a shock which might have proved disastrous but for the intervention of Flaubert.

Maupassant's pessimism should have warned him that disaster lay in the shadows. Matters had gone very well with him of late. His play had been produced, and Flaubert at last seemed satisfied that his pupil's verses could be submitted to the public in book form. Charpentier, the publisher, had been exposed to Flaubert's repeated suggestions, and the poet already dreamed of seeing his first book on the stalls.

Unfortunately for Maupassant, the authorities were then in the throes of a purity campaign. Early in 1879, one of his best but frankest poems, " Le Mur," had been published in a magazine called *La Revue Moderne et Naturaliste*. It was a small but thoughtful effort, and Maupassant's name figured among those of Huysmans, Emile Goudeau, Alexis and Paul Bourget. He could not afford to quarrel with any editor, however obscure, but he had been seriously annoyed by the cuts made in his poem.

"The *Revue Moderne* have sent me your 'Mur,'" Flaubert wrote sympathetically. "But why have they half-destroyed it?"

Harry Alis, the editor, had apologised for his blue pencil in the most conciliatory manner. "At the time of going to press we learn that we are more and more immoral. We are threatened with proceedings. . . . That is why, as a measure of prudence, and so as not to prejudice our case, we are unhappily forced to mutilate M. Guy de Maupassant's beautiful verses. Our contributor will console himself by recalling the adventures of his relative,[1] M. Flaubert, whose masterpiece, *Madame Bovary*, had the honour of being indicted before the Court of Assize."

The editorial fears were only too well grounded. The enterprising M. Alis had reprinted "Au Bord de la Mer," which had previously appeared in *La République des Lettres*. He re-titled the poem "Une Fille," and gave Maupassant's pseudonym, "Guy de Valmont." There seemed nothing very alarming in that, but the Prefect of Seine-et-Oise had warned the Etampes authorities to keep a careful eye on Alis's productions. A month after the publication of "Une Fille" the paper printed a short story by a young American whose moral outlook did not at all commend itself to the authorities. Here was an opportunity to swoop down upon those in control of *La Revue Moderne et Naturaliste*. The prosecution could produce a piece of verse and a page of prose which the local court would not hesitate to condemn as "obscene."

The manager of the journal, closely questioned, reluctantly supplied the names of his authors. The American had left the country, and all the official wrath now concentrated upon the luckless poet. Through him, the authorities hoped to strike a decisive blow at the ebullient Alis, and they were determined to secure a conviction. A summons was duly

---

[1] In his enthusiasm, the editor falls into the common error.

served, and Maupassant had to appear before the bench at
Etampes on a charge of corrupting public morality.

He was seized with panic. Nothing could save him now
from losing his post at the Ministry of Public Instruction !
If he escaped a fine or imprisonment at the hands of the
magistrate, there was still the unpleasant publicity of having
been involved in a scandal. For once his Norman *flair* seems
to have been lacking, and he completely failed to see the box-
office value of the proceedings.

Once in front of the Bench, his courage returned and he
defended himself with some warmth. He explained that
the verses in issue had appeared four years previously in *La
République des Lettres* and he had not authorised the reprint.
The magistrate listened severely and reserved judgment. It
was torture to wait, and Maupassant's lively imagination made
the delay more painful. He felt that the magistrate had not
believed his story and trembled for his miserable salary. This
would surely be an excuse for the Minister to dismiss him, particularly in view of his very modest record as a civil servant!

Flaubert did not at first take the prosecution too seriously.
A quarter of a century before he had also sat in the dock and
the proceedings had not affected his Art ! And what else
mattered ? He was trying very hard to find a publisher for
Maupassant's collection of verses when this unpleasant
business started.

" I tell you, he has talent," he wrote to the wife of his own
publisher. " His verses are not dull, and that is the most
important thing from the reader's point of view. . . . In
brief, *he is my disciple and I love him like a son*."

But the author of *Madame Bovary* knew human nature too
well not to realise that Maupassant might lose prestige,
perhaps even his post, through the scandal.

" I should be delighted, my dear boy, if I were not afraid
of prudishness in your office. That may cause you some
difficulty. Let me know at once how this affects you."

That letter awaited Maupassant when he got back from Etampes.   He at once sat down and wrote a full statement of the position.

"The magistrate was very polite and I think I kept my end up all right.   They have indicted me, but I'm not sure that they'll go through with it, because they know I'll defend myself like a lunatic. . . . My position at the Ministry worries me and I shall move heaven and earth to get a *nolle prose-qui*. . . . I really need a letter from you, full, encouraging, paternal and philosophic, with lofty ideas on the moral value of these prosecutions. . . . You could give your opinion on my poem ' Au Bord de l'Eau ' from the moral and literary point of view (artistic morality is only the Beautiful, after all).

" My counsel — a friend — has suggested that your letter might be published in *Le Gaulois*, as part of an article on my case.   It would be both testimony in my defence and an argument upon which my counsel could base his plea. Your exceptional position — as a man of genius prosecuted for his masterpiece, acquitted with difficulty, then glorified, and definitely accepted as an impeccable master — would be such a help that my advocate thinks that the mere publica-tion of your letter would squash the whole affair.

" Forgive me, my dear master, for inflicting this un-pleasant task upon you.   But what can I do ?   I am alone in my defence, my very livelihood is threatened, I can look for no help from my family and there is no chance of pouring gold into the lap of some great advocate. . . . I am going to pull wires on all the papers where I have friends.   I salute you very tenderly, my dear master, and again ask your pardon.

" Filially yours,

" GUY DE M."

" *P.S.* — If it displeases you to see your work printed in a newspaper, please don't send me anything."[1]

[1] *Lettres inédites de Maupassant à Flaubert*, by Pierre Borel.

Flaubert did not hesitate. This was a fight after his own heart, and his letter duly appeared in *Le Gaulois*. He also advised Maupassant where to recruit sympathisers, and himself tackled everyone who might be of service. Bardoux – who had read " Au Bord de l'Eau " when Maupassant was trying to find a place in the Ministry of Public Instruction – promised to assist. Editors, publishers, politicians – all were solicited by the indefatigable Flaubert.

His letters to Maupassant make no concession to the possibility of failure. If the poet is convicted, " we will engage a great lawyer and make an awful row. In that case, Raoul-Duval would be good; but still, we haven't come to that yet. With a little cunning, we'll be able to stop the whole thing."

That indeed proved to be the case. The prosecutors had not bargained for such a solid opposition, and were only too eager to strike the charge out of the list. And the young poet went back to his office with a light heart. Charmes was as friendly and sympathetic as ever, but Maupassant thought he detected a certain chilliness in the higher officials. Those thin little smiles told him what he might have expected had the proceedings taken a different turn.

Before long these same men would be boasting of his acquaintance. The name of Maupassant would be known to all Paris, from the refined *salons* to the disreputable little *bistros* where he had so often spent his evenings. He would be loaded with commissions for articles, flattered, interviewed and paragraphed.

But all this was hidden from the young clerk who so gratefully found himself back at his desk early in the year 1880. He had an idea for a story based on one of his uncle's anecdotes. It was about the courtesan who had spent a night with a Prussian officer during the invasion – merely an anecdote, yet he had never quite forgotten it. The details had been hardening in his mind for many years, but verses, plays and silly articles had pushed the fat prostitute into the background.

Within a few short months she would come to life again, vivid, pulsating and real, and her little anecdote would be read and applauded by the civilised world. And the only voice of protest would be that of a tired, middle-aged harlot living precariously in Rouen. ("But this isn't true!") Nobody would be very much interested in her denials. The world already knew her, not as Mlle Adrienne Legay, but as the immortal "Boule de Suif."

CHAPTER IV

MÉDAN

ZOLA was marching triumphantly through the drains of Paris. His "cottage" had already begun to show signs of becoming quite a bourgeois country house. With *Nana* on the bookstalls and theatrical managers scrambling to secure the stage rights, he could at last look forward to a period of financial calm.

Every Sunday the young Naturalists would go over to Médan and enjoy the delights of hearing their own voices or bathing in the river. Not that Maupassant had deserted his master. Flaubert was not in the best of health and now stayed at Croisset as often as he could. And Maupassant would find it pleasant to take his yawl down to Médan, where he was sure of a friendly welcome and a feast of words.

The little garden is very neat and prosperous-looking, and Zola has added conservatories and even an outhouse. *Nana* has been painted a pretty green and is still giving excellent service. But it is the house which strengthens Maupassant's private opinion that the good Zola is really a romantic bourgeois in spite of his unorthodoxy on paper.

" Zola works in the middle of an extraordinarily large and lofty room," he writes.[1] " And this enormous study is hung with huge tapestries, and loaded with furniture of every period and of every country. Armour of the Middle Ages – possibly genuine – stands cheek by jowl with astonishing Japanese curios, and pretty pieces of eighteenth-century stuff."

[1] *Emile Zola* (Quantin, 1883).

The great man cannot resist running off to Paris to buy bric-à-brac, and every Sunday the young gentlemen find something new in the house — Buddhas, Venetian boxes and yet another suit of armour. They love this man, and smile indulgently when he shows off some obvious fake. It is all very ingenuous and *nouveau-riche*; and Maupassant laughs up his sleeve. A few years later he will poke good-natured fun at Zola's pride of property in *Les Dimanches d'un Bourgeois de Paris*.

Maupassant enjoyed these Sundays with Zola and the others. The house was always being enlarged or redecorated, and the writer would proudly show his friends every new improvement. He was never happier than when workmen were in the house, and the sight of hammer and saws lying about gave him real pleasure. Sometimes his wife and his mother quarrelled — chiefly about money matters — but the good Zola knew too much about human nature to take sides. His wife could also afford to overlook the presence of a mother-in-law, for the thoughtful Emile had installed a huge linen-room on the first floor. Here Madame Zola settled into perfect contentment as soon as breakfast was cleared !

Apart from Zola's erratic tastes in furniture, Médan was a very pleasant retreat for a tired young clerk. The food was good and abundant (" Zola himself eats like three ordinary novelists ! " noted Maupassant), and there was always plenty of light amusement. Zola, who was very short-sighted, would fire at tufts of grass which Maupassant gravely assured him were birds. Occasionally they would go fishing, but Zola had no better luck at this sport. It was Hennique's monocle which seemed to fascinate the fish !

" As for me," wrote Maupassant, " I used to lie full-length in a boat called *Nana*, or spend hours in bathing, while Paul Alexis mooned about, Huysmans smoked cigarettes and Céard complained of being bored in the country. So we spent our afternoons, but as the nights were magnificent, warm and heavy with the scent of flowers, we used to take a walk every evening on the big island opposite the place. I would row them all over in the *Nana*."

Back in the house, Zola would unfold his legs and tell them about his new novels. It was pleasant to listen to him affirming their literary principles and seasoning all his talk with sharp asides on contemporary fiction. In Paris — whenever, in fact, he was in a crowd — Zola would be timid and rather an awkward conversationalist. But in his own house at Médan, among his eager young friends, he rattled on happily.

Cézanne was sometimes present to argue with Zola, but the young men seemed to have fallen completely under the great novelist's influence.

" The essential characteristic of Naturalism is that it is not exclusively a literary system (like symbolism, for instance), but the application to Literature of a general method." There is a murmur of approval from the circle of young men, and Zola takes breath. " The novel should have no fixed boundary — it has gone beyond all the other forms. Like science, it is the master of the world." Cézanne grunts, and is about to say something, but Emile is now astride his hobby-horse. " The novel should touch every-thing, physiology and psychology, social economy, religion, morals." His voice is shrill with excitement. " All Nature is our domain ! "[1]

Maupassant says very little. He is tired, pleasantly tired after his bathe, and the room is warm and comfortable. There is little he can contribute to this discussion. He is no hand at æsthetic argument, and, after all, he is still a very humble amateur in the world of letters. There is a good deal in what Zola says, he is quite sure of that. As Flaubert's pupil, he has a very healthy respect for the place

[1] Cf. Zola, *Le Roman Expérimental*, p. 375.

of closely observed and documented detail in all works of art. " Ideas should not be superimposed on stories." He makes a careful note of that phrase. " They must be the inevitable result of the characters themselves." Above all, every self-respecting novelist must strike a blow at the tyrant of censorship.

But there were moments, particularly when he was alone, when he felt uneasy. " We must leap into the stars from the springboard of exact observation," said Zola. " The truth mounts on wings to the symbol."[1] The novelist should be above politics and always deal with facts without taking sides. That was good Flaubert, but surely this was a kind of politics to form a group of combatants and give them the name of " Naturalists." As an outlook, a literary attitude, it was very well, but were they not compromising their independence as artists in accepting this collective debt ? Sharpshooters, yes; but not a regiment advancing to battle. Thus Maupassant, still the spiritual child of Flaubert, reasoned in private but continued to sit in the shadow of Zola. The Naturalists had taken his loneliness under their wing, but he still shared, without expressing, Flaubert's suspicions.

Fortunately for Maupassant, he had a mind and personality of his own; otherwise, he might well have refused to link himself with the collective work which the Naturalists now decided to undertake. That is not quite the paradox it sounds. Had he taken up his stand with Flaubert in refusing to accept the tag " Naturalist," he might have lost his greatest opportunity. As it was, by meekly playing second fiddle to Emile Zola he exploited the great man's name and still proved himself much more than an imitator.

Les Soirées de Médan, the book which made Maupassant a celebrity overnight, first took shape in the most casual

[1] Barbusse, p. 170.

fashion. One evening they were sitting about Zola's table talking Literature, when someone brought up the question of the war of 1870. Nearly all of them had had some experience of military service and each had his own definite views. Zola, whose part in the affair had been none too glorious, showed astonishing warmth on the subject of patriotism. His sentimentality did not commend itself to Maupassant, who at once attacked wars and the Deity that permits them. Very politely, but with some heat, he jeered at the killing instinct which the history books distort and glorify.

The other young men did not argue the subject too vigorously: Zola had been rather carried away by his own heat and they waited patiently for the steam to pass off.

" Well, well," murmured Hennique, after an awkward silence, " why shouldn't we do a few short stories on the subject of the war ? "

Why not, indeed ? They had all imagined various plots, and this might be an opportunity to strike a collective blow for Naturalism. Most of the fiction previously written on the last war had been pessimistic stuff, with a strong partisan bias. Here was an invitation to treat the subject from a Naturalist angle.

Zola saw in the idea both an opportunity to make his *credo* known and a means of showing his affection for his young comrades. He gladly agreed to lend them his patronage by contributing a story to the collection and persuading Charpentier to publish the volume.

Maupassant was the humblest member of the party. He had not yet proved his worth, but the subject of his own contribution was already in his mind, and that was more than half the battle. And it was something to know that his own name would be associated with that of Zola, and to feel that a publisher was pledged to accept the book.

It is certainly not true to suggest that Maupassant kept

his share in the volume a secret from Flaubert. He was vague, but that was surely due to his reluctance to weary his master with all the details of spade-work.

"I'm working hard at my story on Rouen in war-time," he writes on December 2, 1879. "Hereafter, I shall have to carry pistols in my pocket when I go through Rouen !"

A month later, however, Flaubert was still in the dark concerning the details of the work.

"Aha !" he writes to Maupassant, "so you're going to publish a *volume* ! And you say ' *our* ' proofs ! Who are ' *us* ' ? I'm longing to see this anti-patriotic effusion. It would have to be very strong meat to turn my stomach !"

A day or two later, Maupassant writes again giving further details and informing Flaubert that three of the stories have been previously published. They are Zola's "L'Attaque du Moulin," published in *La Réforme*; Huysmans's "Sac au dos," which had been printed in a Belgian paper; and Céard's "La Saignée," which had recently seen the light in Russia.

"When Zola learned about these last two stories, he declared that, with his tale, they would make up into a curious book, a little chauvinistic and rather striking. Then he told Hennique, Alexis and me to do a short story apiece. That, of course, would have the selling-value of his name and might bring in one or two hundred francs for each of us."

For some time they had worried and argued about the title. Someone suggested *L'Invasion Comique*, but that might have affronted a section of the public. Instead, they decided upon *Les Soirées de Médan* – a compliment to their commander-in-chief and a shrewd exploitation of Zola's publicity value. Flaubert at first thought the title " stupid," but soon overcame his aversion when Maupassant sent him " Boule de Suif."

" My pupil's story, ' Boule de Suif,' the proofs of which

I read this morning, is a masterpiece. That is the word, a masterpiece of composition, comedy and observation. . . ."

This was high praise from the author of *Madame Bovary*, and the other contributors could not disagree. Zola himself was not present when the story was first read out, but after the publication of the volume he hastened to add his tribute. The five young men had met at Maupassant's apartment, and each read his own contribution. The host came last, and, when he had finished reading, they warmly congratulated him on a masterly piece of work. He was gratified, but Norman common sense told him that a short story is soon forgotten.

For years he had stored that little tale in his head, and sometimes, no doubt, he had sketched out a rough draft on the Ministerial notepaper. Like most of his work, this tale had matured in his mind long before he committed it to paper. The writing of this stark and sober piece had been performed under the worst possible conditions. Sometimes his sight was so troublesome that he forced himself to write while keeping his right eye closed. Acting on Flaubert's advice, he had seen an oculist, but the trouble continued, and he now took ether regularly. When the migraine became really painful he had five leeches applied to his ear.

Throughout the actual writing of " Boule de Suif," Maupassant was harassed by that fussy little bench at Etampes. Although he sat down to write the little masterpiece when his very livelihood was threatened, it would be melodramatic and untrue to suggest that the story was written in a desperate urge to escape drudgery. Poor Maupassant, as we have seen, was overcome with relief when the miserable charge was lifted from his head. He had written " Boule de Suif " because it seemed a good subject for Zola's little book. Once having undertaken the story he could not give it up, an attitude which did not at all appeal to some of his lady friends.

"Madame Brainne has been my despair these last two months," he tells Flaubert. "She complains of my absences, makes scenes, even insults me, but I still call, having arranged to go at dinner-time and leave immediately afterwards. We chat at table and then I run away. She is such a good woman that she has ended up by accepting this kind of call, which leaves me the rest of the evening for work."

Madame Brainne seems to have become very attached to the young writer. She had been kind to him in his struggling days and now adopted a quasi-proprietary air. But even her devotion was not proof against middle-class prudery. "Boule de Suif," which she read in proof, disgusted her, and she did not hesitate to say so. Knowing Maupassant's state of mind – he had not yet recovered from the Etampes episode – Flaubert hastened to reassure him.

"I consider 'Boule de Suif' a masterpiece," he repeats. "Yes, my lad, nothing more nor less than masterly. . . . In brief, I am delighted; two or three times I laughed out loud. Madame Brainne's prudishness makes me sick !" Flaubert continues in this strain, but his anxious eye detects one or two matters which might be "misunderstood." He thinks Maupassant has been too severe on the French soldiery and also suggests that the word *tétons* should be cut out of the narrative.

"Your heroine is charming," he continues, "but I wish her belly weren't so big ! . . . I've some ideas up my sleeve for getting the story known, but I hope to see you soon. I want two copies of the book. Bravo again !"

To the genuine artist, praise is not enough. Before he can congratulate himself on having been completely successful, he must feel that his work is impeccable. Flaubert's whole-hearted applause told the young man that he had succeeded with "Boule de Suif," but he knew only too well how literary judgments differ. Had Maupassant been the model apprentice of the fable he would have contented himself with Flaubert's praise and at once sat down to write more masterpieces. " Do twelve more stories like that and you will be someone," Flaubert had said, but it was not so easy. There was still much to disturb him in regard to " Boule de Suif." His story was one of a collection, and there was no reason to hope that the critics would take kindly to this Naturalist broadside.

Zola's name had persuaded a publisher and it might help to attract readers, but that would not necessarily ensure a hearty welcome to his collaborators. Editors, who despised Zola's work but knew its selling value, were only too eager to welcome his contributions, but they refused to beckon his " tail." It was Zola's signature, not his material, which now sold copies, but that did not mean that his unpleasant little puppies could unburden themselves all over the paper ! In the past Zola had good-naturedly left doors ajar only to find that the editors isolated him and vented their dislike on the " lackeys " who tried to follow him in.

There was another disturbing element. Zola – who did not have to worry about sales – had decided to use the book as a Naturalist plank. Already he had prepared a Foreword which sounded dangerously like a manifesto:

" Of the stories which follow, some have previously appeared, either in France or abroad. They all have a central idea and a similar philosophy.

" We are waiting for the attacks, the insincerity and the ignorance of which contemporary critics have already given us so much proof. Our only concern has been to make known both our friendship and our literary tendencies."

With that challenge to open the book, Maupassant feared that the critics would not enthuse over *Les Soirées de Médan*. And Madame Brainne's attitude was evidence enough that his " Boule de Suif " might not be a welcome addition to bourgeois bookshelves. These were unsettling thoughts, but nothing could be done except wait for the reviews. Fortunately for the young author, he received at this time an invitation to spend Easter with Flaubert at Croisset. The new book was due for publication in a fortnight, and this visit might enable him to forget his doubts.

He was the first to reach Croisset, and helped Flaubert to make all in readiness for the other guests. Never had the country been more beautiful, nor his welcome more sincere. As they discussed both *Les Soirées de Médan* and Maupassant's forthcoming book of verses, the young man felt that all his cares had been left in the train from Paris. Flaubert pooh-poohed his stage fright and shook his huge head whenever his pupil began to enlarge on his qualms. As he spoke, his red waistcoat rose and fell with each breath. Maupassant listened gratefully but with one ear. Through the windows he could see the masts of invisible boats stealing over the Seine. The countryside was quiet, but he felt the earth stirring in its sleep, the fruitful beloved earth of Normandy.

Suddenly Flaubert heaved himself from his arm-chair. " *Mon Dieu,*" he cried, " you must hurry, my lad. They will soon be at Rouen with nobody to meet them ! " And he pushed Maupassant into the cart and stood on the little terrace, shading his eyes with the newspaper which Maupassant had brought him from Paris. Then he turned heavily, all the springiness having suddenly left his body. He was very tired, but none of his guests should see it. If only he had enough money to keep " the boy " beside him ! They could help one another in so many ways, and the young man needed looking after. Only the day before he had written to his niece on this subject:

" Fortin has just examined my disciple. He took an hour over it. (I don't know his opinion yet.) I'm sure Guy is suffering a good deal. He went up to bed at nine o'clock this evening. He's probably got the same nerve trouble as his mother."

Meanwhile, the young man was rattling along the road to Rouen. He brooded on " Boule de Suif " and found himself wondering what Zola would think of the story. But his starved eyes kept straying to the hedges and poplar-trees. Breezes from the river swept over the meadows and his mind began to fill with visions of summer. The Seine would be twittering with girls' voices, and he would take his yawl far down the river. Petit-Bleu, Toma-hawk and the rest would sing all the way down to Argen-teuil, while he rowed. " Exercise, that's what I need; that'll cure me of all my headaches ! " And on Sundays he would row over to Médan and drink tea while Zola un-earthed some ghastly Buddha, ingenuously repeating what the dealer had told him.

Médan ! That jerked him back to reality. If only the next few days were over ! But, fortunately, there would be much to do when he got back to Paris. Final proofs of *Les Soirées de Médan* had to be passed and a dozen matters of policy decided. They would have to push the book under the very noses of the critics !

At the station he greets Zola, Edmond de Goncourt and Gustave Charpentier, who ply him with questions about Flaubert's health. Zola, he notices, has begun to fill out, but his face is still very pale. He seems pre-occupied, and his short black beard rests in his overcoat collar.

That evening they sit down to an excellent dinner. The turbot sauce is a great success and Flaubert has provided plenty of good wine. Dr. Fortin is one of the guests, and he seems to be enjoying himself, but now and then he gives Maupassant a sidelong glance, and turns quickly away when the young man looks up. These headaches are very puzzling. Possibly the trouble is eye-strain, or it may be due to something behind the eyes. . . . But this is not the time for gloomy diagnosis, and the worthy physician turns to his neighbour.

Flaubert has not laughed so heartily for weeks. Old Alphonse from the village is helping to serve, but every now and then he doubles up with laughter and nearly drops all the dishes. Maupassant is in fettle and his droll stories make the others hold their sides.

Someone suggests that their host should read an extract from *Bouvard et Pécuchet*, but he begs to be excused. He is too much of an artist to recite work which is still in the proof stage. They retire very early that night, but Flaubert manages to buttonhole Zola before the latter goes up to his room.

" You will have a good surprise, Emile," he says proudly. " My pupil has written a story which will please you." Then, with a sly dig in the ribs, he adds, " Don't be too jealous if they like his ' Boule de Suif ' more than your tale ! "

The party returned to Paris after luncheon on the following day, and Maupassant soon found himself aglow with literary excitement. That month of April 1880 was to see the publication of " Boule de Suif " and his book of poems, *Les Vers*. It was enough to keep any young writer from his official desk, and Maupassant seems to have assumed command of *Les Soirées de Médan*.

A few days before the date fixed for publication he calls a meeting of collaborators.

" My dear friend," he writes to Céard, " we are all meeting next morning, April 12, at 3.30 in Hennique's office at Charpentier's to send off copies of *Les Soirées de Médan*, which will be out on Wednesday. Please let Huysmans know at once." One need scarcely add that this notice was conveyed on the stationery of the Ministry of Public Instruction and Fine Arts !

A day or two before publication date, Maupassant wrote

an open letter to *Le Gaulois* in which he drew attention to the new volume. He begins with a declaration of the Naturalist method, and continues with a highly fanciful account of how *Les Soirées de Médan* came to be written.

" We sat down and, in the great calm of the slumbering fields, Zola told us that terrible page of the sinister history of war which is called ' L'Attaque du Moulin.'

" When he had finished, we all exclaimed: ' You must write that at once! ' He burst out laughing and said: ' I've already done so.'

" My turn came next day. . . . Zola found the stories interesting and suggested that we should make up a book of them. That volume is now about to appear."

This account was one of Maupassant's jokes. The idyllic picture of the young disciples sitting at Zola's feet and reciting their stories was, of course, pure fiction, but Maupassant hoped to irritate the critics with this pretty snapshot of the Naturalists at work.

Within two days M. Albert Wolff of *Le Figaro* had leapt at the bait and was finding it most indigestible ! Delighted at the success of his move, Maupassant and the other Naturalists sat back to enjoy a full page of free publicity.

" Zola has built a country house where he lives for eight months of the year surrounded by his sycophants. The other four months he spends in Paris in the society of these same youngsters, who call him ' Dear Master ' in the fond hope of hailing him as the Great Citizen of Médan. These young people imagine that the mere presence of Zola at Médan will place this village among the historic places of France. . . . And it is this impudent little band which, in a most insolent preface, throws down the gauntlet to the critics. But we're too old to be caught napping. They say to themselves: ' Let us get ourselves knocked about, that will make the book sell ! ' I hope that my colleagues, grown old in harness, will not be taken in by this schoolboy's ruse."

The worthy critic, in warning his friends, had succeeded in giving the book an excellent send-off, for all the other scribes immediately rushed to their inkpots !

" Wolff's article has filled me with joy," declared Flaubert. " Oh, eunuchs ! "

Within a few days every reviewer in Paris was wiping his pen on the little yellow-backed volume. Jean Richepin of *Le Gil Blas*, disdaining literary criticism, contented himself with coarse personal portraits of the six authors.

" Zola's face is as fat and sallow as a pork butcher's. . . . Huysmans waddles along, skipping about like a cat at play. . . . Céard is a skinny fellow, sickly, sour-looking. . . . Hennique is a tall, elegant youth with an eyeglass over his long nose. . . . Alexis is a pleasant chap, popular with women and a lover of life." This critic, who seemed to judge authors by their biceps, could not bring himself to disparage the " poet who had been led astray at Médan." Of Maupassant, he says: " He is a proud and healthy master, a mad oarsman, a lover of the healthy life. It is a pleasure to see him. He is a Norman, a relative of Flaubert,[1] and a worthy representative of that fertile and healthy race."

While the critics stormed and ranted, M. Charpentier found that his first and second editions dwindled in a manner to delight a publisher's heart. When the tide of reviewing went out, the shore was piled high with readers. Within two days of M. Wolff's outburst, *Le Figaro* itself achieved a remarkable volte-face:

" Each of the writers has done a report, often talented, of something actually seen. Those who experienced the horrors of the war will have the impression of seeing a photograph, when they read this book. . . . In *Les Soirées de Médan* we have an interesting piece of work,

---

[1] The critic, like so many others, goes astray on this point.

written by six men, animated with the desire to set down the truth. And that is something worth respecting to-day."

Zola's name had helped to make the book known, but it was soon apparent that Maupassant had gained most from the publication of *Les Soirées de Médan*. People who had only heard of him in connection with the Etampes affair realised for the first time that a new and important writer had taken the field. Soon everybody was chuckling over " Boule de Suif."

There was very little in the story itself, but the treatment plainly showed the hand of a master. A fat harlot travelling from Rouen to Havre finds herself in most respectable bourgeois company. In the diligence with her are a count and countess, a wholesale wine merchant and his wife, a wealthy mill-owner, also with his spouse, and two nuns. The only disturbing element, apart from " Boule de Suif," is Cornudet, the democrat, who is drawn from the writer's uncle: " For twenty years he had soaked his great red beard in the bocks of all the democratic cafés."

" Boule de Suif " was nicknamed thus because of her bulk.[1] " Small, round and fat as lard, with puffy fingers choked at the phalanges, like chaplets of sausages; with a stretched and shining skin, an enormous bosom which shook under her dress, she was nevertheless pleasing and much in demand, on account of a certain freshness and a bright disposition. Her face was a round apple, a peony bud ready to pop into bloom, and from inside opened two large black eyes, shaded with thick brows; below, a charming mouth, moist for kissing, furnished with tiny shining baby teeth. It was said that she was full of excellent qualities."

Before the coach sets off, the other women are muttering " harlot " in stage whispers. Unfortunately, " Boule de Suif " is the only one who has brought any food with her, and the sight of the provisions is too much for the others.

[1] The name means " Ball of Fat."

They graciously agree to share her food, and the nuns show an excellent appetite.

En route, the party stays the night at an inn. The Prussians are in occupation, and the Commandant at once singles out " Boule de Suif " for his night's entertainment. She declines to share a bed with this Prussian, who cynically refuses to let the others go on to Havre until she has yielded. They can only think of themselves in this crisis and start plotting against the poor girl. The conspiracy seems to break down against the harlot's extraordinary stubbornness, until one of the nuns enters the coalition. Nothing could displease the Almighty, she argues, if the intention were laudable. The wretched girl weakens, but she cannot yet bring herself to accept the Prussian's embrace. At last, seduced by the nun's casuistry, she submits for the sake of her fellow-travellers. Their real hypocrisy is only brought home to her when the journey is resumed. The mask of friendliness then drops and she is snubbed by the people who had so recently cajoled and flattered her. She is once again the prostitute, anonymous and despised, and the ladies are careful not to soil their skirts by contact with her.

The supreme irony of the situation is driven home on the last lap of the journey. This time it is the unfortunate " Boule de Suif " who has forgotten to pack her victuals. Having sacrificed her, the others have no longer any use for the harlot and ignore her completely.

" She thought of her great basket full of good things which they had greedily devoured, of her two chickens shining with jelly, of her *pâtés*, her pears, and the four bottles of Bordeaux; and her fury suddenly ebbing, as a cord drawn too tightly breaks, she felt ready to weep. She made terrible efforts to prevent it, making ugly faces, swallowing her sobs as children do, but the tears came and glistened in the corners of her eyes. . . . Madame Loiseau indulged in a mute laugh of triumph, and murmured:

" ' She weeps for shame.'

" The two good sisters began to pray again, having wrapped in a paper the remainder of their sausage."

At first sight, there seems little in the story to explain Maupassant's enormous success. It was an amusing anecdote, of course, and there was enough " plot " and suspense to keep the reader interested. But the real triumph lay in the author's superb handling of the situation. In this short story, Maupassant had proved himself not only a master of French prose but a penetrating and sober analyst. There was a delicacy and balance so perfect that even Flaubert could express nothing but admiration for the technique. This was a moral tale without any moralising, and a striking piece of irony without the slightest concession to staginess. The whole episode stood out, stark and alert with a sense of reality.

Apart from his narrative skill, Maupassant displayed astonishing power in his character studies. Each of these people was etched in to the life. With a few frugal strokes, he had brought out everything that was vital and distinct about his characters. They all seemed urgent with their experience, gloriously alive, and the author had moved them across the stage with the confidence of a brilliant producer.

" Boule de Suif " was so faultless in construction that only a practised writer could see the immense talent behind this simple tale. Céard, Huysmans and the others had raved over the story, but it was men like Zola and Flaubert who realised that Maupassant was now eligible for the highest honours in Literature. As a critic and observer who never seemed to be criticising, he had won his place in the Naturalist vanguard, but the sheer vigour and sweep of his style showed that he was already fully equipped with the tools of his craft.

Meanwhile, the reviews poured in. The critics did not entertain too many illusions on the Naturalist theory, but

I M

they could not overlook a writer whose story was on everyone's tongue.

" ' Boule de Suif,' by M. de Maupassant, has made a great success," wrote one gentleman, " and not without good reason. M. de Maupassant, whose verses I have had occasion to castigate, is a very distinguished writer of prose. A style so concise, restrained and concentrated that it might almost be called ' sober ' is here employed by a remarkably observant mind. It is the purest Flaubert. . . ." Even Madame Brainne, who had been so shocked by the proofs, now declared herself "enchanted" with "Boule de Suif"!

While editors were beginning to bombard Maupassant with commissions for articles, he had the added satisfaction of seeing his book of verses in print. *Les Vers*, which was now on all the bookstalls, had been dedicated to his master in the most affectionate terms: " To Gustave Flaubert, the illustrious and paternal friend whom I love with all my heart, to the faultless master whom I admire above all others." Delighted as he was with " Boule de Suif," it was this slim volume of poems which gave Flaubert his most personal pleasure. And rightly so. He had given Maupassant many valuable lessons, and all the world could see the harvest in " Boule de Suif "; but that story somehow belonged to Zola. It had ripened at Médan under the auspices of a group movement which Flaubert did not favour. But these poems were another dish. He had supervised their growth and lopped off the weeds. This book was dedicated to him, and contained the poetry, not of a movement, but of Gustave Flaubert's pupil.

Writing to Maupassant on April 25, 1880, he expresses all the pride of a successful teacher.

" MY DEAR YOUNG MAN,

" You are right to love me, because your old man is devoted to you. I read your book [*Les Vers*] at once, though, of course, I knew three-quarters of it already. We shall go through it again together. What pleases me most of all is that it's personal. No smart stuff, no posing, nothing Parnassian, nor Realistic (or Impressionistic, or Naturalistic).

" Your dedication has stirred a world of memories in me – your uncle Alfred, your grandmother, your mother. And your old man's heart is heavy and the tears are in his eyes. . . ."

Gustave Flaubert was not the man to hug his memories. His pupil was beginning to attract notice, but there was still work to be done. The young man's short story, however excellent, did not mean that his future was assured. " Do a dozen more like that," he had said, and meant it. Now that *Les Vers* was on the market they must fight for its success, for Zola's name was not on the fly-leaf this time !

" Next week bring me a list of the idiots who write reviews, so-called literary. Then we will set up ' our batteries.' But remember good Horace's maxim: ' *Oderunt Poetas.*' . . . Eight editions of *Les Soirées de Médan* ? My *Trois Contes* has only gone into four. I shall be jealous. Well, I'll see you at the beginning of next week."

For once, the public taste upset the good Horace and Maupassant had the satisfaction of knowing that two editions of his poems had already been exhausted. The prosecution at Etampes, " Boule de Suif " and other pleasant aids to publicity were now bearing fruit. *Le Gaulois* and other papers suggested articles, letters of congratulation swept into his post-box and the whole world seemed to thrill in unison to his success.

There was no money, as yet, to show for his triumph. His was only a sixth part of the royalties in *Les Soirées de Médan* and he might not expect more than two or three hundred francs from the verse. Like a true Norman, he could not really appreciate his success until the money was actually chinking in his palm.

It was still a little difficult to focus his victory. The critical applause had stunned him with pleasure and he seemed to be in a state of dazed certainty. He was somebody now, he knew that, but his flesh peppered with goose flesh each time he picked up a new review of *Les Soirées de Médan*.

But Flaubert would tell him how he really stood. The old man would cut through all his doubts with a circular saw and advise him on all these requests for articles. He had already sketched out some ideas which he hoped to mention when he next visited Croisset. The dear old fellow would certainly laugh over the story he had in mind about the strumpets who attend a first Communion service. . . .

Five days after he received Flaubert's letter, Maupassant was at Croisset. But they neither laughed nor planned new campaigns. Maupassant had drawn the curtains and closed the little white shutters. For Flaubert was dead. The house was silent and the young man walked up and down the dining-room trying to crystallise the tragedy. It was so unexpected, so ironical. His little triumph was now as hollow as a jug. Without Flaubert to share the future, he felt isolated. But, almost immediately, he corrected himself. Nothing is sacred to a writer; while he was washing the body of his master and preparing it for burial, his eyes were busily storing details. Flaubert himself had given him the habit of observation, and, as he waited for the other mourners, his mind was probably littered with fragments of the article which he would write on the dead man upstairs.

The giant lay asleep in his coffin, a large coffin, and Maupassant's was the last hand to touch his flesh. All night the young man sat with his master, reading and re-reading the letters which Flaubert had sent him. His thoughts dwelt upon that Easter dinner when Flaubert had laughed like a rowdy schoolboy. Only six weeks ago. It was so sudden, but Maupassant could not help seeing a certain appropriateness in that end. Flaubert had not clung pathetically to life, knowing that his powers were failing. He had died as he had lived, abruptly, and without making himself an object of pity.

The mourners greeted Maupassant with an instinctive sympathy. All the young men who had so often sat and joked with him in the Rue Murillo were there – Céard, Hennique, Huysmans, Alexis. Through a kind of cold stupor, Maupassant saw other faces: Charpentier, Goncourt, journalists, writers, publishers. . . . Only a few weeks before, Flaubert had come out of this house and kissed each of his visitors on both cheeks.

They slowly followed the coffin to the parish church of Canteleu. Before they reached the little cemetery, Zola and Daudet silently joined the procession. The hearse crunched slowly over the bare white road as if reluctant to separate Flaubert from his beloved Normandy. It was a green, fresh spring morning, and the beautiful countryside unrolled slowly before the dead man. Nobody in that sad procession ever forgot the frightened cow who suddenly appeared over a hedge and began to moo, gently, suspiciously. . . . " It seemed like a distant voice, like the sobbing of this countryside that our mighty dead had loved so well," said Emile Zola. " I shall always hear that beast's lament."

All the futility and hopelessness of life seemed to be symbolised in that moment. The clumsy gravediggers heaved and strained at the ropes, but the coffin could not enter the grave. And Flaubert's body was left, wedged sideways in the grave, until more men came to shift the heavy coffin.

They crowded about Maupassant, shaking hands and

mumbling the old hopeless phrases of sympathy. Flaubert's niece sobbed painfully but Maupassant could not cry. He felt a numbing sense of loss, but beyond that no emotion. He would mourn Flaubert to the end of his days, yet on this day he could not weep. Only when he was back in Paris did he permit himself to speak of the dead man.

But the young heart rarely hoards its grief, and Maupassant had much to distract his mind from the terrible tragedy of Croisset. He was a celebrity now, not merely a wretched clerk whose verses sneaked into obscure weeklies when the editorial back was turned. With " Boule de Suif " selling heavily, and his volume of poems already mounting into the third edition, he could rightly claim to have entered Literature " like a meteor." Within the short space of two months, April and May 1880, his name had appeared on two popular books – an astonishing success for a hitherto unknown author. But publishers cannot be dunned by young writers, and Maupassant had not yet reached the stage when he could say, " It is my pet ambition to ruin a publisher or two ! " That came later. For the present, he was still grateful to those who published his work and offered him advice.

M. Pol Neveux[1] cites a letter to Zola which gives a vivid impression of Maupassant's state of mind at this time. Writing from the Ministry of Public Instruction and Fine Arts, he says:

" DEAR MASTER AND FRIEND,

" I beg you to do me the service which you first promised – that is, to write a few words about my volume of verse in your article for the *Voltaire*. . . .

" Laffitte has asked me for a story which I'm doing – I've refused to fix the fees, as I want you to advise me on that subject. Like Huysmans, I've just got on *Le Gaulois*. We

---

[1] *Correspondance, Boule de Suif* (published by Conard), p. 143.

are each doing a weekly article and should pick up 500 francs a month.

" I can't tell you how I think about Flaubert; he haunts me. I keep on thinking of him all the time. I hear his voice, recall his gestures; I can still see him in his big brown dressing-gown, with his arms in the air as he spoke. . . ."

And Zola and the others showed their sympathy by recalling a thousand debts of kindness which they owed Flaubert.

That summer Maupassant took stock of the situation. His agreements with various journals would bring in enough to keep him in modest comfort. Regular work, security – the dream of every young author – were now his. By writing a few articles and stories he might earn himself the leisure to do the more ambitious work which he had had in mind for so many years. " A full-length work," Gustave Flaubert had advised, but that would have to wait until he could afford to sit down and write for three months without seeing a sou. No, it seemed far safer to concentrate on short stories, which could be dashed off quickly and paid for while the editorial memory was green. Dashed off ? That was not what he really intended. He was Flaubert's pupil, and, as such, owed a responsibility to his master's reputation. The plots were already in his mind, but he would need leisure to work out the details before dipping his pen in the inkpot. He could write quickly – " Boule de Suif " had proved that – but his work needed a long time in the cellar. To think out detail, to polish his narrative, he must leave the Ministry of Public Instruction with its files and petty annoyances.

Maupassant moved with Norman caution. Literature is notoriously precarious, and he had only to remember Flaubert to realise that even the greatest talent was not always proof against the ignorance and prejudices of the public. The author's livelihood depended entirely upon his output. If he failed to maintain that output through ill health or a sudden desiccation of ideas, he might starve. An unpleasant scandal, a book which failed to please – anything might unseat the hapless artist.

He could not be certain that he was really a brilliant writer. He had written an excellent short story and put together a few pleasant rhymes, but that did not entitle a man to turn his back on a very safe and respectable position. More than one author had found it impossible to repeat the success of a first book. As a civil servant he would automatically be eligible for a pension, but he knew, only too well, what an impoverished writer could expect at the hands of the Ministry of Public Instruction. In his case, the whole problem was further complicated by the puzzling illness which maddened him with pain but seemed to leave him none the worse when the attack passed. Were these headaches the first warning of blindness, or merely the effects of overstrain ? Night after night he had discussed his symptoms with the little druggist at the corner of the street, and now his bedroom had begun to look like a pharmacy !

It was a difficult problem, and Maupassant decided to compromise with his doubts by asking for a year's leave of absence. If matters did not turn out satisfactorily, he would then be saved from the fate of the one-book author. Fortunately, Charmes was sympathetic and contrived to soothe the ear of Jules Ferry, the new Minister. The young man, thus encouraged, put forward his plea with all the delicacy and tact of a model Government official.

" My health is poor and the profession of letters is precarious," he wrote.[1] " If some illness or some piece of bad luck obliged me to take such a step, I should like to be able to find here once more my post and my salary."

[1] Cited by R. H. Sherard in *The Life, Work and Evil Fate of Guy de Maupassant* (Werner Laurie).

He was duly given leave, and could at last taste the full luxury of being his own master. Flaubert would have completed his delight in the new freedom, but there were many compensations. It was autumn, and the Seine looked fresh and yet so mysterious. He could now take his boat down the river, knowing that the week-end trippers were all ashore and beginning to shiver in their summer under-wear.

Liberty was sweet, and such a temptation after being imprisoned for ten years between the hands of a clock. The little room in the Rue Clauzel seemed quite a different place now that he no longer brought back official dust on his shoes ! He still rose early, from force of habit, and wrote all the morning. His afternoons were free for rowing or walking or talking, but it was not pleasant to do these things in one's own company. All his friends were padlocked to their ledgers and reports, but he could find a welcome in several drawing-rooms where a man might stretch his legs and listen to the latest scandal. And, quite often, boudoir doors were left ajar.

He knew every sound in his shabby apartment-house. Sometimes, when he was feeling ill and depressed, he would long for the solitude of a villa in the country. But in the evenings his depression seemed to leave him, particularly if he had rested on his sofa during the afternoon. And when the pale day had wasted itself, life flowed back into the jaded house. The little midinettes would run up to their rooms, their wooden heels clattering on the stairs.

Their voices reached his ears, quickening within him an instinct for the warm friendliness of the streets. They were kicking off their shoes now, scenting themselves, coaxing the frowsy hair into little curls, sheathing their bodies in stuffs soft to a lover's touch. He smiled as he thought of how he used to prowl the boulevards late at night, when harlots are cheapest. Now he could call upon respectable married women whose husbands were not over-exacting. The siege was longer, more sophisticated, and he could not always accustom himself to the petty details of a long campaign.

But the days of hired love were over. Henceforth, women offered their bodies with all the vulgar enthusiasm of autograph-hunters.

PART TWO

CHAPTER I

FLEURS DU MAL

MAUPASSANT'S disease has always interested doctors and psychiatrists. Mental aberration is a fascinating study, and the more distinguished the victim the deeper are the footnotes. In the case of the great French writer there has been so much poppycock and guesswork that no self-respecting biographer can afford to go far beyond the established facts.

That Maupassant was infected with syphilis as a result of his early dissipation is now denied only by those pious perjurers who cannot pay tribute to genius without equipping it with a moral halo. As it is more gentlemanly to inherit the disease than to acquire it in the heat of youth, these authors fill their pens with whitewash and write a few reluctant lines on Maupassant's " heredity and over-indulgence in athletics." That attitude is not only misleading but thoroughly unsatisfactory from the viewpoint of anyone seriously interested in Maupassant's literary development.

The disease which condemned him to a sad and premature death was due to infection by the enterprising spiral-shaped germ called *spirochæta pallida*. It was the same agent which destroyed such minds as Heine, Baudelaire, Jules de Goncourt and Nietzsche. Much is known about the disease to-day, but in Maupassant's time empiricism was still in the saddle. The effects of physical agents on the mind are still being investigated, but in the case of syphilis the medical text-books are flooded with evidence. Maupassant's medical history does not differ from that of many humbler

Syphilis

victims, and there is no longer any justification for turning a blind eye upon his case.

We know now that general paralysis of the insane is due in practically every case to long-standing infection by the *spirochæta pallida*. Syphilis can be hereditary, of course, but there is little evidence to indicate that Maupassant received this legacy from either of his parents. His father was a sensual philanderer but he proved more fortunate in his amours than the luckless writer. The mother has been the real source of all the rumours on this point. She was highly strung and neurotic, and, after her son's tragic end, nearly killed herself with an overdose of laudanum.

Without discounting this legacy of neurasthenia, one can say without fear of contradiction that Madame de Maupassant did not suffer from the disease which ended her son's life. This background of " nerves " undoubtedly aggravated the writer's sufferings, but the seat of the mischief was not in Madame de Maupassant's blood. " He has his mother's nerve trouble," friends would say, but all Maupassant's symptoms were consistent with a far deadlier source of infection.

" Trop d'exercice, trop de putains," Flaubert had written, and the last word alone is operative. The oarsman does not contract syphilis from rowing, unless he puts in at riverside brothels, where a woman submits to the embraces of half a dozen anonymous lovers during one night. Many men have survived a dissipated youth and become respectable fathers and good citizens, but poor Maupassant was not so fortunate. And he paid the penalty in years of terrible suffering when life offered him fame and prosperity; everything, in fact, but the medical succour for which the world had still another quarter of a century to wait.

The hereditary basis of the writer's nervous disorders is easily traced. As with many Normans, his physical gusto did not altogether conceal the underlying streak of morbid pessimism. In spite of his frenzied rowing and full-blooded practical jokes, he is still his mother's son; and, like Flaubert, he shouts to try and silence the gloomy whispering in his soul. But he lacks Flaubert's self-control in all but his prose. His character is weak and he cannot deny himself the pleasures of the moment. Even before he becomes a candidate for general paralysis he has taken his fill of the world's vices.

This weakness of character explains much that occurred after he became infected. Spoilt as a child by an indulgent and impulsive mother, he faced manhood with a shallow philosophy which mocked God and glorified sheer physical comfort. So proud was he of his biceps that the mere hint of illness made him a coward. At Etretat, on his visits to his mother, he would spend whole evenings with M. Leroy, the chemist. Hypochondria found in him a willing victim, and no lay student of medicine possessed more books and articles on disease.

His mother loved him and smiled indulgently when she heard of his vigorous patronage of the farm lasses. At home, he was completely free of all parental restraint. His father, we know, brought mistresses into the house and was in no position to lecture his sons. Maupassant whored and drank before he was out of his teens. He was accepted by the rough fishermen as one of themselves, and, when the nights were foggy and cold, the lad took his nip from the brandy flask like the others.

In Paris he had known short commons for the first time. They had unnerved, instead of strengthening, him. There is no greater snob than the impoverished aristocrat. His noble birth becomes a kind of psychological overdraft upon which he throws himself when all else has failed him. We know that Guy de Maupassant expressed his unhappiness in a reserved and bitter contempt for his fellow-clerks. Later, when the dreaded germ was lodged in his blood, this contempt deepened into a megalomania which shocked all those who tried to approach him.

Although Maupassant definitely became infected as a result of his dissipation, it is well to remember that the germ fell upon fertile soil. Much of the writer's life after the age of thirty can be explained in the light of his disease, but it is interesting to note how his temperament reacted at the various stages of its development.

" In personality," says an American review, " he was really a faun with sensual features and Crô-Magnon jaw, the sort of man who would brazenly take leave of companions in the street or on the river to visit a *bagnio* or a waterside brothel."[1] Such a man embraces a tainted woman and the result is madness or death. But it is not quite so simple as the rule-of-thumb doctors would have us believe.

The medical data may be briefly recapitulated. Unchecked syphilis often leads to general paralysis, the symptoms of which are clearly defined. In the early stages the victim is restless, irritable and over-anxious. He is eager to sample all the pleasures of the moment and is a prey to eroticism and obscenity. He is excitable, but this usually takes a beneficial form, for the pale germ makes the brain blossom before destroying it. The mind is often so stimulated that it leaps into the dazzling regions of genius. The germ acts like a drug, filling the feeble flesh with a brief spark of exhilaration and a sense of well-being. It seems to be indifferent to the body; its objective is the mind. For years the unhappy victim may not alter in appearance but his brain is already pierced by this poisoned dart. At first it is a caress, a mere stimulus of the brain cells which stir to sudden activity. Cases have been recorded of quite mediocre intelligences which have suddenly displayed great

[1] *Journal of American Medical Association*, July – December 1917, p. 1555.

brilliance.[1] With a talent like Maupassant's, the result showed itself very quickly. Only when the end came did a saddened world understand that he had left a few flowers in place of the harvest that might have been.

The second or expansive phase of general paralysis usually sounds the warning note. The patient is impulsive, self-satisfied and bombastic. He is Napoleon, has millions in the bank and can do anything. This grandiose delusion of self-importance is usually accompanied by slovenliness in dress and a fondness for simple-minded antics. The victim is alternately exalted and depressed, and suffers from racking headaches.

The final stage makes the passage from deterioration to utter breakdown. The sudden flash of brilliance is succeeded by an obvious weakening of the faculties. The first exhilaration of happiness has been crushed by a terrible gloom peopled by fancies and hallucinations. The victim waits for sleep, but nightmares surge about his pillows. He has lost his accuracy of statement and his handwriting becomes erratic. He suffers horribly in body and spirit, but it is a slow death. Sometimes twenty years may pass between that first fatal embrace and the moment when the victim is received into a strait-jacket.

Poor Maupassant was born half a century too soon. Had he become infected in the twentieth century, the wages of sin might have meant no more discomfort than a series of intravenous and intra-muscular injections. As it was, he was condemned to a miserable death without a chance of saving himself. The pathological basis of his disease had not been established, and, while the terrible *spirochæta* flowed in his blood, he was taking cold baths, swallowing pills, and sometimes wearing two or three pairs of glasses at a time! After his death, the doctors shook their heads

[1] For an excellent study of this subject, vide *Sous le Signe de la P.G.*, by Paul Voivenel and Louis Lagriffe.

KM

wisely and announced that they had always been aware of the writer's sad fate. But during his lifetime he was chasing from one spa to the next, undergoing treatment for every possible disease except the one which still defied the scientists.

It is this sad burden of incurable disease and inevitable eclipse which makes Maupassant's career such a tragedy. Seen in bleak retrospect, his career will supply a text only to the most hardened moralist. "He paid for his viciousness," some may say, but surely no man reaped such a sad harvest from his wild oats. He became infected in the prime of manhood, but his real suffering only began when he was famous and rich.

With the publication of "Boule de Suif," Maupassant was at once enthroned as a master of the short story. It seems incredible that ten thousand words of prose should have made his reputation, but he had merely fulfilled the precept of Bouilhet, his first mentor. "A hundred lines of verse, perhaps less, are enough to establish a writer's name, if they are perfect and contain the essence of a man's talent and originality," the poet had said, and "Boule de Suif" was a perfect illustration. There was now no question of waiting patiently for Zola to suggest another Naturalist subject. Like Flaubert, Maupassant had never been comfortable in his association with a "school" or group of writers. The artist should not compromise his independence, he told himself, and quietly resolved to go his own way. He could now stand on his own sturdy legs.

Maupassant was a realist and understood his limitations. Many another author would have been tempted to use his success as a path to more dazzling fields. He might have rushed back to his bed-sitting-room and resurrected the plays which so many producers had rejected. The theatre was very fascinating, and offered such enchanting temptations to an author's vanity ! Again, he might have written breathless little sketches for the newspapers and minced up Parnassus once a year with a slender volume of verses under his arm.

It says much for his Norman common sense that he concentrated on the medium which the public had already approved. " Boule de Suif " had pleased Flaubert and other good critics, and Maupassant was far too prudent to risk his hard-won success. Unlike Flaubert, he had a hearty respect for the box-office and was determined never to return to his desk at the Ministry. In his heart, however, lurked a snobbish distaste for the profession of letters. Its only justification lay in a really solid success, and, to this Norman, that meant a shower of gold pieces.

Maupassant took up his pen with tremendous confidence. Flaubert was no longer at his elbow, but he had learned his lessons and was now fitted for work. The older man had constantly reproached him for idleness, but Maupassant seemed to have left all his discontent behind him. Determined to consolidate his position, he set himself a strenuous time-table. From seven a.m. until noon he worked steadily, giving up the remainder of his day to friends and exercise. But he worked even when he was away from his writing-table. Flaubert had so trained him that observation had become instinctive, almost a second sight. What he saw he noted mentally, analysing reflections and shaping his phrases so that, when the time came to record them, he had but to transcribe from memory. He had so drilled his faculties that his mind's eye seemed to click like a turnstile.

Naturally enough, the writer turned to scenes which had already stamped themselves on his mind. He could claim to know four types very intimately – whores, peasants, clerks and rowing men. He would take his stories from

life and try to achieve a sharp and photographic outline by
defining scenes and characters with vital accuracy. The
characterisation would be photographic, but to achieve
natural-seeming simplicity he must first organise and then
suck his subjects dry. To avoid becoming a mere photographer he had to catch the light and yet somehow convey
depth, for, unless controlled, colour would deaden his
canvas instead of giving it vitality. Finally, he decided
that he could be a good Naturalist and still teach Zola that
brushwork could be clear-cut without robbing the canvas
of its power !

In the light of this reasoning, he began to empty his brain
of short stories. He was earning bread-and-butter money
with his articles, but the reviews were only too eager for
more tales. On February 18, 1881, his story " En Famille "
made its appearance in *La Nouvelle Revue*, which had
previously rejected one of his earlier poems. Now that
" Boule de Suif " was such a success, the worthy editress,
Madame Adam, was ready to swoon at the mere sight of a
new manuscript from his pen.

The tale itself was a satiric trifle. A petty bourgeois
family, headed by a wretched clerk, swoops upon an in-
heritance from the old mother whom they believed dead.
Unhappily for her greedy relatives, she comes out of her
trance and upsets all their little schemes. Not a great
theme, nor a very original one, but it was told with perfect
simplicity and point. It is a study in pettiness, and
the newly emancipated clerk chose a typical hack as his
butt.

Madame Adam was not the only critic to revise an earlier
opinion of the new writer. A year or two before, Turgenev
had said to Léon Hennique: " Poor Maupassant ! What
a pity it is that he will never have any talent ! " " Boule de
Suif " had come as a pleasant surprise to the Russian, who
now hastened to encourage the young man. " I have read

your story in *La Nouvelle Revue* with the greatest pleasure," he wrote.

A month later, " L'Histoire d'une Fille de Ferme " appeared in the *Revue Bleue*. It was another triumph of condensed writing. This time Maupassant wrote a tale of a farm drudge who has an illegitimate child by a lustful plough-boy. She is seduced by her master, who marries her without knowing of her previous escapade. She visits the baby secretly, fearful of her husband's displeasure, but, on discovering the truth, he is only too eager to adopt the child.

This unpretentious tale is written with a masterly touch. Again we have the remarkable clarity and delicate analysis of " Boule de Suif." The story is told simply and without the slightest moral bias. It is only in the completely satisfying impression conveyed by this tale that one becomes aware of the positive hand behind all the effortless reading. For this story, Maupassant chose a peasant setting which he brought to life with a few economical strokes. How quickly he conveys the physical atmosphere of the farm !

" Three inquisitive hens were picking up the crumbs under the chairs, while the smell of the poultry-yard and the warmth from the cow-stall came in through the half-open door, and a cock was heard crowing in the distance. The farmyard, surrounded by trees, seemed to be asleep. The tall grass, among which the tall young dandelions rose up like streaks of yellow light, was of a vivid green, the fresh spring green. The apple-trees threw their shade all about them, and the thatched houses, on which grew the blue and yellow irises, with their sword-like leaves, smoked as if the moisture of the stables and barns was coming through the straw. . . .

" She took up a bundle of straw, threw it down into the ditch and sat down upon it; then, not feeling comfortable, she untied it, spread it and lay down upon it at full length, on her back, with both arms under her head, and her limbs stretched out.

" Gradually her eyes closed, and she fell into a state of delicious languor. She was indeed almost asleep when she felt two hands on her bosom. . . . "

" Le Papa de Simon " is another tale which he wrote at this time on the subject of the adopted child. It was a theme to which he returned more than once in the course of his career.[1] His pre-occupation with this subject may well have been due to a guilty conscience. He was never tight-fisted with his mistresses, and several writers have laboured the rather obvious conclusion.

While these stories were appearing in the Press, Maupassant worked out the details of another theme which interested him. As with " Boule de Suif," this story was based on a true-life episode which had been reported to him by a friend. For this tale, the immortal " Maison Tellier," he was indebted to Charles Lapierre, the manager of a Rouen paper called the *Nouvelliste*. Maupassant, who had met him through Flaubert, listened attentively to what a thousand other men would have chuckled over and quickly forgotten. One of the brothels in Rouen, a house in the Rue des Cordeliers, had been shut for several days. On the door was scrawled a notice: " Closed on account of the Confirmation." It seemed that the lady in charge of the establishment had been invited to attend her niece's Confirmation in her native village. Fearful of complications in her place of business while she was away, she decided to take the girls with her. Hence the cryptic notice on the door !

That anecdote amused Maupassant enormously. He knew the red-light district of Rouen and appreciated the irony of the story. Soon his mind swirled with little scenes

[1] Cf. " Mademoiselle Perle," " Un Fils," " Rosalie Prudent," " L'Inutile Beauté," " Mouche," " Pierre et Jean," etc.

which all circled about that brief notice. He could picture the discomfiture of the regular patrons of the brothel when they found themselves deprived of their comfort. Petty tradesmen they would be, men who led bourgeois respectable lives all the week round and sneaked off regularly for their one evening of hired pleasure. He could see all the girls in his mind's eye, and the brothel itself presented no difficulties to a man of his character and experience.

In " Boule de Suif " he had flayed the bourgeoisie with irony, and this anecdote seemed to present an excellent opportunity to repeat the dose. This time, however, he could reach the same objective with a series of sly digs at conventional standards. He would again use the harlot to prove his point, but the whole story could be written in a light semi-humorous vein. And it would not be difficult to stress the real pathos of this situation. He could show how this excursion brought out all the simple faith in these wretched girls. They would kneel in church and sob like children, but, when this religious emotion was over, they would go back to the brothel and once more entertain the respectable citizens who so impatiently awaited them !

It seemed an excellent subject, but his friends disagreed with him. Fortunately, Maupassant had already decided not to be swayed overmuch by the opinions of fellow-writers. A young author always expects encouragement when he demands advice ! Maupassant was eager to pump anyone who might make his story more life-like, but, beyond that, he refused to submit his work for the approval of a School.

While puzzling over the precise form which his story should assume, he decided to take a holiday, a luxury which he had long denied himself. Now, with his first royalties clinking in his pocket, he could no longer resist. A month or two earlier, his mother had been in Corsica for reasons of health, and he followed her there in September 1880. Six months earlier, he was still a petty clerk, bowing low at the approach of any politician or wire-puller. Flaubert was alive then and the printers were setting up the type for half a dozen short stories.

All this was over, and Maupassant took his little vacation with the pleasant knowledge that he could pay his hotel bill with a few articles for the Paris Press. He stayed at a good hotel in Ajaccio and soon made the acquaintance of Léon Gistucci, the nephew of his mother's doctor. This young man wrote verse, and Maupassant found him a pleasant companion for walks and sea-bathing. It is to Gistucci that we are indebted for an intimate glimpse of the writer's early sufferings. One afternoon the young Italian called on Maupassant at the Hôtel de France. To his surprise, he found him in bed with his head bandaged. His eyes were closed and his face deathly pale. Only a day or two before, Maupassant had much impressed the Italian by his strength and endurance as a swimmer.

" It's nothing," Maupassant explained with a sickly smile. " It's only migraine."[1]

Reassured, Gistucci sat down at a table littered with newly written articles on Corsica in which the unhappy author had been recording his impressions. *Le Gaulois* printed four of these articles, but Maupassant had stored away material for several more stories. Flaubert had taught him the value of taking notes and he was now expert at card-indexing material which might prove of value.

Back in Paris, he resumed work, but seemed in no hurry to rush his new tale into the printer's hands. To achieve perfect objectivity, he had forced himself to release his mind from the first heat of what artists call " inspiration." Biting

---

[1] These headaches were evidently the work of chronic syphilitic meningitis. That would now be definitely established by means of a lumbar puncture, but in 1880 doctors could offer little comfort to sufferers of " migraine."

into every aspect of the story, he chewed very slowly before rejecting what seemed inessential to its development. For years he had been learning how to do descriptive sketches in prose, but discipline was needed before he could achieve a really decisive cohesion. With his palette ready to burst into life, he must refuse to take it up until his mind's eye had seen and grasped every patch of light and shade.

" Boule de Suif " had been such a triumph that everyone was anxious for details of the new masterpiece. But Maupassant had already begun to retire into himself. " The first part is staged in a bawdy house and the second in a church ! " he confided vaguely.

Only his mother knew of his great faith in the new tale.

" I've almost done my story about the harlots at Communion," he writes to her in January 1881. " I think it's quite as good as ' Boule de Suif,' if not better."

There were many distractions. He had not yet developed his morbid passion for privacy, and was only too eager to show himself in the fashionable *salons*. It was all so delightful and refreshing after the dingy office in the Rue de Grenelle ! Every afternoon tender bits of gossip melted between his tongue and palate before being digested in his brain. And it was very amusing to hunt down these elegant ladies who talked so demurely of " friendship " !

It was a gay and friendly world which opened its doors to the young writer, but he was not entirely blind to its curious moral standards. Sometimes he would return to his apartment and jot down a random thought which had crossed his mind at the tea-table.

" They make use of religion as an umbrella. If it is fine, it is a walking-stick; if sunny, a parasol; if it rains, a shelter; and if one does not go out, why, one leaves it in the hall ! And there are hundreds like that, who care for God about as

much as a cherry-stone, but who will not hear Him spoken
about."[1]

For *Le Gaulois* and other journals he was still writing
ironic little sketches which kept his name before the public
and stimulated interest in his next book.   But sometimes his
articles showed that he wielded a fighting pen.   In June
1881, Maxime du Camp, one of Flaubert's oldest " friends,"
saw fit to publish a most disparaging article on the dead man.
An attack on literary grounds might have been overlooked,
but this author concentrated upon Flaubert's epilepsy.   That
was too much for Maupassant, who retaliated with two
indignant articles in defence of his master.   He was
admirably seconded by Henry Céard, whose stinging reply
to du Camp appeared in another journal.

Maupassant had recently returned from Africa.   Like
Flaubert – indeed, like most Normans – he was always
tormented by this need of change.   Later, when the disease
had him in its grip, this need became an obsession, but at this
time his longing for travel seemed natural in a young writer.
He was drawn to Africa by " an imperious need, by a
longing for the unknown desert, like the presentiment of a
nascent passion."[2]

He had sailed across the Mediterranean in the middle of
that summer, dazzled and warmed by the hot sun.   Algiers
fascinated him, but he was eager for the desert.   Three
weeks of his stay he devoted to a tour across the Zar'ez
region, accompanied by two French officers.   The rough
journey itself was a tonic after the cramped life in Paris, but
he did not give himself up entirely to physical enjoyment.
He was now a writer, not a mere tourist, and everything
he saw was carefully laid aside in his mind.   The desert
seemed to take a load from his shoulders but this sensuous
surrender did not prevent him from noting a hundred details

---

[1] *Bel-Ami*.   Opening passage of chapter xii.
[2] *Au Soleil* (1884), in which he set down his impressions of Africa.

of insect and animal life which the young lieutenants overlooked.

Harlotry had always interested him. Here was psychology and physiology, and the disciple of documentary fiction could not easily withstand its appeal. The Ouled Naïl, a tribe of desert prostitutes, gave him an insight into strange perversions which he recorded as gravely as a student at a lecture.

Three months later he was back in Paris, armed with a copious bundle of travel notes. Unlike so many authors, he was not at all tempted to abandon a subject simply because his brain was crowded with new and more exciting material. His whole literary method depended upon a cautious approach to the theme, and he was content to wait three years before publishing his African impressions. Flaubert had often warned him that talent was " a long patience," and, while he would have been the last man to admit it, Maupassant owed something of his restraint and orderliness to his early life in the hated civil service.

" La Maison Tellier " was at last written and in the hands of a publisher. It was dedicated to Turgenev. Maupassant had always felt tenderly towards this soft-voiced writer from the Steppes who had come to be regarded as something like a literary agent for French authors. Thanks to him, Zola had obtained some very lucrative contracts with Russian editors when he was finding it hard to live on his writings. Turgenev not only suggested subjects to Zola but frequently collected the money due from backward editors !

This gentle Russian had a genius for helping lame pens over stiles. His good nature was often proof against his own literary tastes, but he could sometimes be scathing. His remark about the heroine of *L'Assommoir* is delightfully malicious:

"What difference does it make to me," he asked George

Moore, "if she perspires in the middle of the back or under the arms ? "[1]

Goncourt and Taine had both benefited by Turgenev's sponsorship of their works in Russia, but the Russian's affection for Flaubert went far deeper. Maupassant was always touched and delighted by the sight of these two men slanging each other. Both men were giants, physically and intellectually, but Flaubert made a Rabelaisian figure in his floppy, unbuttoned vest and red Algerian cap, while his friend looked like a snowman in some fairy-story.

The two old bachelors were on the best terms. Turgenev used to address the great Norman as " my ferocious ancient," while Flaubert would describe his friend as " a soft pear." They were both lonely, and their friendship went back fifteen years to the days when they broke bread with Zola, Goncourt and Daudet at the Café Riche. Once a month they dined there together under the mighty chairmanship of Flaubert. They usually remained at table from seven p.m. until two in the morning, lowering huge dollops of *bouillabaisse* and slitting French Literature from head to toe. And they had all cursed those in power and planned to storm the bookstalls much as Maupassant and his friends did a few years later.

When Maupassant first met him Turgenev was a charming patriarchal figure, silver-haired, with the slow, child-like smile of a dreamer. The Russian had first endeared himself to him through his great kindness to the " ferocious ancient." Turgenev's gout often crippled him and precluded his very welcome visits to Croisset. Poor Flaubert would be grievously disappointed, but there was always something to remind him of his friend's goodwill. Turgenev used to send salmon and caviar, and the great Norman

---

[1] Cited by A. Yarmolinsky in *Turgenev* (p. 321), a fascinating study of the Russian novelist at work and play.

would sit down to table with a copy of one of Tolstoy's novels propped up against the cognac bottle. Only Tolstoy could take his place beside Flaubert in the ranks of contemporary novelists; so Turgenev thought, and he took good care to ensure that these two masters read each other's works.

A common affection for Flaubert had brought Maupassant and Turgenev together in friendship. The tragedy at Croisset deepened this feeling. With the publication of *Les Soirées de Médan*, Turgenev frankly admitted that he had misjudged his friend's pupil and was eager to make amends.

Maupassant had always been an admirer of Turgenev, with whom he had much in common. The Russian had once laid down his *credo* in his advice to a young author: " The author must be a psychologist, but in secret; he must sense and know the roots of phenomena, but offer only the phenomena themselves — as they blossom or wither." That was Maupassant's own principle, although he had not yet consciously formulated his creed. Like Turgenev, he despised anything that weakened the strength and beauty of language, and both men believed that a writer should serve his own vision of the truth, not a system or school of thought.

Maupassant had begun to realise that his work showed more kinship with the Russian's style than with Flaubert's. Like Turgenev, he was a brilliant anecdotist who successfully seized an incident and projected it on paper without trimmings. And neither of these great short-story writers suffered from Flaubert's worship of cadences. Truth of detail, yes, and care in construction, but Art for Art's sake could be carried too far. Realism was surely the end rather than the means.

Turgenev was proud and eager to assist his young friend; unfortunately, in this instance he misled Maupassant into

committing one of his very few faults in " local colour."
In " La Maison Tellier " there is a brawl between English
and French sailors. The Frenchmen shout the " Marseil-
laise " and the drunken English retaliate with " Rule,
Britannia!" This last touch was supplied by Turgenev,
whom Maupassant had consulted with a request for an
English song appropriate to the occasion !

With " La Maison Tellier," Maupassant arrived at a
most important decision. Charpentier had published his
verses and also *Les Soirées de Médan,* but to remain
under his imprint might well mean being subordinated
to names like Zola, Flaubert, Goncourt and Daudet. He
had started brilliantly, but he was still a new name and
needed the enthusiastic publicity which a smaller publisher
would be more likely to give him. Norman shrewdness
warned him that it might prove far more profitable to stand
at the head of Havard's list than half-way down that of
Charpentier.

As he had anticipated, Havard received him with open
arms. Maupassant submitted " Le Papa de Simon,"
" En Famille " and " L'Histoire d'une Fille de Ferme,"
together with the new story " La Maison Tellier," and the
publisher's letter has fortunately been preserved.[1]

" My Dear Author," wrote Havard.

" I am sorry I was away when you called, but I have read
and much enjoyed the stories you left with me. As you say,
' La Maison Tellier ' is hot and very daring; it is, above all,
a burning ground which should arouse much bad temper
and sham indignation, but it is saved by its form and talent:
if I'm not greatly mistaken, you will score a big success.
(I'm not speaking of literary success, which is assured in
advance, but sales success.) As for " Papa de Simon," I
think it is a little gem. Since you are anxious to get the
book out quickly, I sent the three stories to the printer as

[1] A. Lumbroso's famous dossier.

soon as I had read them, and I hope you will be good enough
to arrange an appointment so that we can fix a date for
publication."

To give full measure, Maupassant provided four more
stories which Havard incorporated in the same volume.
They were four tales of the Seine, anecdotes of rowing
which the writer had carried in his mind for several years.
The best of these was " Sur l'Eau," but its chief interest lies in the skilful treatment of the supernatural, a
subject which fascinated Maupassant. And in this tale of
a man whose boat is arrested by a woman's skeleton lies
a remarkable power of description and a horror of life.
Here, for the first time, is that morbid pessimism which was
to reappear so frequently in the writer's later work.

But there seemed to be little cause for melancholy. " La
Maison Tellier " appeared at the end of the year and was at
once acclaimed as a masterpiece. A dozen editions were
exhausted within two years, and Turgenev did Maupassant
an excellent service by making his work known in Russia.
We know from his correspondence[1] that Turgenev paid
a special visit to Tolstoy with a copy of " La Maison
Tellier."

In Paris, the book was selling enormously, although some
found it " hot and very daring." Zola, delighted with this
Naturalistic success, had written an enthusiastic review
which the *Figaro* declined to print, although the editor
relented three months afterwards. " The subject of the
tale that gives its name to M. de Maupassant's volume is
particularly shocking for modest readers," he told Zola,
and absolutely refused to accept advertisements for the
book !

Loti thought " La Maison Tellier " the most perfect
masterpiece in the French language. Without fully

---

[1] *Ivan Tourgueneff d'après sa Correspondance avec ses amis français*, p. 268.
Tolstoy translated some of the French writer's work into Russian.

endorsing this judgment, one can appreciate a fellow-writer's admiration for the brilliant technique of the story. Maupassant had spent many months on this tale of 6,000 words, but the result almost approaches perfection. By changing the setting from Rouen to Fécamp, he found it easier to snapshot small-town vice. He knew every corner of Fécamp, and it is this familiarity which gives the tale such remarkable colour and conviction. But it is in its utter economy of expression that this story scores most heavily. Here is a " moral " tale in the fullest sense of the word, yet there is not one word of moralising to disturb the organic growth of the story. As in " Boule de Suif," we have the same distinct pleasure of recognition, unsharpened by caricature.

The story itself is known to every lover of great Literature. Maupassant's work does not lend itself to quotation – in itself a tribute to his sense of structure – but one may perhaps be pardoned for citing the opening passage of " La Maison Tellier." The note of the story is richly struck and the reader's attention fixed from the very first sentence:

" Men went there every evening at about eleven o'clock, just as they went to the café. Six or eight of them used to meet there; always the same set, not fast men, but respectable tradesmen, and young men in the Government or some other employ; and they used to drink their Chartreuse, and tease the girls, or else they would talk seriously with Madame, whom everybody respected, and then go home at midnight ! The younger men would sometimes stay the night.

" It was a small, comfortable house, at the corner of a street behind Saint Etienne's church. From the windows one could see the docks, full of ships being unloaded, and on the hill the old grey chapel, dedicated to the Virgin.

" Madame, who came of a respectable family of peasant proprietors in the department of the Eure, had taken up her profession just as she would have become a milliner or dressmaker."

And after the emotionalism and sentiment of the Communion comes a masterly climax, perfectly pitched in its irony. Maupassant did not favour the surprise twist, so dear to modern writers, but his endings are always sharp and dramatic. In " La Maison Tellier," as in most of his tales, the last paragraph is a crisp commentary on the whole situation.

The girls are back in the house to which the patrons have hurried eagerly :

" At last, at one o'clock, the two married men, Monsieur Tourneban and Monsieur Pimpesse, declared that they were going home, and wanted to pay. Nothing was charged for except the champagne, and that only six francs a bottle instead of ten, the usual price. When they expressed surprise at such generosity, Madame, who was beaming, said to them:

" ' We don't have a holiday every day.' "

There seemed no end to his stock of stories and anecdotes. The other young Naturalists who remembered him as Flaubert's pupil were astonished at his remarkable output. The civil servant was hemmed in by doubts. His poems and exercises had been shaped with all the painful care of an apprentice whose master will reject anything short of perfection. Now, as if by a miracle, all that hesitancy had vanished and Maupassant was shedding masterpieces just as a Norman apple-tree sheds apples. It seemed incredible, but the explanation was not so difficult. With " Boule de Suif " he had proved that his apprenticeship was at an end. In that magic moment, weakness and indecision fell from him, and he was ready to shake the wonderful apple-tree with a firm hand. All these years he had stored little anecdotes and plots, waiting patiently for the technical

Lm

perfection of a Flaubert. When " Boule de Suif " lifted the latch with her sausage-like finger, a hundred shapes were already pressing against the door, gasping for ink.

Money was pouring into his lap. Five hundred francs (then about £20) for any short story or article from his pen ! It was hard to realise at first that in a few hours he could earn what the Ministry had paid him for three months of drudgery. Sometimes he wrote a story in three hours,[1] a performance which Flaubert would never have attempted, but all the details and many of the phrases had already been worked out before he set pen to paper.

The Midas touch did not tempt him to do slipshod work. He was Flaubert's pupil and the master's hand was still heavy upon him. The author of *Madame Bovary* might, perhaps, have been a little shocked at the speed and facility of the young man's output. Much of Maupassant's journalism was ridiculously overpraised. His short stories were all fluent, simple and beautifully pointed but, to an observant eye, there were occasional signs of repetition. Again and again he returned to the brothel for inspiration, assured in advance of his readers' approval. Too often he dipped his pen in false sentiment, allowing cheap satire to make his points. Everything he wrote had his smooth authentic touch but he did not always scruple, when editors panted, to use the same tricks.

Maupassant had known too many privations to remain immune to temptation. His little apartment suddenly seemed dingy, and he soon decided to move to a much more comfortable flat in the Rue Dulong. He did not launch out with the lavish hospitality which later became habitual, but his food was now prepared by a cook who could study his palate. Some of his friends lifted quizzical eyebrows but only the uncharitable could charge him with extravagance. He had missed so many dessert courses during those hard

---

[1] " Mouche " is an excellent example.

early years of the soiled *à la carte* tariff; now, at last, he had reached the *table d'hôte* era !

The change of residence implied much more than additional elbow-room. Gone were the days when a friend might burst into his room and settle into an arm-chair for two or three hours of bawdy gossip. He was not now the apprentice with a weekly task which could be fitted into an odd evening. Flaubert no longer welcomed him in the Rue Murillo with a blue pencil in his huge fist. He was now behind his own counter, with editors clamouring for to-morrow's " copy." That meant hard work and an utter change in his mode of life.

Those who called on him between seven a.m. and noon were refused admittance. The cook had her orders and was capable of shutting the door in the face of an impor-tunate visitor. Only in the evenings did his old friends discover that she had a pleasanter side to her nature. Then the table was laden with delicacies and the visitors demon-strated beyond all doubt that a good cook may amply atone for the host's deficiencies.

Deficiencies ? There were already vague suggestions that Maupassant was most at home in the princely drawing-rooms of the Faubourg Saint-Honoré. Every afternoon, it was said, he sat at the feet of a princess like a lap-dog. Had the gossips been privileged to attend these tea-parties, they might have changed their view of the proceedings without, however, forfeiting their malice. They would have seen this rugged Norman sipping his tea with a faint and rather perplexing smile.

He had the smooth manners of a courteous civil servant whose politeness rarely lapsed into warmth. He could not be called a brilliant talker, but there was a certain charm in his sceptical asides when someone pressed him for an opinion. His judgments were always astringent, gently disparaging, but he never dabbled in petty gossip.

Sometimes his face looked like a country bumpkin's under the huge bronze candelabra, and people found it difficult to believe that this was the brilliant author. Only when a lady with her dress cut very low leaned towards him did he seem to show anything like interest. " So fascinating ! " the ladies whispered to each other. " You feel he's watching you all the time ! He's just like a sad-faced bull."

Maupassant was such obvious prey. He was fascinating and dangerous, and rumour multiplied his conquests. A woman's curiosity cannot resist the challenge of a professional woman-hater, and Maupassant had so much to offer. His fame as an author attracted the snobs, but he was also a gentleman and a strong lover. And these perfumed and leisurely ladies were not slow to appreciate the rare phenomenon of brain and biceps in their *salons* !

Poor Maupassant persuaded himself that he was merely using the drawing-rooms as Zola used his public-houses. He was the documentary artist, observing life at first hand. He did not know, refused to believe, that a latent snobbishness had gathered force within him. Soon these women would mock him when his back was turned and snigger at the rumour that he knew the *Almanach de Gotha* by heart.

But the future was mercifully hidden. Society lay before him, trussed and skewered, like a plump turkey. His mantelshelf was littered with scented invitations to receptions, teas, banquets, secret rendezvous. He listened in reverent silence to the subtle flattery of princesses, conscious of the irony of the compliments he paid them in return. And he smiled as he thought of a phrase which would have shocked and delighted these pretty ladies.

" Marriage is an exchange of bad humour by day and bad smells at night ! "

If his literary friends mocked at his social antics, they could not withhold admiration from the remarkable work which appeared over his signature. Soon after the " Maison

Tellier " collection came a third batch of stories with all the splendid qualities of his earlier work. He was a pessimist, people said, but which other writer possessed his knack of telling a story ?

The new book of tales was first published by a Belgian publisher. A luxury edition, it was quickly exhausted. Two years later, the French publisher, Havard, reprinted the stories together with several new ones by the same author.[1] The volume sold very well, but some people began to ask themselves whether Maupassant took all his photographs from behind a sofa in the Maison Tellier. These tales were brilliant snapshots, but the author seemed to see nothing but flesh. Was this brilliant mind lying down in its own filth ?

The title-piece, " Mademoiselle Fifi," was in itself an excellent tale which invited comparison with the magnificent " Boule de Suif," Maupassant had again drawn his heroine from the brothel and pitted her against the Prussian invader. This time, however, the Prussian is an unpleasant sadist who gloats over France.

" All the women in France belong to us," he crows. The harlot is rabid with patriotism. " I am not a woman," she taunts him hysterically. " I am only a strumpet, and that is all that Prussians want." The officer slaps her full in the face and she stabs him to death.

This melodramatic sketch — it runs to barely 5,000 words — made Maupassant more popular than ever. People still remembered the war and appreciated the jingoism of " Mademoiselle Fifi." Those who had disliked " Boule de Suif " for its irreverent treatment of the French Army

---

[1] The Belgian edition (Kistemaeckers) included " Mademoiselle Fifi," " La Bûche," " Le Lit," " Un Réveillon," " Mots d'amour," " Une Aventure parisienne " and " Marocca." The French edition consisted of these tales in addition to " Madame Baptiste," " La Rouille," " La Relique," " Fou ? " " Réveil," " Une Ruse," " A Cheval," " Deux Amis," " Le Voleur," " Nuit de Noël " and " Le Remplaçant."

were now ready to acclaim the author as a brother and patriot ! Maupassant merely smiled into his thick moustache and pocketed the royalties. He had his views on this patriotism, but the time had not yet come to express them.

While Havard was gleefully selling off " Mademoiselle Fifi," Maupassant was already blotting the last pages of his new book. This was *Une Vie*, his first novel, the full-length work which Flaubert had long urged him to undertake. As far back as 1877 he had mentioned " a novel " to his mother, but, apart from one or two sketches,[1] the book remained in his mind until he was ready to write.

The appearance of the new book astonished all those who knew the author. He seemed to be a writing machine. Short stories and articles poured from his pen, yet Paris continued to hum with rumours of his love-affairs. They knew, of course, that he had given up his rowing and barred the door to all interruptions, but this industry was phenomenal. That tremendous vitality which had formerly expressed itself on the Seine now found vent in his inkpot. At 6.30 a.m. he would take a cold bath, followed by a very light breakfast. Half an hour later he was at his writing-table. Often his servant despaired of keeping the study clean, for Maupassant would usually walk from the washstand to his table with towels dripping water. Books, papers and newspapers were propped against every piece of furniture, but there was nothing untidy about the work done in that room. Sometimes, during the afternoon, his servant would steal a glance at the pile of foolscap on the table. Page after page of that neat sloping handwriting with never a correction !

We know now that a deadly germ was lashing his brain into this extraordinary activity. As if conscious of his doom,

---

[1] " Le Saut du Berger " (*Gil Blas*, November 1882), " Le Lit " (ibid., March 1882) and " La Veillée " (ibid., June 1882) were all incorporated in the novel.

the great writer seemed eager to waste no time. But nobody could foresee the inevitable tragedy and raise a finger in his defence. Every new book seemed a fresh triumph, an assurance of still greater fame. The novel, *Une Vie*, had appeared as a serial in the *Gil Blas* between February and April 1883: and, from the first instalment, Paris applauded and eagerly awaited its publication in book form.

Twenty-five thousand copies of this novel were sold in eight months, although the book trade was in such a low state that Havard had become alarmed for his business. But nothing could stem Maupassant's success. " Five hundred francs for a short story," the editors had said. " A franc a line for every line of your novels," they now promised him. Authors wrote from half a dozen countries, begging for permission to translate his work; women wrote hysterically offering themselves or their daughters; critics who had rapped him over the knuckles for " Boule de Suif " now lavished praise on him.

Zola applauds, gratified that " Boule de Suif " was born, if not bred, at Médan,   Céard, Huysmans and the others try hard not to feel that unworthy pang of envy which is so difficult to resist. But Goncourt, waspish and easily offended like an old maid, cannot quite reconcile himself to the younger man's success. He is one of the doyens of this Naturalism, yet Zola and Maupassant are knee-deep in the laurels. He cannot openly show his displeasure, but his pretty journal pricks up its ears at the slightest warning. And Goncourt sits over his chronicle with pen poised, ready to transfix this upstart!

The whole world envied and admired Maupassant, but nobody was aware of his suffering. It had seemed natural to confide in Flaubert and there was none to take his place. His mother was herself an invalid and he could not bring himself to worry her with his own ailments; it would have been too cruel. Madame de Maupassant seemed to have taken a new lease of life with her son's glorious success. In his triumph she saw the fulfilment of her own thwarted hopes. To all who would listen to her — and they were many — she boasted of having always dreamed of a great literary career for her son.

It was a mother's greatest glory. This woman, so sensitive and neurotic, suddenly saw her life as a beautiful drama. There were many moments now when she ransacked the past for literary souvenirs of her beloved son. Who could blame her for seeing her life as a struggle against odds which had acquired glorious significance through her son? She had kept doggedly on the traces of her brother, honouring his memory with a fastidious reverence: here, at last, was her moment of triumph. Maternal vanity conditioned all her thoughts; only one thing was lacking to complete her bliss — she wanted her son by her side. If he would not share her villa, she offered him a plot of land she owned behind Etretat.

Maupassant could not alarm his mother with accounts of his illness. She would fuss and treat him like a child, wrecking his nerves within a very short time. And Hervé would be more likely to pour out his own woes than listen sympathetically to his brother. He had left the Army, but seemed reluctant to enter the Diplomatic Service, in spite of his mother's wishes. Sickly at birth, he had developed into a burly young man who enjoyed nothing better than a good bout of fisticuffs. He seemed determined to earn his living in the open air, preferably by horticulture, and was now eager to discuss ways and means with Guy.

It was even more difficult to confide in his elegant friends of the Faubourg Saint-Honoré. He was too proud to confess that sometimes the pressure on his temples became unbearable. They admired him for his strength, marvelling that a talent like his should be allied with such a physique.

How could he tell them that he spent many afternoons on his sofa with a looking-glass in his hand ? It would not be easy to admit that at night his body shivered among the warm bedclothes, while he screwed up his sleepless eyes, oppressed by vague fears. Sometimes he would get up in the early hours of the morning and stare into that mirror. He often sat for hours like that, leaning on his elbows, trying to focus the message in those morbid, haunted eyes.

He had given up his violent rowing on the Seine. He no longer smoked, and drank very little, but nothing seemed to cure him of these violent headaches. Ether helped, of course, but often that also failed him. He was now taking cold douches, but reason warned him that his spells of giddiness were only half-physical. The pain would leave his head only to take command of his spiritual being. Then his strength slid from him and he was sick with a paralysis of the will. All became futile and hopeless, and an invisible evil seemed to dwell in his body, knotting it with inertia.

While *Une Vie* is selling in thousands, Maupassant is terrified by the fear of blindness. An oculist who examines his eyes on March 19, 1883, assures him that there is nothing abnormal apart from a slight astigmatism.[1] A month later he is back in the surgery: his left eye is very bloodshot. " Overstrain," he is told, and recommended to wear spectacles for work. But the " migraine " seems indifferent to his new spectacles. Prescriptions pour thick and fast and he is ready to spend hours talking to a suburban pharmacist. Have there not been cures by such men when all the fashionable doctors have failed ? He is ready to try anything.

Soon every doctor in Paris knew that Maupassant was interested in nervous diseases. " He is collecting data for his new novel," they said knowingly. Nobody suspected

---

[1] Every doctor knows now that progressive optic atrophy is frequently allied with syphilitic infection.

that far behind the spectacles the spiral-shaped germ was already piercing his brain. The documentary novelist was buttonholing doctors, chemists, hypnotists. " Tell me ! " It was a cry of anguish, but the doctors would not, could not, help him.

His face sometimes wore a distressed and uncertain smile while he flirted with the pretty ladies over the tea-table. This was always interpreted as the pose of a cynic and sensualist. They could not know that he was often groping for an excuse to take his leave, eager to lie down on his sofa with his eyes closed and the scent of ether in his nostrils.

When *Une Vie* was published, Guy de Maupassant had the freedom of every drawing-room in Paris. Flattery he loved, and a princess's confidential whisper meant far more to him than the most laudatory review of his work. But a lady might cool her dainty heels in her boudoir while he listened gratefully to the opinions of a first-year medical student.

CHAPTER II

" LA GUILLETTE "

MAUPASSANT had become what we now call a best-selling author, but there was still an undercurrent of disapproval among the critics. Everyone appreciated the quiet force of his writing but it was being said that his range was limited. " Why give oneself so much trouble to study beings so unworthy of interest ? " asked a writer. Maupassant defended his work with a characteristic plea for artistic freedom.

" The modern writer aims at the accurate observation of the truth. . . . There are no classes among women. They count for nothing in society except in relation to those who marry or protect them. In taking them for companions regular or irregular, are men always so scrupulous about their origin ? Why should we be more so in taking them as literary subjects ? "

This plea did not silence his critics, but he was not yet ready to take his microscope into the Faubourg Saint-Honoré. He had already shown that he could step out of the Maison Tellier and still maintain the masculine firmness and vigour of his style, but he needed time to focus the Society in which he had only just begun to move freely.

For his first novel, Maupassant returned to the scenes of his childhood. He was still the short-story writer, and the novel itself is composed of a series of loosely bound episodes which recall his early manner. As in his short stories, however, the author convinces by his astonishing sense of local colour and the studied simplicity with which he builds up character.

A short-story writer is not always a great novelist. The

mediums are very distinct and the virtues of one are frequently found to be vices in the other. Maupassant had proved himself a great short-story writer, but now he clearly showed that he could elaborate a central idea and still make his transitions effective.

The epigraph, " L'Humble Vérité," strikes the keynote of this novel. Maupassant told a simple story of a woman from girlhood to old age. Like the writer's mother, she marries and is quickly disillusioned by her sensual husband, who is modelled on Gustave de Maupassant. The tale then takes a sharp turn from autobiography and closes with a picture of the old woman saddened by poverty and the ingratitude of her son. The author, with characteristic irony, shows his heroine abandoned by all save the sewing-maid whom her husband had seduced.

Apart from the honeymoon scenes, the whole action is staged in the country which Maupassant knew so well – the coast of Normandy between Yport and Etretat. It is a sad epic of suffering which he unfolds in *Une Vie*. To modern eyes, the structure of the tale seems loose, but the faults in construction are easily redeemed by the sheer interest of the story and the skill with which the author has painted life-like scenes. Unity of background gives the tale a certain cohesion, but the writer's etching-needle has scratched into every page.

The whole tale is studded with perfect vignettes of Maupassant's own early life and background:

" Women sat in their doorways mending linen; brown fish-nets were hanging against the doors of the huts, where an entire family lived in one room. . . . They walked home chattering like two children, carrying the big fish between them, Jeanne having pushed her father's walking-cane through its gills. . . . A love of solitude came upon her in the sweet freshness of this landscape and in the calm of the rounded horizon, and she would remain sitting so long on

the hill-tops that the wild rabbits would bound by her feet."
Like his heroine, Maupassant had "planted memories
everywhere, as seeds are cast upon the earth, memories
whose roots hold till death." These souvenirs were to be
renewed in one after another of his books and stories.

Maupassant had not forgotten the scenes of his youth,
nor had he outgrown his early prejudices. In "Boule de
Suif" he had drawn a most uncomplimentary picture of
two nuns. Now, with a larger canvas, he made a much more
elaborate attack on the clergy. He portrays two types of
priest, the benevolent, easy-going abbé and the fanatic, but
neither is calculated to enforce the reader's respect.

It is the Abbé Picot, the good-natured village priest, who
introduces a libertine as a suitable match for the pure and
sensitive heroine. In a few sharp sentences, Maupassant
hits off this bluff man of God.

"He was very stout, very red, and perspired profusely. . . .
The priest was well versed in the art of being pleasant,
thanks to the unconscious astuteness which the guiding of
souls gives to the most mediocre of men who are called by
the chance of events to exercise a power over their fellows."

But it is the harsh intolerant Abbé Tolbiac who represents
the type detested by Maupassant. He is "a young priest,
very thin, very short, with an emphatic way of talking, and
with dark circles round his sunken eyes." This man is a
fanatic, hated and feared by all who still believe in the joy
of life. His disgust for all ordinary human pleasure is soon
made clear to the unfortunate villagers.

"Inflexibly severe toward himself, he was implacably
intolerant toward others, and the one thing that especially
roused his wrath and indignation was love. The young men
and girls looked at each other slyly across the church, and
the old peasants who liked to joke about such things
disapproved his severity. All the parish was in a ferment.
Soon the young men all stopped going to church."

Maupassant's anti-clerical attitude certainly lost him no popularity in France. The novel was soon being translated, but Russia, strangely enough, seemed most reluctant to see a translation of *Une Vie*. Turgenev himself, hard at work on the translation, failed to find a publisher. As compensation he paid Maupassant a thousand francs: " To present four hundred roubles to a man of talent, who is, moreover, my friend — my means permit that."[1]

A few months later Turgenev was on his death-bed. Charcot had diagnosed the disease as angina, but the unhappy man was really a victim of cancer of the spinal cord. Maupassant, who saw him five days before the end, was horrified by the change in the gentle Russian giant. His powerful body seemed to have collapsed like a deflated balloon, and he looked shrivelled and waxen. " How can I live with legs like a grasshopper's ? " he cried plaintively. Death was near, yet just out of reach, and poor Turgenev screamed with pain.

" If you are my friend, give me a revolver," he had begged Maupassant.

Flaubert. . . . Turgenev. . . . He was now alone. Zola was a good man, but somehow he had never felt warmth for him. There was something of the little bureaucrat in Zola which made him want to laugh. In his mind's eye he always saw a caricature; a heavy, clumsy bourgeois with his pince-nez and umbrella, stammering helplessly as soon as he became excited. A lion on paper, Emile was nothing but a timid little rabbit in a drawing-room. What made it worse was the good man's hankering for honours; and Maupassant's eye, rarely charitable, noted how he pined for the badge of respectability. How obstinately he offered himself to the French Academy ! Already succumbing to an unhealthy snobbishness, Maupassant found it difficult to

---

[1] Cited by A. Yarmolinsky (*Turgenev*), p. 320.

forgive Zola for this very human weakness. Himself a parvenu, the younger man now saw something coarse and undignified in this craving for official recognition on the part of the author of *L'Assommoir*.

His heart had never really been in the School of Médan. The young men had joined hands in a common cause, but underneath all their ideals lay a very healthy instinct for self-preservation. They were sincere young writers with a hearty respect for liberty of thought and honesty in its expression, but beyond that their roads lay in different directions. As Flaubert's pupil, Maupassant believed in the independence of the artist. He and his friends had been sharp-shooters in the defence of Natural-ism, and only a sentimentalist would have expected them to go on wearing uniform when the enemy had long since departed.

Hating discipline, Maupassant did not care to do more than indulge in a little guerilla warfare; anything else repelled him. With typical Norman shrewdness he saw that he had gained everything from *Les Soirées de Médan*. It would have been personally distasteful and commercially unsound to have continued to pin the colours of Naturalism to his pen.

It is not suggested that Maupassant gave up fighting for his principles simply because he was now in mufti. Every-thing he wrote showed how well he had assimilated the theories of the neo-realists. His spiritual loyalty to Zola was particularly brought out soon after the publication of *Une Vie*, when he contributed a splendid appreciation of Zola's work to the *Revue Bleue*. Now, however, he was writing as an independent man of letters, not as the disciple or collaborator.

That year, 1883, was one of the busiest in Maupassant's short literary life. Apart from the article on Zola, he had written a long and highly sympathetic study of Turgenev and a very considerable amount of journalism. He could not easily resist the temptation to scribble prefaces and sketches and, knowing how quickly he wrote, editors loaded him with commissions.

Maupassant now brought out *Une Vie* and *Les Contes de la Bécasse*. He seemed inexhaustible, and his name never dropped from the bookstalls. As a short-story writer his signature represented a kind of trademark of literary quality, and his work could be commissioned with perfect confidence by editors who were going to press within a few hours. Sometimes he made trouble, but they could overlook much for the quality of his articles and stories. He did not like to have his photograph reproduced – a strange obsession for a young author ! The editors shrugged their shoulders. He seemed to be a very good business man and often demanded payment in advance. Perhaps, they argued, this photophobia was merely a pose to achieve notoriety.

These editors were wrong. Maupassant had a morbid horror of having his portrait published. "Our work belongs to the public, not our faces !" he once said. Like every author, he had his poses. With him, however, the pose was more often than not a caricature of himself, and he always poked fun at those who tried to dramatise the author's life. "Writing ?" he would murmur. "Well, it's not much, but it's better than stealing !"

Again and again Maupassant posed as the aristocrat and dilettante who looks down on his trade and is determined to sell his honour dearly. It was the gesture of a fashionable man of letters who had begun to have grandiose ideas about himself. The blue blood of his admirers had gone to his head where the *spirochæta pallida* had already established a base.

But his attitude was not all pose. He had had a surfeit of fashionable *salons* and already dreamt of a villa in Normandy.

The life of the drawing-rooms had begun to irritate him, but he could never resist the flattery of his princely devotees.

"I dined at the Circle, then went to a reception at Prince X's. . . . Nothing but Highnesses – except me – reigning in the *salons* of their noble subjects," he confides in a letter.

"My dear friend, I don't want to meet another prince, because I do not like to be standing up for a whole evening, and these boors never seem to sit down. . . . And what marvellous comedies are enacted there ! It would give me infinite pleasure – yes, infinite – to relate them, but I have friends, charming friends, who are devoted to these buffoons. The Prince de X——, the Princesse de N——, the Duchesse M——, the Duc de B——, are so nice, that truly it would be wrong to do it: I can't, but it tempts me, it eggs me on, it gnaws at me. . . .

"At all events, that has enabled me to lay down a principle, more true – believe me – than the existence of God:

"Any man who wants to preserve the integrity of his thought, the independence of his judgment, to see life, humanity and the world as an impartial observer, above all prejudice and religion, must cut himself off from what are called worldly relationships, because universal stupidity is so catching, that he cannot associate with his fellow-creatures, see them, listen to them, without becoming infected with their stupid ideas and ideals."[1]

Poor Maupassant realised the danger without being able to save himself. His success had been too violent, too heady, for him to resist the noble sycophants. Had Flaubert lived, he might have shaken his former pupil by the coat-collar and reminded him of the dangers of sacrificing his independence. But the atmosphere of Croisset was so different from that of the Faubourg Saint-Honoré, and Maupassant became more entangled in the silky web of

---

[1] *Amitié Amoureuse* (349th edition), pp. 40-3. Cf. Pol Neveux, p. 153.

Mm

flattery. He fondly imagined that he could cut loose whenever it suited him, but he had lost his peace of mind in those beautiful drawing-rooms where he tried so desperately to forget his fears and doubts.

Flaubert might have saved Maupassant from the enervating life of the *salons*, although nothing could have checked the young man's frequent visits to the pretty boudoirs. A far stronger force than Gustave Flaubert was pricking the unhappy man's lust. Sensual he had been since his early youth, but now he was indulging in the wildest sexual excesses. The worst voluptuaries in Paris had marked him down for destruction, women who spent half the day in adultery and the remainder on the confessional stool. Five out of six husbands in Paris were cuckolded, and the *mari complaisant* had indeed become so common that the term was almost without significance.

Maupassant had hired too many women to be able to resist the call of this soft seductive flesh. In their arms he felt proud and strong and sure of himself. One wretched woman had already signed his death-warrant in some riverside den, but the ladies who yawned lazily between their coroneted sheets hastened the end.[1]

Exhausted by the demands of editors and mistresses, Maupassant refreshed himself in the country. Soon after the publication of " La Maison Tellier " he hurried off to Brittany with a knapsack and a walking-stick. He detested the tourists who jot down their stupid impressions after sampling all the *table d'hôte* comforts on the beaten track. In Paris nobody had a greater taste for bourgeois comforts, but as soon as he trod the little white paths leading down to the sea, the old moodiness dropped clownishly from his shoulders. The man who worried incessantly over his

---

[1] One of these voluptuaries, a beautiful Polish Jewess, was a particular favourite with the writer. Her husband also ended his days in a strait-jacket.

health now tramped about in the rain, sleeping in a barn and sharing his hunk of dry bread with a peasant.

He walked along the Breton coast, passing through Sucinio, over the weird rocks of Carnac, to Pont l'Abbé and Penmarch. Disdaining to score the bull's eyes aimed at by every tourist, he wandered from the highways, taking the country's legends in his stride. Wherever he went, the peasants seemed ready to share both their cheese and their simple philosophy with this sturdy tramp.

In Paris he pulled on his rôle of sophisticated writer like a glove, but the life had become too exhausting. He was suffering from his old eye trouble and became increasingly irritable. As a reaction from his complicated life in Paris, he needed the physical and simple régime which only the country could offer him. With *Une Vie* selling handsomely, he decided to build a chalet on the plot which his mother had supplied. He was tired of trains and the smell of coal-dust irritated him. At the end of a long journey, what was there but " hotel dinners, long *table d'hôte* meals among tiresome or grotesque people " ? But if dining in a crowd was annoying, eating by himself depressed him ! Tourists he despised, yet how often he reached a strange city with a chill at his heart !

" Those heart-breaking evenings in an unknown town. . . . Oh ! I know those gloomy aimless walks in strange streets. I am more afraid of them than of anything else."

He hated to be alone, but Paris was impossible all the year round. With a country house at Etretat he would never again know loneliness ! His mother was near and there would be so much to occupy him. When he wearied of writing, he could live the life of a country gentleman, shooting, entertaining his friends, exercising his body.

The new chalet was christened " La Guillette," although he had toyed with the idea of calling it " Maison Tellier " as a souvenir of the volume which had provided most of the necessary funds ! It was a splendid place and Maupassant personally supervised all the plans. The chalet was a compact but picturesque affair with red tiles, a beautiful creeper and a balcony linking the two wings, giving the effect of a terrace. Surrounding it was a pleasant garden, blazing with flowers, but Maupassant was far more interested in his vegetables and fruit.

It was a good walk from the station, and the writer often threw his bags into the ancient carriage which his mother had sent, following on foot. " La Guillette " was a fair distance from the sea, but the view over the fertile valleys was magnificent yet restful. Behind the white cliffs sloped the rich country he knew and loved so well. These valleys smiled coquettishly, gay with furze. They twisted sinuously, their skirts catching the reflected light of the sun.

In the garden stood a bowl of goldfish which he visited regularly every morning, armed with a plate of bread. This soon became known to the birds, who came fluttering about him eager to anticipate his call on the goldfish ! This duty performed, he would go back into the house, bathe his eyes and write for several hours. After lunch he usually had a little revolver practice. He had built a shooting-gallery and could riddle a leaf on a tree at thirty paces, a little trick which always caused jealous husbands to hesitate before avenging their honour. It must be said for Maupassant that he never abused his skill, and there is no proof that he ever fought a duel.[1]

Maupassant had also laid out a beautiful bowling-green which he kept in perfect condition. When he was alone, he would go fishing or swimming. His local reputation as a swimmer always pleased him; it was so reassuring to feel that he could swim the six kilometres round the " Aiguille "

---

[1] He wrote a few stories on duelling, of which " Un Lâche " is the most dramatic, and in *Bel-Ami* the hero fights a duel with pistols.

rock and back without undue exhaustion, a feat which only his brother, Hervé, could emulate.

There was good sport to be had in the district, and he could always ride or join his old friends the fishermen, with whom he remained on excellent terms. They were all proud of " Monsieur Guy," and, to them at least, he was still the high-spirited lad who used to help pull in their nets by moonlight. Often he would call on some ancient mariner and remind him of old times. He never tired of listening to their stories, and they sat for him unconsciously while he encouraged them to repeat details which had seemed so unimportant to them.

Shooting he particularly enjoyed, and, when there was nothing better to aim at, he went out after rabbits. But there was often a chance of shooting sea-fowl, and it is this sport which he describes so vividly in one of his stories:

" Through the close ranks of the reeds – a multitudinous, whispering company – narrow channels had been cut down which flat-bottomed punts were poled, stealing silently through the still water, brushing past the reeds, frightening the fish which took refuge among the weeds, and the wild-fowl which dived, their black, pointed heads suddenly disappearing from sight. . . .

" Our cone-shaped shelter looked like a gigantic diamond with a fiery heart, sprung up suddenly on the frozen water of the marsh. . . . A strange, forlorn wandering cry passed through the air above our heads. The wild-fowl were being roused by the light of our fire. Nothing thrills me like this first clamour of living creatures, as yet invisible, flying swift and far through the darkness, before the first wintry ray of light has illumined the horizon. That cry, that fugitive cry, borne upon the wings of a bird in that icy hour of dawn, is to me a sigh from the soul of the universe "[1]

The house was beautifully appointed, and Maupassant

[1] *Love.* Translated by Marjorie Laurie (Everyman Edition).

had insisted on all the latest comforts. The furniture itself was carefully chosen with an eye for elegance and luxury but without ostentation. He was spending money lavishly but all his books were selling excellently and he could already rely on about 20,000 francs a year from royalties. For a short story or article, which often represented a morning's work, he was paid 500 francs. Had he been writing to-day, Maupassant would have made a fortune from his pen; as it was, he seemed very satisfied, although his unhappy publisher was always being pestered for up-to-the-minute statements of sales.

Sometimes Havard protested that he was not making nearly as much as the author imagined. Rarely a day would pass without some inquiry as to the number of copies sold. Not content with letters, Maupassant would never miss an opportunity to call on the publisher with some irritable demand for greater activity. For an author who professed such contempt for the vulgar trade of Literature, he seemed remarkably anxious to sit in the box-office. But Havard could well afford to keep his temper. " You are the only author whose books I await impatiently," Alexandre Dumas *fils* wrote to Maupassant, and the general public heartily supported that judgment.

Only once did Havard raise his voice in protest. He had brought out a new edition of the poems which Charpentier first published in 1880. The verses had sold very well and Havard imagined that Maupassant's name would dispose of the new edition. He was disappointed, and his grief was not lightened by Maupassant's vigorous demands for " more action."

" I have spent nearly 5,000 francs on production, and 2,000 francs on publicity, and I'm still a long way from covering my expenses," he pointed out. " I think you should be more conciliatory on this score and help me to bear the blow."[1]

[1] Cited by Maynial, p. 146.

But it was not merely greed for gold which made Maupassant such a nuisance to his publisher; he never hoarded the money. He was simply a sick man who was surrounding himself with material comforts. In Paris he lived quite modestly, worked hard and received far more hospitality than he gave. It was quite another matter when he was in residence at "La Guillette." Then the house was rarely empty, for his noble friends found it a delightful change after the hothouse atmosphere of their *salons*.

Maupassant did not spend all his money on his own pleasures. He was a good son, and his mother saw nothing unseemly in availing herself of his generosity. She had so long been forced to live on a small income that it was almost impossible to resist Guy's open purse. Her private income had practically vanished when her son leapt into fame, and she would most certainly have known real poverty but for his good fortune. She now took a villa at Nice and made frequent demands on him, as Gustave de Maupassant noted, a little resentfully.

With Guy's name blazoned on every bookstall in the world, Hervé could no longer postpone his long-cherished dream of becoming a market-gardener. Guy duly set him up as a horticulturist at Antibes, at the same time settling 1,200 francs a year on his niece.

Some of the local peasants also knew that "Monsieur Guy" had a kind heart. One old woman named Marie Seize used to waylay him with such a tale of woe that even Zola would have been shocked to hear that anybody could live in such degraded poverty. Whenever they met, Maupassant gave her twenty francs, but at last decided that he was being imposed upon. "Don't give her another sou if she calls again," he told his valet.

Marie was not so easily diverted. She had mastered the technique of her own peculiar business, and Maupassant could not help acknowledging her talents. One afternoon, when he refused to hand over the usual stipend, she threatened to tie up all her brood and drown them. He prevented this calamity with the inevitable louis. A few days later, Marie again fixed her bleary eye upon him.

" Monsieur de Maupassant," she wheedled, " we have no coal and . . ."

Maupassant turned to his valet.   " Give her twenty francs." He had a kind heart, but, tempted sufficiently, he would have sacrificed much more to play the rôle of open-handed dupe.

CHAPTER III

MOTHS

THE valet, François Tassart, had entered his employment soon after " La Guillette " was built. He was
not only a good cook but an intelligent and sympathetic
companion. He stayed with the writer until the end, and
his *Souvenirs* give an excellent picture of Maupassant's sad
decline.

His first impressions remind us that in appearance
Maupassant gave no indication of what he was suffering.

" A hefty chap, florid, with a big fair moustache and very
wavy chestnut hair. His nightshirt was open, revealing a
powerful neck, and he wore tight trousers and Turkish
slippers."

Maupassant was not the man he had imagined. He was
kindly, considerate and absolutely unaffected. He points
out his chalet with real pride.

" Look, there's my house, ' La Guillette.' I love the
place." Then he looks out to sea. " How beautiful it is !
What a lovely colour ! It's violet ! "

The two men were soon on excellent terms. François
was given a most unusual bedroom — the inside of a wrecked
fishing-boat ! This also served as the master's bathroom,
but François seems to have settled down very comfortably.
He soon became accustomed to his master's habits. The
day after his arrival, Maupassant took him out into the
garden and proudly displayed his plants. When it came to
watering the lawn or picking fruit, Maupassant insisted on
handling everything by himself.

" He was remarkably quick at picking strawberries,"
notes François.

Maupassant was not long alone. That evening a beautiful woman came to dinner. While François is discussing the visitor with the cook, Maupassant calls for a light. François hurriedly lights a lantern and conducts them to the gate.

" Don't wait for me," says Maupassant, jumping into the lady's carriage. " I have my keys."

A few days later, François learned that his master was not always so charming to his lady friends. One evening he had returned from a reception *chez une Altesse*, accompanied by a young blonde woman. She had stayed for some time but the writer was soon bored. Instead of taking the very broad hint she called every morning in the hope that Maupassant would see her. François had instructions not to disturb his master, but the lady persevered. At last Maupassant lost all patience. " Do what you like about her, but don't bother me," he told François. " She keeps saying that she's leaving for Vienna, but doesn't go. Chuck her out if you have to ! "

François soon discovered that women occupied the greater part of his master's leisure. Not all his visitors were lights of love. One of Maupassant's dearest friends was his neighbour, Madame Leconte du Nouy, who would often chat with him in the evenings. Sometimes, when his eyes were really painful and he was afraid to go to bed, she would read to him while he lay on a sofa on the balcony with his eyes closed.

Often they would discuss life, and Madame du Nouy was never tired of cross-examining the famous writer on his love-affairs. After his death she wrote a book, *Amitié Amoureuse*, which she dedicated to Madame de Maupassant. The hero, Philippe de Luzy, was based on Maupassant, a fact which robbed the authoress of his mother's friendship but sent the circulation of the book soaring.[1]

[1] It is now in its 349th edition. *En Regardant passer la Vie*, in which Madame du Nouy collaborated with M. Amic, is another valuable guide to Maupassant's social life.

There was no thought of death on those soft nights on the terrace of " La Guillette." Like every victim of hypochondria, Maupassant's mood would swiftly change from abject fear to a sense of glorious physical exhilaration. When the pain lifted from his head, he would again become the handsome male, conscious of his health and strength. Here in the country he enjoyed bragging of his conquests over the hysterical Highnesses. He talked, as he wrote, with the quiet force of a man who has already turned inside out all his intuitive knowledge of life.

" These women, whose slave he seemed, did not stand so high in his esteem as they thought," records Madame du Nouy. " He was not their dupe; their past hovered over the present, casting a dazzling light upon it. He described them to me body and soul, made me know and judge them."

One can imagine how much the lady enjoyed these confessions of a misogynist ! It is so pleasant, so subtly flattering, to hear one's own sex indicted !

Maupassant told her of a woman who was determined to impress her personality upon him by eating nothing but rose-petals in his presence !

" How can you love them after analysing their mean sentiments, their pose of philosophic erudition, their baseness of soul, the pettiness of their conduct ? " demanded the lady on the terrace.

" I do not love them, but they amuse me," he said gravely. " I find it very funny to make them believe that I am the victim of their charm."

It was not a pose but the creed of a brutal sensualist.

" Woman is only an eternal harlot, unconscious and serene, who gives her body without disgust, because it is the merchandise of love." He seemed to relish that sentiment, for he rolls it on his tongue in one after another of his stories.

" Well, Guy, what about me ? " his mother once asked in mock anger.

"You are not like the others," he answered very seriously. This unhappy man could never see his lack of logic. Schopenhauer had planted the seed of misogyny and Fate forced it deeper into the soil. Seeing all women with the eyes of a sensualist, Maupassant denied what he had never sought. He took without giving and was disgusted with what he received. Knowing only harlots, he despised all women. He was that type of perverted idealist who spits on the altar rather than see it defiled by another. All his life he demanded sex without sentiment, and ended by denying himself the tenderness of women.

"My eyes say to my heart: hide yourself, old man, you are grotesque," he wrote, and gave his readers the clue to all his distorted philosophy. The candle had burned brightly at both ends and the darkness was often terrifying.

He could not always reconcile what he knew with what he hoped. He never departed from his view that women have only two functions in life – physical love and maternity – but several of his heroines are the objects of his pity. Jeanne Lamare, Miss Harriet, Christiane Andermatt, the Comtesse de Mascaret, all move slowly before the reader, each adding her protest against man's injustice. But it is only part of the author's protest against the injustice of life itself. If woman suffers through her utter dependence on the male, the latter also knows the hollowness of physical love.

Society disgusted him, yet he continued to frequent the fashionable *salons*; women disgusted him, yet the rustle of a skirt was enough to set him off on the old chase.

"I have never loved," he confesses. "I think I judge women too critically to be susceptible to their charm." He did not realise that physical over-indulgence had left him morally impotent.

He had no faith in life but was terrified of death. The first despair is already to be seen in his book of travel, *Au Soleil*, which appeared in 1884. Three years had passed since his visit to Africa, three years in which he had established himself as a successful writer. He had a house in the country, a luxurious flat in Paris, a valet, and he was already negotiating for the purchase of a yacht. But having all the flesh-pots only intensified his pessimism. A man who struggles for something has little time for introspection. Maupassant had everything but the cure for these agonising headaches. When drugs failed him, he knew the fear of death; that fear obsessed him. He wanted to laugh and sing and joke, hoping to shout down the little despairing voice within him. And it is that voice which whispers into all his writings from this time onwards. He has denied God and love, but he cannot deny death.

In his book of travel, he captured all the hard light of Africa. The sun glows through every paragraph, but the morbid horror of death prefaces this beautiful picture of a holiday in the sun.

" Whatever we do, we shall die ! Whatever we believe, whatever we think, whatever we attempt, we shall die. And it seems that we shall die to-morrow without knowing anything, although disgusted already with what we do know."

He was afraid to die, but the doctors merely smiled when he discussed his symptoms. Imaginary invalids are common in the ranks of writers, and Maupassant always had his nose in medical works. He was probably the kind of man who is not satisfied until he has actually contracted some illness. Every doctor knows that type of patient – he is a stock figure in the work of medical men all over the world. This writer was leading a fast life and complaining when Nature exacted her penalty. He suffered from pains in the head, but that was surely not surprising, if only half the stories were true ! He took drugs, pursued every petticoat in sight, wrote like two ordinary men and expected to be completely fresh and healthy at all times ! As it was, he had muscles like a wrestler and enjoyed a reputation for remarkable athletic feats. The doctors shrugged and pocketed their fees. If his head ached he must wear spectacles; there seemed to be nothing else wrong with him. As he seemed so anxious to sample patent medicines, they wrote out prescriptions and recommended watering-places suitable for such varied complaints as asthma and rheumatism.

His condition did not improve. His eyes were very painful, particularly when he overworked or stayed too long in a crowd. He wore his spectacles while he was writing, and the worthy François did what he could to make his master comfortable when " the trouble " came. Cold showers seemed to do him good, and the valet soon became an expert masseur.

They had become accustomed to these sudden attacks of migraine. " Rub some vaseline into the nape of my neck," Maupassant would groan. " If I'm not better by eleven o'clock, I'll breathe a little ether." Vaseline, showers, massage, vapour baths – poor Maupassant was eager to try every new prescription. As soon as the pain passed, he would strut about the room, confident that he was cured at last. Life was once again glorious and exciting !

" These douches are excellent," he would remark to François. " What a pity Flaubert never went in for hydrotherapy and friction ! He would not have gone so young. But then, he never cared for that kind of hygiene. Just think ! He was only sixty when he died; he was still strong and vigorous and I'm quite sure this kind of douche would have prolonged his life."

François was not at first perturbed by these attacks of migraine. It was ridiculous to suppose that they were chronic. Few of Maupassant's friends were aware of his suffering and he certainly did all he could to conceal it.

Doctors were often at his dinner-table, but it was widely assumed that he was picking their brains for his books. In a sense that was true. Only when the tragedy came did the public bury its nose in his masterpieces for revealing accounts of his suffering.

As yet there was no indication that he was marked down for early death. Rumours usually start belowstairs, but there was still nothing to disturb François. When he entered Maupassant's employ, the valet asked the cook a few questions.

" He is an excellent boss," said Désirée. " A good boy, a child of the country, whom everyone calls by his first name. And nobody can swim like him."

His melancholia he seemed to reserve for his books. Those who romped and debauched with him paid little attention to his gloomy outpourings on death. It was all very *fin de siècle*, a kind of spiritual indigestion after a surfeit of pleasure. Zola, Ibsen and all the Realists had it, this feverish malaise and sense of discouragement which had become almost fashionable.

At Etretat, Maupassant was usually full of boyish high spirits, and the whole countryside laughed at his practical jokes. Sometimes he would organise a party of guests and lead them in a wild dancing procession. These parties usually began at midnight, when all the guests were aglow with alcohol. Maupassant would drag out a barrel-organ which he had unearthed somewhere, and his cousin, the painter Le Poittevin, usually took command of this instrument. With lanterns lit, the party would set off, laughing and dancing like schoolchildren. Outside a farmhouse they would serenade the peasant and his family, persuading them to get up and prepare some onion soup. Then the party danced merrily under the apple-trees to the strains of the barrel-organ.

" The cocks woke up and crowed, the horses pawed

restlessly in their stables, and the cool country air fanned our faces, filled with the scent of grass and new-mown hay ! " wrote Maupassant in an article which appeared in the *Gil Blas*.

He seemed indefatigable in his efforts to amuse his guests, a high-spirited crowd of artists and Society folk. Maupassant had no use for serious literary men who would talk endlessly of style and æsthetics. He preferred to live his literary life in his study and to relax as soon as he had blotted his manuscript.

People loved to come to Etretat, where there was always plenty of sport and amusement. Maupassant had a genius for hospitality but his social success was primarily due to a careful choice of guests. Sometimes Zola and one or two other writing men were invited for luncheon, but these visits were not frequent. For the most part, he only asked people he really wanted, the worldly easy-going set whose hospitality he enjoyed in Paris or Cannes.

The food was always excellent, and Maupassant arranged his menus with the care he gave to his stories. He personally supervised all the preparations for entertaining his guests. There were bathing-parties, excursions to local beauty-spots, bowls tournaments. For those who liked the simple pleasures, he provided a pretty seesaw on which many flirtations were initiated. At night, beautiful firework displays or amateur theatricals were often staged.

One of his most successful entertainments was a lottery which he conducted with remarkable wit and gusto. The prizes caused their winners a good deal of embarrassment, and one unfortunate young woman had the greatest difficulty in separating a very alarmed rabbit from her beautiful gown ! For Maupassant the evening was only marred by the undesirable presence of curious spectators.

" Did you see them hanging over the hedges ? " he complained to François. " I'm sure there were quite 1,500 of

these nosy-parkers. . . . If I had a very big house, properly
fenced in, I'd be much better off, believe me." He then
sketched out his plan for a house in which a hundred guests
could stay in comfort !

Grandiose ideas were already forming in his head, the
early warnings of the coming storm, and some of his practical
jokes showed evidences of hysteria. He always loved
" farces " but often they went too far. Once, when two
women fainted in the excitement of a firework display, he
revived them by discharging some crackers close to their
ears !

He went to extraordinary lengths to ensure the success of
his pranks. On one occasion he paid off an old score by
making a young beauty look completely ridiculous. He had
invited four ladies to meet a handsome Spanish marquis who
was supposed to be very wealthy. Maupassant had carefully
prepared the ground by informing his guests that the
marquis was looking out for a desirable companion. The
ladies decked themselves out in their best and prepared for
battle.

The marquis turned out to be an eccentric young man.
He absorbed champagne like a sieve, threw off his coat
before the *entrée* was served, and took little naps between
courses. When he awoke, Maupassant skilfully directed
the conversation with a few innocent questions about his
plans. The marquis took the cue and enlarged upon the
type of establishment he had in mind. It seemed that he
intended to take a luxurious house in Paris. Who was the
best tapestry-maker in France ? Who would help him to
fill a good stable ? The little ladies were eager to help him
with these and many other problems ! Their pretty heads
were already whirling with visions of life with this handsome
nobleman. Meanwhile, Maupassant filled their glasses and
egged on the gallant marquis. Before he left that night, the
Spaniard had shown marked preference for a delightful little

Nm

woman who had used all her arts to qualify for the honour of being taken home by the fascinating stranger. Needless to state, she was the one whom Maupassant had marked out for his revenge !

The marquis played his part beautifully, and carried off the unsuspecting lady, nearly falling down the stairs in his enthusiasm. Only when the couple had gone did the host console the disappointed competitors by informing them that the marquis was not serious.

" Before dawn he will quietly leave a louis on her mantel-piece and hop off ! "

Another of his favourite jokes was to disguise a young actress as a man and see " him " flirt with the married women. So perfect was the disguise that the stranger usually succeeded in making rendezvous with the ladies ! Even François was deceived into declaring that the " young man was very charming."

Often his jokes were crude and far-fetched. One noble lady had long resisted his advances and he could not easily reconcile himself to his failure. She was a witty person who enjoyed a joke as much as he did. One morning her servant delivered a package to Maupassant. She had sent twenty-four little dolls, six dressed like harlots, six like widows in mourning and the others like nuns. We do not know the significance of this particular gift, but Maupassant lost no time in turning it to account. The donor was childless, in spite of her popularity, and Maupassant hit upon a rather heartless way of snubbing her. That evening he and Francois ripped up some old handkerchiefs and padded out the widow dolls so as to show that widowhood and maternity were by no means incompatible. He then sent back the immoral widows with the brief note: " All this in one night ! "

Maupassant's love of practical joking was so well known to his friends that his efforts sometimes misfired. Once he sent a lady a basket full of frogs. François had his orders and managed to keep a straight face when the lady asked questions. Maupassant often sent presents, but this time his friend was suspicious and refused to open the beautiful basket. Poor François tried hard to be faithful but the lady finally forced him to divulge the contents. Instead of taking offence, she burst out laughing, ordered her carriage and emptied the basket into the lake of the Bois de Boulogne ! The valet returned rather crestfallen, but Maupassant roared with laughter.

" I might have known that she would think of nothing but saving their lives ! "

His friends seem to have been most indulgent. It was almost impossible to be a guest at " La Guillette " without being the victim of some hoax. One can well imagine the feelings of a duchess on being addressed with " Bonjour, petite cochonne ! " by the author's parrot. The guest's discomfiture would be completed by a pet monkey who seemed to share his master's profound contempt for conventional morality.

Maupassant's visitors would frequently be amazed to discover that they had missed their last train back to Paris. The host had thoughtfully stopped all the clocks in the house ! On these occasions, nothing delighted him more than to spend the night laughing and chatting with his guests. It was a childish, unkind sort of prank, but the offender made himself so pleasant that nobody could complain. And none suspected that Maupassant would have gone to more extreme lengths to avoid being left alone, particularly at night.

It will be noted that women were usually the victims of his practical jokes. In many cases he was taking his revenge for being jilted, for he was by no means as irresistible as his great public imagined. But his reputation as a woman-hater tempted many to seek his acquaintance. He was never averse to start a new affair and had soon mastered all the wiles of the seducer. Madame Leconte du Nouy has shown that " Philippe " wielded an insincere pen when he could not break down the doors of the boudoir. He favoured the direct method, but his experience of gilded *salons* had taught him that some women cannot be won over a cup of afternoon tea. They were all the same, of course, but many of these well-born hysterical ladies saw their pillows through a haze of sentiment. Some were dreamy and passionate, seeking to cloak their adultery with romantic dreams. They had to be humoured with pretty speeches and poetic sentiments. Only when the citadel had fallen, did these deluded women discover that their hero was a satyr.

As Maupassant always favoured married ladies, he could break off an affair at his own convenience, knowing that his victim would not dare to risk a scandal. He was quite indifferent to the feelings of women who confused biology with sentiment. A woman who puffed desperately at the fag-end of her illusion was nothing more than a fool and a hypocrite.

He once received an unexpected visit from a lady driven half-mad by his indifference. She arrived at " La Guillette," prepared to enforce her arguments with a revolver ! Maupassant was not at home when she called, and François spent an uncomfortable half-hour trying to persuade her to leave. Meanwhile the excitement had proved too much for the visitor, who suddenly fainted. When she recovered her senses, she was in a very different frame of mind.

" François, I beg of you, let me see M. de Maupassant or I shall die. I swear that I shall not harm him ! "

Maupassant himself interrupted this melodramatic scene and seemed quite undismayed by the presence of this visitor.

" Don't worry," he told François, " I'll see to everything." A few hours later the lady took her departure.

"We are now good friends again," she told the astonished valet.

A far more practical person was the lady who had called a week or two before this incident. Maupassant was also out on this occasion. "Well, give him this note as soon as he comes in," said the visitor. Then she took a sheet of paper and printed in block capitals the word "Cochon."

When Maupassant saw the message he burst out laughing and exclaimed: "May the devil take them all!" Then, with a whimsical smile, he added: "This young marquise, who writes so well, is the daughter of a former Minister under the Empire. But I don't want to see her; she gets on my nerves."[1]

It would be easy to condemn Maupassant, but one cannot readily do so without taking into account the character of those who pursued him. When circumstances demanded it, he would trim his logic with bunting, but he was franker and more honest than the voluptuaries who accused him of heartlessness. He, at least, had the courage of his lack of conviction. Every woman in Paris knew that he despised wedlock as "the acme of bourgeois imbecility." He had connived at too much adultery to risk his own hand in marriage. In the story "Au Printemps" he set forth in the clearest possible terms what he saw beyond the altar:

"You say to yourself: 'How sweet life would be with a wife!'

"And so you get married, and she calls you names from morning till night, understands nothing, knows nothing, chatters continually, sings the song of 'Musette' at the top of her voice (oh! that song of 'Musette,' how tired one gets of it!), quarrels with the grocer, tells the porter all her domestic details, confides all the secrets of her bedroom to the neighbour's servant, discusses her husband with the

[1] *Souvenirs sur Guy de Maupassant*, François, p. 74, *et passim*.

tradesmen, and has her head so stuffed with stupid stories, with idiotic superstitions, with extraordinary ideas and monstrous prejudices, that I — for what I have said applies particularly to myself — shed tears of discouragement every time I talk to her."

Such a declaration merely stimulated feminine curiosity. His conversation was notoriously coarse and brutal and he was known to take a sadistic delight in breaking hearts. These facts only fanned the flame for the moths. Every woman painted him differently in her own heated imagination. The nymphomaniacs saw in him a worthy playmate. Hard, experienced beauties were attracted by his wealth, fame and social position. The third estate consisted of silly and romantic girls with vague maternal instincts. They endowed him with Byronic qualities and dreamed of redeeming him with a pure unsullied love !

Small wonder that Maupassant was often confronted with a choice of twenty invitations for dinner ! Those who lacked the necessary social equipment tried to arouse his interest by writing to him. Sixty or seventy admiring letters were quite a commonplace every morning. So contemptuous had he become of these correspondents that he rarely troubled to look beyond the first few words. They usually revealed what the writer was at such pains to camouflage.

Soon after the publication of *Une Vie* he opened a letter which really touched his imagination. It was absurdly enigmatic, but not without a certain impudent charm:

" Monsieur:

" I read your works, I might almost say, with delight. In truth to Nature, which you copy with religious fidelity, you find an inspiration that is truly sublimer, while you move your readers by touches of feeling so profoundly human, that we fancy we see ourselves depicted in your pages, and love you with an egotistical love. Is this an unmeaning compliment ?   Be indulgent ;   it is, on the whole, sincere.

" You will understand that I should like to say many fine and striking things to you, but it is rather difficult all at once.   I regret it all the more as you are sufficiently great to inspire one with romantic dreams of becoming the confidant of your beautiful soul, always assuming your soul to be beautiful.

" If your soul is not beautiful, and if those things are not in your line, I shall regret it for your sake, in the first place; and then I shall set you down in my mind as a maker of Literature, and dismiss the matter from my thoughts.

" For a year past I have intended to write to you, and have been many times on the point of doing so, but – sometimes I thought I exaggerated your merits and that it was not worth while.   Two days ago, however, I suddenly saw in the *Gaulois* that someone had honoured you with a flattering epistle and that you had inquired the address of this amiable person in order to answer him.   I at once became jealous, your literary merits dazzled me anew and – here is my letter.

" And now let me say that I shall always preserve my incognito for you.   I do not even desire to see you from a distance – your face might not please me – who knows ? All I know of you now is that you are young and unmarried, two essential points even for a distant adoration.

" But I must tell you that I am charming; this sweet reflection will stimulate you to answer my letter.   It seems to me that if I were a man I should wish to have no dealings, not even by letter, with an old fright of an Englishwoman, whatever might be thought by

" Miss Hastings.[1]

" Madeleine Post Office."

---

[1] *Letters of Marie Bashkirtseff,* translated by Mary J. Serrano (Cassell). Cf. *Further Memoirs* (1901) (Grant Richards).

Maupassant was intrigued by this strange epistle. There was a naïve charm about this correspondent which made him wish to make her acquaintance. He did not know then that she had had a long experience of writing to literary idols. She was a highly talented Russian girl, this Marie Bashkirtseff, who so demurely sheltered behind the pseudonym " Miss Hastings." Like Maupassant, she was fighting against disease, and both were greedy for excitement. This girl, however, lived in a state of feverish exaltation. A dreamer and a talented painter, she had a passionate longing to mate spiritually with all the great creative artists. She had amassed a remarkable stock of erudition, but wore her blue stockings with a certain coquettishness and seemed determined to hunt down a genius who would turn her quivering virginity into glorious womanhood.

This girl's mind had been nurtured in the soft romantic air of Russian idealism. Physically she was not Maupassant's " type." He liked older and more experienced women, particularly those with dark passionate features. She was then only twenty-three and looked younger, but there was a Slavic melancholy in her face which appealed to some men. Her small oval face was perfectly framed in golden hair which, with her sad dark eyes, gave her the air of a serious child. Her lungs were riddled with tuberculosis, and she had all the intense but fragile charm so often found in consumptives.

This ardent and susceptible young woman had a passion for pen-and-ink flirtation. She loved to be serenaded from beneath the balcony of the post office. A more unlikely mate for a man like Guy de Maupassant could not be imagined !

Marie Bashkirtseff certainly had more success with Maupassant than she probably anticipated. Believing himself worshipped from afar by this intriguing young woman (had she not described herself as " charming "?), he decided to correspond with her. He did not know that

Marie had already stormed the post-boxes of Zola, Dumas *fils* and Goncourt !

Maupassant would have chuckled over her letter to Emile Zola, knowing how that writer disliked this particular kind of nuisance.

" I have read all that you have ever written without missing a single word," she wrote breathlessly to the author of *L'Assommoir*. That letter concluded with a most delicious piece of impertinence which Maupassant would have relished.

" I do not suppose that you will answer me. They say you are in private life a complete bourgeois."

Zola had ignored her, but Alexandre Dumas *fils* could not resist the temptation to snub this delicate creature.

" What I ask is that you should be for once the spiritual director of a woman who desires to consult you as she would a priest," she had written.

Dumas brusquely assured her that novel-reading had turned her head ! From behind her pillar-box she fired the last shot.

" Sleep well, monsieur, and continue to be as much a bourgeois in private as you are an artist for the public. . . . Apropos of divorce, I now announce to you that of my admiration from your person."

" Miss Hastings " was delighted to hear from Maupassant, who gravely assured her that he could not be her confidant without knowing more about her appearance. " Sixty women write to me regularly," he announced.

Her next letter still held him at arm's length.

" To my great regret, then, it seems that we must remain as we are – unless I should some day decide to prove to you that I do not deserve to be No. 61. . . . If you need only a vague description to induce you to disclose to me the beauties of your withered and scentless soul, take this: fair hair, medium height, born some time between 1812 and

1863. And intellectually ! – no ! I should seem a braggart and you would guess at once that I was from Marseilles.

"*P.S.* – Excuse the blots, erasures, etc., but I have already copied my letter three times ! "

Maupassant's curiosity was now completely aroused. This woman, whoever she was, had clearly determined to puzzle him. He retaliated by striking an attitude of sophisticated boredom:[1]

"It's all the same to me," he groaned, "men, women, events. Everything can be divided into boredom, jokes and wretchedness. I spend two-thirds of my time in being terribly bored. The other third is spent in writing stuff which I sell to the highest bidder, while grieving at having to ply this abominable trade. . . . I do not ask if you are married. If you are, you will reply 'No.' If you are not, you will say 'Yes.'"

But the girl was too clever, or too cautious, to be convinced by this plea for understanding.

"Those old stories about your profession being a hard one ! You take me for a bourgeois who takes you for a poet and you endeavour to enlighten me. . . . So you are bored, and you look upon everything with indifference, and you have not a spark of poetry in your soul. . . . If I were not married could I read your abominable books ? "

Maupassant could not help admiring this little tease who tricked out her personality with all the skill of a practised coquette. She was such a *poseuse* herself that it became very difficult to pin her down.

"Why do I take the trouble to earn money," he asks plaintively, "when there is no pleasure in spending it. . . . In truth, I prefer a pretty woman to all the arts. . . .

[1] How different is the tone of this correspondence from that with his *real* friends! "You know the regular way to recognise women of the world at the Opéra ball," he says in another letter to her. "One pinches them. The girls are used to it, and simply say, ' Stop it.' The others get angry."

" The more I go on, the more I notice that even the shadow of pure love is preferable to all glory.   But does that shadow exist ? "

Unfortunately for Maupassant, the young lady was too busily interested in herself to peck at the bait of " pure love."   She had hoped to indulge in a beautiful friendship which would fit nicely into her diary of notes on famous men, and this writer seemed determined to add her name to his sordid list !   The two poses met and exploded in mid-air.

" I may confess that your odious letter has made me pass a very bad day," she says frigidly.   " If you still keep them, send me my autographs; as for yours, I have already sold them in America at a fabulous price."

But she cannot easily give up this literary flirtation.

" And do you not desire a little romance amid all your Parisian materialism ?   A spiritual friendship ?   I do not refuse to meet you, and I am even going to make arrangements for doing so without giving you notice."

They did meet, and it was obvious that she would not be an easy conquest.   Her ideal of manhood was a blend of artist and conquistador.   To him the affair meant nothing more than a gay waltz with an exotic partner.   His responsibility would have ended when the music stopped. But Marie's boudoir was too clearly the *poste restante*.

With his usual flair for taking notes from life, Maupassant had already decided to build a short story around her.   In this tale, " En Voyage," he paid tribute to the beauty of the " Countess Marie Baranow " who was dying of a lung disease.   The story appeared in book form in the autumn of 1884.   A few days later Marie Bashkirtseff was dead.

CHAPTER IV

HORLA

MAUPASSANT published five books in the year 1885. It was a remarkable achievement for a man who spent so much time in the pursuit of pleasure, but that year has a terrible significance for the student of his career. It marks the peak of the writer's output – in quantity if not in artistic value – and it leaves him on the threshold of general paralysis of the insane. The following year he publishes only two books and never again more than three. But between the rich harvest of 1885 – a harvest partly induced by toxæmia – and the time when Maupassant was scratching out every other line of his prose, the treacherous development of his illness can be clearly traced.

It is Maupassant's restlessness which first strikes the would-be chronicler. Every creative artist needs the stimulus of travel, but with Maupassant the urge to keep moving was clearly pathological. No sooner has the biographer photographed his subject in the Rue Clauzel than he must fold up his tripod and hurry to the Rue Dulong, thence to the Rue Montchanin, the Avenue Victor-Hugo and finally the Rue Boccador. Poor Maupassant hated the smell of paint, but that unpleasant odour was always in his nostrils. Every other page in François's diary has a reference to some imminent change of hearth. The master's travelling cases are never dusty, yet each new haven seems to be permanent.

Back from Normandy, Maupassant suddenly decides on a two months' visit to the south, where his mother and Hervé are already installed. He takes a beautiful apartment in

Cannes with a view over the sea.   Everything delights him
and he is enchanted at having escaped a chilly winter in
Paris.   The beautiful coast, the soft caressing winds and
the red-roofed villas awaken a hundred joyful dreams in him.
The road zigzags from Cannes to Golfe Juan, with a
beautiful snapshot at every turn.   From Nice, he can see
Antibes in the sunset outlined against the Alps.   He is at
once enthusiastic and resentful, wondering if he can possibly
stay away from Paris for more than two months. . . .

For a few days all went very well.   Every evening his
mother and Hervé came to dine with him, chatting pleasantly with all the gaiety and affection of relatives who do not
see each other often enough to become bored or quarrel-
some.   The conversation usually turned on Guy's success.
It seemed only yesterday when he was suffocating in his
little office, debating whether to accept Flaubert's loan of a
few francs for the railway fare to Rouen.   Now he travelled
with his cook and valet, and talked of buying a yacht to
sail him to Italy or Africa.

These things pleased his mother, but she was even
happier when he talked to her of his work.   They
would argue for hours over the structure of some story,
and Maupassant was often in her debt for some
suggestion.

" Well, that's perfect," he exclaimed after one of these
discussions.   " Now my story will fall on its feet like the
porter's cat."

The day after his arrival in Cannes, he organised an
elaborate practical joke.   This time his victim was a certain
count who loved to dabble in financial affairs.   Knowing his
weakness, Maupassant called a meeting of a dozen financiers
and suggested that they should form a company to take over
the Island of Santa Margarita.   The unfortunate count was
solemnly elected President, and the others – who were all in
the plot – talked in millions.   Everybody smoked huge

cigars, and the conspirators, taking their cue from Maupassant, did all they could to gratify the presidential vanity.
The bubble only burst when M. le Comte discovered that
the island was Government property and not for sale !

The Côte d'Azur soon bored Maupassant. " We're
leaving," he suddenly announced to François. " You can't
walk two yards without having to take your hat off to the
Highnesses who swarm here. They invite me to dinner all
the time. It fatigues and depresses me."

He is glad to be back in Paris. Barrows of violets are in
the streets, his new book of stories will soon be on the
market and he rejoices at seeing the faces from which he had
fled so recently. His cousin, Le Poittevin, has built a
luxury hotel in the Rue Montchanin, and Maupassant takes
a suite on the ground floor. Three decorators set to work at
once but the writer does not like the men. He can never
forget that a house-painter robbed him of a tie-pin and a
ring which he had inherited from his grandfather ! Once
these workmen are out of the place, he recovers his spirits
and takes a great interest in furnishing and decorating the
rooms. He has a passion for buying gewgaws, and, like
Zola, cannot resist the wheedling voice of an antiquary.
The result is somewhat confusing. The vases, statuettes
and figurines are vivid reminders of the size of his bank
balance, if little else.

" I can breathe here," he exclaimed, when the last piece of
furniture had been settled to his taste. Some of his aristocratic friends tried to share his enthusiasm, but it was
generally held that the suite was over-heated, over-scented
and over-furnished.

Whatever their private views, his friends were more than
eager to accept his hospitality. Now began the period of
elaborate menus and gilt invitation cards. Maupassant and
François would spend anxious hours plotting how best to
tempt the palates of people whom the writer professed to

despise. To the very end he believed that he was making use of them for literary purposes; as he was, to an extent. He did not know, or refused to believe, that one cannot breathe the foul air of perfumed *salons* and escape infection.

He still played pranks in the drawing-rooms, and nothing could ever rob him of his impulse to pull a tempting leg, however noble. On one occasion he horrified a crowded *salon* by solemnly defending cannibalism.

" But surely you haven't . . . ? " the voice of his hostess ebbed in sheer horror.

" Oh, yes ! " he replied gravely. " I once tasted part of a woman's shoulder." Then, with the air of a gourmet savouring the delights of the past, he sighed: " It was so good I had to have a second helping."

He did not know that the fashionable ladies laughed at him when his back was turned. They had lionised him at first, but the novelty was becoming a little threadbare. To keep his place in Society an artist must be either a great wit or a very accomplished diplomat. Maupassant was neither. Even a lion grows old, and this author was seen in too many *salons* to remain a prize for ever.

It is not suggested that Maupassant was dropped by the princesses who had welcomed him so eagerly during his first triumphs. Invitations still rained upon him, but the attitude of those who sent them had changed. It was known that he preferred the company of rich Society men to that of writers and artists. The snobs at once decided that here was a parvenu who could not live without them.

Maupassant's vanity was proof against the irony which often bristled among the pretty compliments. His mind, like his writing, was direct and honest, and he was no match for the accomplished wantons who invited him to their *soirées*. He had a superbly intuitive sense of the weaknesses of these women, but his mind's eye became afflicted with a kind of paralysis when they flattered him. What these cruel voluptuaries did not know was that their true ally was not so much the writer's vanity as the tiny germ which fed it.

He made many enemies in these *salons*. Discarded mistresses do not make polite tale-bearers, and there were many to spread unpleasant gossip about Guy de Maupassant. Nobody seemed to suspect the truth, but some of these elegant ladies were watching him while he sat brooding over the tea-table. They had seen him fly into sudden fits of anger, then become hysterically gay and coarse-tongued. He was taking drugs, this former oarsman, and sometimes one of his numerous mistresses would surprise him during a sick period. He would stop short in the middle of a sentence, look round hurriedly as if somebody stood at his elbow. What could a woman think when he suddenly stared into space as if listening to voices? And in 1885 – when this burly lover was only thirty-five – these ladies smiled behind their fans as he talked disdainfully of love. A tiny rumour was slowly trickling from one boudoir to the other. Maupassant is not the man he was. . . . Muscles are not everything. . . . He needs women because he is afraid of the dark. . . . He cannot sleep alone. . . .

Poor Maupassant did not suspect that he lost pride and honour in these beautiful dressing-rooms, but he had no illusions about the type of woman who tapped his foot under the dining-table while she smiled at her husband's stale jokes. He was to portray her as " swayed by semi-hysterical nerves, torn by a thousand contradictory whims that did not rise to the dignity of wishes, losing all illusions, yet having tasted no real joys . . . who without ardour in any direction, without enthusiasms, seems to combine the caprices of children with the exhausted vitality of old cynics." He saw them unsentimentally, and bragged of using these high-born ladies for his pleasure; but the converse was equally true.

Maupassant himself created the legend of magnificent

conquests in the highest circles, and other writers have been content to accept him at his own valuation. They have ignored two very simple but highly illuminating facts. Firstly, Maupassant was for several years developing *folie de grandeur* which afterwards showed itself in such a tragic and decisive fashion. Secondly, an impotent man, or one worn out by his excesses, is apt to disarm suspicion by bragging of his triumphs.

One need only report an incident at the house of a Madame d'A—— to realise how low Maupassant had fallen in the esteem of his " slaves." He had been invited to a party at which he understood fancy-dress was to be worn. When he arrived, he was greeted with howls of laughter, for everyone else was in immaculate evening wear ! No doubt he dismissed the whole affair as the type of practical joke which he might have played on the others. But it was the work of those who could afford to risk his displeasure, knowing that he had no head for the social heights. If the irony did pierce his vanity, a coroneted note of apology always set matters right.

His life in these gilded palaces was by no means lost to Literature. He had forfeited his peace of mind but not his artistic integrity. Like Gaston de Lamarthe, the hero of *Notre Cœur*, Maupassant was " armed with an eye which gathered portraits, attitudes and gestures with the rapidity and precision of a photographic camera, and endowed with a novelist's sense and insight as natural as a hunting-dog's scent." It was this talent which the critics had accused him of debasing. Taine, who admired his work, had gone so far as to challenge him to enlarge his canvas. " Peasants, harlots and the bourgeoisie are not everything," he had written in March 1882. " Some day you will no doubt reach a few cultivated people, the upper bourgeoisie. Paint man like an artist, and at the same time reconstruct him like a dialectician."

OM

Maupassant waited more than two years before he was prepared to answer that challenge. He had, as usual, chewed his data until he was absolutely certain that there was no danger of literary indigestion. Now that he was ready to describe the world of fashion, he did so with the implacable rationalism of the great artist. Snob he might be, but nobody could accuse him of posing his subjects for a flattering studio portrait. He had gone into the brothels and pilfered human documents which the world recognised as universal. For the last three years he had rubbed shoulders with princesses. To the direct literary realist the change of subject meant little.

It would be a betrayal of Maupassant to suggest that *Bel-Ami*, his second novel, has worn as well as some of his other work. Bel-Ami, the central character, achieves material success by sacrificing everything and everybody to his own ends. Maupassant follows this scamp through a succession of sordid adventures until he has become a great power in the world of finance and politics.

For a satire on journalism and the corrupt society of a half-century ago, this novel is superb. The upstart hero seduces every woman who can be of use to him; he lies and cheats when nothing else will serve and finally rings down the curtain with an impudent touch of blackmail.

As a piece of " naturalism," *Bel-Ami* has rightly been acclaimed a masterpiece. Each portrait and scene has the finality of a crack of the whip. It is only from a distance that one has a certain sense of disappointment. The sheer pictorial quality of the novel carries one along, but the mind is left somewhat stunned, as if too many blows have been directed at the same point. There is, perhaps, *too* much seduction, and the villainy tends to be overdone.

Lacking the real social purpose of a Zola or a Balzac, Maupassant nevertheless succeeded in painting a picture which, in part at least, reflects many of the evils of present-day Society. As a writer he was not insensitive to his age, but if the reader can avoid looking too closely at the back-cloth he will recognise the corrupt Press and the low side of high finance. In that recognition lies Maupassant's achievement as a novelist. By disciplining facts into intuition, he managed to find the universal in all his subjects.

The author's pessimism strays into every book, but in *Bel-Ami* we feel for the first time the agony of disillusion. In his writing Maupassant is often thinking aloud, and to study any one passage closely is almost like eavesdropping.

" Solitude now fills me with horrible agony – solitude at home by the fireside at night. It is so profound, the silence, the silence of the room in which one dwells alone. It is not only the silence that surrounds the body, but the silence around the soul; and when the furniture creaks, I tremble all over. . . ."

Yet his despair went deeper than a mere horror of loneliness. Lacking all faith in the hereafter, he was obsessed with the thought of death. At thirty-five most men are in their prime, but Maupassant already knew the fear of incurable disease and half-guessed the cause. On the wall of the Restaurant du Pont at Chatou he once scrawled a few couplets which tell us more than a dozen learned tomes on his psychology.

> *Prends garde au vin d'où sort l'ivresse.*
> *On souffre trop, le lendemain.*
>
> *Prends surtout garde à la caresse*
> *Des filles qu'on trouve en chemin.*

He was to pay dearly for his own wayside amours. As yet, however, he refused to succumb to his own logic. Each new doctor seemed a saviour. Lying neatly to his hand were a hundred hopeful signs that his unpleasant headaches were not chronic. His entire medical history was a history of compromises with his doubts. He swallowed at a gulp the most remarkable mixture of drugs and poppycock ever absorbed by a sufferer, but there were moments of real despair when he knew instinctively that he was doomed. He might flex his muscles and brag of his exploits as lover and oarsman, but the tiny bacillus still danced in his blood. People who remembered how Maupassant used to throw out his chest and strut about a *salon* like a wrestler saw in this the eve of his *folie de grandeur*. The truth lay far deeper. It was easy to shout down his dread when he was surrounded by a crowd of flatterers and voluptuaries, but in the loneliness of his room he was no longer anæsthetic to fear. To this sensitive mind, solitude was fatal to illusion.

Another man might have drugged himself continually with physical delights, but Maupassant could not reconcile himself to a life of pleasure. He was a writer and never fully enjoyed his day unless it were prefaced by a good morning's work. Wherever he found himself, that four hours' stretch of writing before luncheon was one of his most regular habits. This taste for systematic work he owed to Gustave Flaubert, but his industry was only partly due to the artistic urge for self-expression. His books were selling, but his scale of living demanded a very high output. Luxury had become essential to him, and that meant a businesslike attitude towards Literature. Although short stories brought in 500 francs apiece, they did not buy yachts and country houses. Only novels with enormous world sales could pay for such luxuries, and they involved steady work.

" I am in the throes of getting installed in my new apartment," he writes to his mother. " It will be pretty, but expensive, expensive, expensive. But I'm placing great hopes in my novel [*Bel-Ami*]." This business of sales was not his only anxiety. A hired beauty might drive off the fears which hemmed him in at night, but there was nobody to stand by his elbow when he sat at the writing-table. In *Bel-Ami* he describes the sinister shadows which surround him:

"A day comes, and it comes early for many, when there is an end to mirth, for behind everything one looks at one sees death. . . . I now see death so near that I often want to stretch out my arms to push it back. I see it everywhere. The insects crushed on the path, the falling leaves, the white hair in a friend's head rend my heart and cry to me ' Behold it ! ' It spoils for me all I do, all I see, all that I eat and drink, all that I love: the bright moonlight, the sunrise, the broad ocean, the noble rivers, and the soft summer evening air so sweet to breathe."

François has barely settled into the new apartment before he is packing his master's bag for another holiday. This time Maupassant has decided to row down the Seine from Paris to Rouen, accompanied by a friend. He seems gay and excited by the thought of rowing for four days, and François notes the professional ease with which his master handles the boat.

On his return he cannot stay another day in Paris. He is happy at last and looks a picture of radiant health. He shakes hands with the gardener, congratulates him on the beautiful flowers and settles down to work. Everything delights him. He waters the garden, feeds his goldfish and calls on all his old friends. In a neighbouring village, Saint-Jouin, he spends many a happy afternoon drinking cider at an inn kept by " La belle Ernestine." She is a bluff, jovial woman and her inn is crowded with souvenirs of the famous. Alexandre Dumas, Offenbach and Swinburne have all leaned their elbows on her table, but she most enjoys a joke with this sturdy son of the country who laughs so loud and brings so much amusing gossip from Paris.

He is not long alone at " La Guillette." Soon the
house is crowded with gay and fashionable friends who
demand amusement. Life becomes rather strenuous for
Maupassant, who must look after his guests while he works
out the details of a new novel. Soon the old evil attacks
again, and François massages him. He is suddenly worried
about his diet, gives strict orders to the cook and becomes
morose at table. Salads every day, no spinach, no carrots,
no cabbages : he has read somewhere that such things are
harmful ! Alexandre Dumas *fils* always laughs at his
symptoms and tells him he has a bad stomach. That is
enough to make Maupassant spend hours in the kitchen
discussing the preparation of his food. He becomes finicky
like a rich old maid with a diet sheet, but his head still aches
painfully and he cannot sleep at night. And François soon
grows accustomed to being awakened in the early hours
with a request for camomile tea.

When the pain became unbearable, the writer inhaled
ether or took hashish. He had a highly developed sense of
smell and many of his stories refer to odours which had
excited his imagination. He loved " the old melancholy
odour of letters that have been packed away," and few
writers have had a more delicate sense of the smells of
streets, fields, houses and furniture. Often the smell of
grass or seaweed would remind him of some forgotten place,
and the inevitable story would soon crackle like a dry leaf
in the wind.

One odour had become very familiar to Maupassant —
the warm, oppressive breath of the Turkish bath. When
the *salons* were particularly tedious, he would take refuge in
the hot rooms and try to relax his limbs. Here he was
conscious of the admiring glances which the other *habitués*
threw at his magnificent biceps. They would have scoffed
at the suggestion that he suffered from headaches which
" grind the head and drive you mad."

A huge negro with a woolly head would massage him, and Maupassant loved nothing better than the sound of expert hands clapping on his flesh. Afterwards, when his body tingled pleasantly, he would have a very cold shower and lie down in the large resting-room. But he could not stay long in that alcove of nodding heads. Some of the greetings he acknowledged, and those who could not boast of his acquaintance would find ways of forcing themselves upon him. Some wished to congratulate him on the success of his new novel, *Bel-Ami*, while others deplored their nudity and borrowed pencils from the attendants. But M. de Maupassant refused to sign autographs and hurried to his cubicle, leaving in his wake a flurry of surmise.

" They say that *Bel-Ami* has already gone into fifty editions."

" He must be making millions. He was only a clerk a couple of years back. Who is he, anyway ? "

" I hear that his mother and Flaubert . . . "

" I don't believe it ! But a friend of mine knows as a fact that he and the Comtesse de —— are . . . "

From Etretat he hurried back to Paris, eager for the noise and excitement of the city. For a while all went well, but as soon as the migraine attacked he decided that Paris disagreed with him. It was too noisy and the Eiffel Tower bored and disgusted him. Early in 1885 he set out for Italy in the company of two painters. If we are to believe the account of one of his companions, Maupassant belittled everything he saw and grumbled all the time. That was certainly not the attitude displayed in his accounts of the tour, and one is tempted to suggest that he was deliberately irritating the painters, who gaped at everything. At all events, he wrote several articles for the *Gil Blas* in which he enthused over Venice, Pisa and Florence. He was fasci-nated by Naples and explored the stinking, feverish city with

the thoroughness of a Zola. For hours on end he would
wander through the streets, striking up acquaintance with
complete strangers.

To give him a different impression of Naples, several of
the local artists and writers invited him to formal luncheons
at the *trattoria* Pallino, but Maupassant preferred to mingle
with the crowds. In Paris he needed the glittering *salons*,
but he had crossed the border to forget them. He disliked
" talking shop " at all times, and· nothing seemed more
futile than to waste his valuable tour in social courtesies. It
was not only tiresome but bad business to sit at the head of
a table listening to pretty speeches. A realist like Maupassant had to travel with his eyes wide open, and everything
he saw was recorded and duly sent off to the French newspapers.

His companions noticed at times how nervous and irritable he became. He seemed to have discarded both good
taste and good sense when he turned his back on those who
were at such pains to entertain him. They did not know
that his apparent rudeness was due to an overwhelming
need of rest. Light dazzled his eyes, and the recurrent
attacks of migraine sent him panic-stricken to his sofa.
He would close the shutters, bolt his door and gulp down a
good draught of potassium bromide. If the attack passed,
he would at once rejoin his friends, assuring them that he
had been at work and did not wish to be interrupted.
Otherwise, he might be there for hours, seeing the furniture
sway about him, and tortured by a mounting uneasiness of
body and spirit.

As usual, he returned to Paris with a sense of enormous
relief. He was in excellent spirits and caressed his pet cat
Piroli like an old friend. Like his hero, Olivier Bertin, " he
adored animals, especially cats, and could not see their silky
fur without being seized with an irresistible sensuous desire
to caress their soft, undulating backs and kiss their electric

fur." Before leaving for Italy he had given François strict orders that the cat was not to be left alone in the apartment.

" If you are away for more than a day, take her round to my cousin and see that the maid looks after her properly."

Maupassant had made himself comfortable and was sitting in his dressing-gown when the cat jumped on his lap and tore at the newspaper he was reading. Not satisfied with this exuberance, Piroli leapt upon the mantelpiece, upsetting that old relic, the skeleton hand. Nothing could mar the writer's pleasure at being back in Paris. The apartment had been redecorated according to his wishes and he declared himself delighted with what had been done. While he and François were chatting, the inquisitive pussy had peeped into his trunks and was playing with a lump of sulphur which the writer had picked up somewhere. Suddenly she began to miaow and run about frenziedly. The sulphur dust had got into her eyes ! Maupassant at once took her on his knees and tried to comfort her:

" Poor little one, beautiful pussy."

When the cat was a little calmer, Maupassant stretched himself languidly.

" François, you will put out my evening clothes," he said. " I'm dining with Madame ——, then we go on to the theatre. The lady wants me to meet M. Raymond Deslandes (director of the Vaudeville Theatre). Everyone tells me to go in for play-writing, but I don't want to very much. . . . Whenever I go to a play, I come out horrified. If it weren't for the charming people that one meets there, I'd never set foot in the place."[1]

These " charming people," how they bored him sometimes !

" Society women get on my nerves," he once declared. " Some of them have intelligence, but their minds are all made in one mould like a rice pudding. They always serve

[1] *Souvenirs sur Guy de Maupassant* (6th edition), p. 41.

you with the same dish.   I love rice but I hate eating it every day."

That attitude did not prevent him from patronising the fashionable *salons* whenever he was in Paris or Cannes. He seemed to find little pleasure in the company of literary men although there were, of course, exceptions.   The writer whose company he most enjoyed was Alexandre Dumas *fils*. "I am on very good terms with him," he once stated in an interview, "but we do not ply the same trade.   And we certainly do not talk Literature.   There are so many other things."

CHAPTER V

LITERARY MEN

MAUPASSANT did not like discussing his work. " I write when I want to, but I don't want to talk about it," he told M. Jules Huret in an interview. Dumas had polished manners and could be relied upon to make any dinner-party a rollicking success. An excellent raconteur, he would force a laugh from the most unpromising soil, and his stories, always gay and *risqué*, appealed enormously to Maupassant. But it was his refusal to talk " shop " which really made him so welcome at his friend's table.

With Paul Bourget, Georges de Porto-Riche, Taine and other literary men he was also on amicable terms, but his feeling for Zola had changed. He respected but could no longer feel much warmth for the master of Médan. They sometimes lunched together, but both men were relieved when the meal was over. They would try hard to remain polite. Literature was never discussed, out of deference to the host, and Zola realised how much had happened since those Thursday evenings when Maupassant was one of his admiring circle of young men. Now Maupassant could scarcely pick up one of Zola's novels without a feeling of exasperation. He disliked his propagandist tendencies and considered that he tried deliberately to shock his readers. To this disciple of Flaubert, Zola's work betrayed a deplorable self-consciousness and more than a little vulgar sensationalism.

Apart from these literary misgivings, Maupassant found it difficult to like Zola. After the elegant company to which he had grown so accustomed, Zola seemed rather ridiculous and bourgeois. He had developed a paunch and, with it, a taste for all the solid middle-class luxuries. To Maupassant, the other's pathetic desire for such fripperies as the Legion of Honour and a seat in the Academy seemed quite ridiculous. He good-naturedly offered to help Zola attain his wish but he could never again admire him.

While the two men sandwiched polite small-talk between their courses, Maupassant felt constrained, and a little regretful for those exciting evenings by the river at Médan. After all, it was to Zola that he indirectly owed his present position in the world of letters. Yet the good Emile offended his eye, and it was embarrassing to entertain him. He breathed heavily after eating and wiped his lips with the gesture of a provincial paterfamilias. When he hoisted on his overcoat and smiled over his pince-nez, Maupassant found it difficult to restrain an inward smile of relief. As soon as the visitor had gone, he would throw himself on his couch and call weakly for some tea.

" Monsieur Zola is a great writer," he once murmured to François, " but I don't like him." It is sometimes far simpler to write a book on a man's work than to sit through a meal facing him.

Maupassant was not the only one to notice the change in Zola. Even Cézanne, Zola's oldest friend, had fallen away. They had struggled and starved together in their youth, and Cézanne, always candid, did not shrink from telling Zola that success had changed him for the worse. To this slovenly Bohemian artist, Zola seemed like some fat tabby snoring contentedly on the rich carpet among his ghastly pieces of bric-à-brac.

In a sense, Zola and Maupassant had both suffered for their success. Literary friendships have often too little bone and too much printer's ink. It is easy to grumble together when there is no fuel and the concierge becomes the common enemy. Cézanne and Zola had been like brothers, ready to split their last crust, but such a bond

cannot easily survive the success of one of the parties.
To remain permanent, friendship of this kind demands
enormous tact and affection, and artists too often become embittered by lack of recognition. It is one thing
to share poverty and quite another to sit at the table of
one's more successful colleague. The latter may exert
all his charm, but his old friend will often feel like a poor
relation.

Zola achieved literary fame at the cost of many good
cronies. Cézanne had bowed himself out with a laugh, half-
amused, half-contemptuous, and others followed. Huysmans and Céard soon broke the ranks of discipleship, and
Edmond de Goncourt, whom Bauer aptly termed "the
Fraternal Sniveller," could not stomach Zola's success.
With his old-maidish eagerness to take offence, he began
to squabble, first adopting a martyred air and finally
dissociating himself altogether from Zola's Naturalism.
The real gulf, however, lay between the numbers of copies
sold by the two writers. As time passed and the public
continued to patronise Zola, Goncourt battened on every
possible excuse for expressing his displeasure, even suggesting – quite without justification – that Zola had jumped his
claim with a novel. Zola at once denied the charge, but
Goncourt assumed a damaged smile and declared that he was
"hurt" but not really angry.

Maupassant was no more fortunate with men of
letters. His success had been even more spectacular than
Zola's and he soon found himself threatened by a hundred
petty squabbles. Unlike Zola, he took no steps to conciliate
those who sniffed out patronage from the most innocent
words. He had little use for men who resented the luxury of
his life because they were not invited to share it.

Rightly or wrongly, Maupassant had soon decided that he
could do without the close friendship of literary gentlemen.
He did not like the petty intrigues of cliques and knew too

much about human nature to ignore the hypocrisy and opportunism which circle around a successful author. Flaubert had taught him that a writer's job was to *write* and the rest counted for nothing. Most of all he despised the mutual back-scratching that lay behind so many official distinctions. Where was the dignity of letters when a powerful writer like Zola rushed forward to beg for baubles which lesser men had been given merely because they had friends behind the scenes ?

The artist, particularly the Naturalist, should be free: he should turn his broad back on these claims. Flaubert had been pitilessly opposed to cliques, against anything that involved the artist in obligations and endangered his independence. Maupassant had not agreed with him over the Médan group, but now he appreciated the full force of Flaubert's argument.

" Three things dishonour a writer," Maupassant once announced. " Membership of the French Academy, the Legion of Honour and writing for the *Revue des Deux Mondes*." He relaxed in favour of the *Revue des Deux Mondes*, and his last novel appeared in that paper, but he had been far from eager to take this step. As for his other principles, there was no question of compromise. The Minister Spuller begged him to accept the Cross of the Legion of Honour, but Maupassant remained firm. When Alexandre Dumas *fils* and others approached him with regard to the Academy, he firmly declined to consider the matter.

" No, it's not for me," he told a disappointed friend. " Later, who knows ? But I want to be free now."

He was equally determined in rejecting Catulle Mendès' suggestion that he should become a freemason. In all such affiliations he saw both a menace to artistic liberty and an encroachment on his leisure. Illness already robbed him of precious hours which should have been given to work or recreation; he could see no reason why he should sacrifice any part of his time to long-winded discussions on Art and Æsthetics.

Maupassant was not a " man of culture." His stock of erudition was small, and he seemed quite indifferent to the value of foreign languages. Flaubert had urged him to read more, but he was always fonder of love than of books. Nor must it be forgotten that his eye trouble made him reluctant to read overmuch. He needed his sight for writing, and in time it became difficult for him to spend even a morning at his desk.

Critics recognise to-day that Maupassant's success as a writer was largely due to his marvellous observation. Had he been a scholar it is highly possible that his work might have suffered. Maupassant never stops to argue about the significance of what he is discussing. He is rarely tempted to display his learning, because he lacks book knowledge. And it is his very lack of both inventiveness and erudition which makes him at once so powerful and readable. His stories are bits of human life, arranged and interpreted by the hand of a remarkable craftsman who preferred to take his data from life rather than the library shelves.

Such a man had no inclination for the abstract discussions in which literary men so often delight. Whenever he wished to discuss Literature he found it simpler – and far more lucrative – to send his articles to a newspaper. But he was by no means the egoist which some journalists have made him out to be. He did not hesitate to acclaim merit, and nobody could accuse him of being a slave to literary fashion. When all the critics were thumbing their noses at the up-start symbolists, it was Maupassant who came forward in defence of the movement.

He was condemned as a snob by men who envied or misunderstood him, yet there is a remarkable lack of evidence to show that he was unkind to fellow-authors and

artists.   He loved to spend his leisure with rich elegant
company, and it must be admitted that his pose of the nobleman playing a bourgeois trade irritated men who respected
his achievement as a writer.   Later, when the terrible
tragedy overwhelmed him, many of his critics reversed their
opinion.   What they had condemned as arrogance was
merely the nervous irritability of a man normally kind and
good-natured.

Maupassant was always friendly and courteous to authors
in need of encouragement. Paul Hervieu, Edouard Rod
and many other young writers had the satisfaction of
seeing their first efforts welcomed by him in the *Gil Blas*.
Whoever wrote to him, whether on business or merely for
advice, was certain of receiving a signed reply.   One need
only quote a letter which Maupassant sent to a young poet
who had sent his verses with a request for his opinion.
That letter, which Pol Neveux cites in his collection, shows
Maupassant's graciousness as a correspondent.   It is also a
valuable index to his own literary outlook.

" Monsieur,

" To lay down the principles of an Art is not an easy
matter, mainly because writers vary in temperament and
need different rules.   I think that, in order *to create*, one
must not reason overmuch.   But one must observe and
reflect on what one has seen.   *To see*: and to see properly,
that is the whole thing.   By seeing properly, I mean seeing
with one's own eyes, and not with the eyes of the masters.
An artist's originality is first shown in little things.   Masterpieces have been written on insignificant details, and on
commonplace objects.   One must look for a significance
which has not previously been noticed and try to express it
in a personal manner.

" The man who will astonish me in his treatment of a
pebble, a tree-trunk, a rat or an old chair, will certainly be
on the way to Art, and qualified later to treat great subjects.

" Poets have sung so much of dawns, sunlight, dew, and the moon, damsels and love, that the newcomers can't help imitating someone when they treat these subjects. . . . You certainly have poetic gifts and an intelligence sensitive to ideas and objects. In my humble opinion, you only need a deeper reflectiveness in order to exploit your medium to the fullest extent – avoiding, above all, so-called poetic ' thoughts,' and seeking poetry in exact or even despised things where few artists have been able to discover poetry.

" But, above all, do not imitate, forget everything you have read; forget it all and (to mention an absurdity which I always think absolutely true), in order to become really *personal*, admire nobody !

" It is not easy, in fifty lines, to talk about such matters without seeming pedantic, and I'm afraid I haven't quite avoided that danger – I shake you cordially by the hand.
                                    " GUY DE MAUPASSANT."

He had no patience with interviewers who tampered with his private life in the interests of vulgar journalism. All his life he had rebelled against the popular assumption that an author must repay his readers by blowing kisses like a prima donna. If a journalist succeeded in evading François, Maupassant would receive him courteously but the worthy editor would be poorly rewarded. For such visitors, Guy de Maupassant always wore his irony in his buttonhole.

Before condemning him for segregating himself from literary men, one must first hear the evidence of François, the writer's valet and a most trustworthy witness. He tells us that the appearance of a new novel from his master's pen invariably resulted in an invasion of young writers, all eager to congratulate the author and procure his blessing. Sometimes Maupassant would lose patience.

" They tire me ! I need my mornings for work, and for

Pm

a long time they have been overdoing it. I will not admit them in future except by appointment. I ask nothing better than to be of some use to them, but in most cases what I can tell them is of no value."

It was quite true. Very few of these young gentlemen would have been prepared to serve the long and patient apprenticeship which Flaubert had imposed upon the author of *Une Vie*. He could only repeat what Flaubert had taught him about style: " Whatever the thing we wish to say, there is but one word to express it, but one verb to give it movement, but one adjective to qualify it. We must seek till we find this noun, this verb and this adjective, and never be content with getting very near it, never allow ourselves to play tricks, even happy ones, or resort to sleights of language to avoid a difficulty."

Maupassant discovered that it does not pay to have too many dealings with fellow-writers. Good advice is misconstrued as patronage and anything like dignity is soon dismissed as a pose. In certain cases, however, Maupassant seems to have acted with an extraordinary lack of tact. His breach with Goncourt is a good instance. He had persuaded the older man to accept the presidency of a Flaubert Memorial committee. Early in 1887 a performance was given at the Vaudeville Theatre, the proceeds of which were to be devoted to the fund. The following day the *Gil Blas* printed a violent article slanging Goncourt for not making up the 3,000 francs still needed. Maupassant later wrote a letter supporting the article, and Goncourt at once resigned. A month later he withdrew his resignation on being assured by Maupassant that he had not even read the article in question !

But the real point at issue between the two writers was Maupassant's preface to his novel *Pierre et Jean*, in which he set out his literary creed:

" There is no need for the strange, complicated and

Chinese vocabulary which is forced upon us to-day, under the name of artistic writing, to fix all the nuances of thought. . . . Let us try to be excellent stylists rather than collectors of rare expressions. The French language is a pure spring which precious writers have been unable and never will be able to disturb. . . . The nature of this tongue is to be clear, sensitive and logical."

As an expression of his own *credo* this passage could not be bettered. No writer had done more to preserve the purity of the French language, and it was fitting that he should make this plea against extravagant refinements of style. But it was more a criticism than a manifesto. It was, in fact, a frank indictment of the technique practised by those pioneers of Realism, the Goncourt brothers. With them polished sonorities and the cult of form were all-important. Now this stripling of Naturalism came forward and solemnly gave notice of his disapproval ! Jules de Goncourt was dead, but his brother Edmond was ready to defend himself against what he considered a breach of taste on Maupassant's part.

As soon as Maupassant had written that fighting preface, he sent a letter to Goncourt protesting his personal loyalty and admiration. That merely served to turn the knife in the wound, although he had intended to soften the blow for Goncourt. At all events, the older writer chose to regard this gesture as the clearest evidence of Maupassant's hypocrisy.

" In the preface to his novel, Maupassant – in attacking ' artistic writing ' – has aimed at me without actually naming me. In connection with the Flaubert Memorial subscription I found him to be lacking in frankness. To-day, he attacks me and at once posts a letter declaring his admiration and attachment. He forces me to conclude that he is a very Norman Norman."[1]

Maupassant's honesty and frankness were obviously too much for this subtle gossip. Goncourt liked Maupassant while he was still a young puppy grateful for caresses, but this author who outsold everyone on the bookstalls was quite another proposition. He could not restrain his jealousy of Emile Zola, and this upstart's success was even less palatable. In the public estimation, Zola and Maupassant were the only two Nauralist writers who really counted as literary forces, and Goncourt – who had been in the vanguard of the movement while Maupassant was a schoolboy – saw himself dismissed as an amateur.

" Why," he mutters in his *Journal*, " is Edmond de Goncourt considered ' a gentleman,' a dilettante, an aristocrat who toys with Literature, when Guy de Maupassant is held to be a true man of letters ? Why ? I should like to know."

He might well ask himself that unpleasant question. Posterity has supported Maupassant's judgment and Goncourt is remembered only for his malicious *Journals* and the Prize Fund which he endowed to encourage " youth, boldness and talent." The founder could not be accused of excessive generosity towards fellow-authors in his own lifetime, but it is fair to admit that the members of the Goncourt Academy have not been swayed by the influence of Edmond de Goncourt. It is perhaps ironical that the Goncourtians have shown little inclination to reward writers who imitate the impressionistic style of the founder ! They have indeed exerted a salutary influence on French Literature by frequently selecting books of a classical form, which would have gratified Maupassant.

His attack on Goncourt's style has been the subject of much discussion. Some writers have cited Maupassant's " covering letter " to the victim as evidence of his approaching insanity. It is a little difficult to dismiss this gesture as a heartless joke on the part of the younger man. Maupassant had expounded his literary philosophy and felt compelled to strike a blow at writers who, in his opinion, debased the French language. Having reached this conclusion, he was not the man to dilute his essay simply because another writer might take offence. No genuine artist could do that with a clear conscience, although a cleverer man, and one more accustomed to literary cliques, would have known that his conciliatory gesture might be misconstrued.

The two men continued to greet each other cordially, but Goncourt was now an enemy. Throughout his *Journal* we hear echoes of his bitterness towards Maupassant. He never again resisted an opportunity to sneer at the unfortunate writer whose medical history was to tally so closely with that of Jules de Goncourt.

" Maupassant looks a little less vulgar than usual. . . . The only book to be found on his drawing-room table is the *Almanach de Gotha* . . . his apartment is like a pimp's. . . ."

He had accused Maupassant of lack of frankness, but that criticism was reserved for his *Journal*. In January 1892, when Maupassant was as helpless as a child, M. de Goncourt again flicked open the pages of his malicious notebook.

Maupassant would never have stooped to attack a writer simply because of his personal dislike. We have seen how he paid tribute to Zola's work although he did not care for his company. Had Goncourt criticised his writing publicly it is likely that Maupassant would have continued to remain on good terms with him. He had a high ideal of artistic integrity and, from our knowledge of men like Goncourt, one cannot blame him too severely for avoiding the cafés where such writers gossiped and slanged their absent colleagues.

He was sometimes to be seen in an editor's drawing-room, but all too frequently the coroneted invitation took precedence of all others. At first he had patronised the *salon* of

Madame Commanville, Flaubert's niece, but soon he was
to be found regularly in the Faubourg Saint-Honoré with
Paul Bourget. The latter's aristocratic nature appealed to
Maupassant, but they differed in many respects. Both took
their microscopes into the princely drawing-rooms, but
Bourget's method was far more subtle and scientific. He
lacked Maupassant's impersonality and photographic force
but his psychological studies have the same Naturalistic
accuracy. Like Flaubert, he has a passion for verifying the
smallest detail, and once attended a specialist's clinic for
over four months to gather data on a certain disease. Both
writers were often criticised for their limited range, but
Maupassant was at least innocent of the charge that was
levelled against his friend – " he does not trouble about
souls with less than 100,000 francs."

Maupassant did not share Bourget's enthusiasm for all
things Anglo-Saxon. One summer he was invited to stay a
few days in Hampshire by Baron Ferdinand de Rothschild,
whom he had entertained at Etretat. After a pleasant stay in
the country he had suddenly announced his intention of
visiting Oxford, which Paul Bourget had advised him not to
miss. Accompanied by some rather half-hearted friends, he
arrived in what Bourget termed " the only mediæval town
of the North." The weather was execrable and the party
saw the famous spires through a mist of drenching rain.
Shivering with cold, Maupassant turned in at the Mitre for
luncheon in the hope that the weather might improve.
Afterwards the party went out into the famous High, but
it was still raining and Maupassant was anxious to see
all the sights as quickly as possible. They hired a carriage
but the driver was drunk and hiccoughed as he pointed out
the beauty-spots. Maupassant was bored, disgusted and
irritable. That evening he returned to London, saw a play
at the Savoy Theatre and went back to Paris early next
morning.

" I'm too cold, and this town's too cold," he explained in a note. " *Au revoir*, and a thousand thanks."[1]

François tells us that his master came back in an ugly temper.

" Is my bath ready ? I want it immediately. I'm absolutely worn out, a mass of aches from head to foot. I can't feel my body any more; these English devils, that so-called high society have put me into this awful condition, they're so dull and annoying with their silly nonsense ! What unbearable people ! So I cut short my visit and only stayed eight days. If it weren't for a Flemish woman whom I met in that dull country . . . I'd certainly have been back in forty-eight hours."

Maupassant had become very irritable and everyone pitied him for being such a sufferer of indigestion ! He still complained of headaches but the ophthalmoscope could detect nothing more unusual than astigmatism. His companions were sometimes shocked by his hysterical laughter and amazed at the sudden fits of depression which usually followed.

" Nerves," they murmured, and Maupassant agreed with them. The only cure, he told himself, was constant change of scene. With this object he bought the beautiful yacht *Zingara*, which he re-christened *Bel-Ami*. The new toy was delightful, " pretty as a bird, small as a nest," and he began to make beautiful plans. She was riding at anchor off Antibes and the beautiful Riviera lay before him. Within a few hours of Paris, here was the sun and warmth which had become so essential to him. When he needed company he could invite his friends for a cruise and sail into distant parts, far from the world of head waiters and *wagons-lits*.

" Railway waiting-rooms smell of filth, wherever they are," he once remarked to François.

Nobody could have suspected that this well-dressed

[1] Cited by Ed. Maynial, p. 193.

yachtsman was haunted by the fear of death. On that
beautiful day when he engaged his crew, the Mediterranean
smiled back at the sky and Antibes drowsed contentedly like
a child in a hammock. The sails seemed to run over the
waves and Maupassant handled the yacht with the skill and
pride of a born sailor. He had finally engaged a sailor called
Bernard and his brother-in-law, Raymond, and these men
became very attached to him. They admired his seamanship
and his strength, but, above all, they loved him for his great
kindness and courtesy. To these men he was a sailor like
themselves; if he could spin yarns and make money out of
them, so much the better.

For a while Maupassant remained in this paradise. Not a
cloud darkened the sky. Every morning he would work in
the villa he had taken on the road between Antibes and
Cannes. From his window he could see the white sails of
his yacht. At luncheon, he would laugh and joke with a gay
crowd of Society folk, but his real pleasure began when he
went aboard his *Bel-Ami*. All the afternoon they would
cruise around the ravishing bays, sometimes going as far as
Nice. He seemed to be as pre-occupied with navigation as
the two sailors, but they would have been surprised at the
thoughts which were passing through his mind.

" And I thought," he writes in *Julie Romain*, " that from
Cannes, which is full of determined *poseurs*, to Monaco,
which is full of gamblers, hardly a soul comes to this part of
the world except to swagger and fling money about and to
display, under this glorious sky, in this garden of roses and
orange blossom, every form of mean vanity, senseless
pretension and vile covetousness and to reveal the soul of
man for what it is — abject, arrogant and greedy."

Hardly is he settled on the Riviera before he is again on
the P.L.M. express. The fashionable idlers bore him and
he is anxious to be back in Paris again, eager to talk business
with Havard and read the proofs of his new volume of

stories. The *salons* which he had found so insufferable a few weeks before now seem like old friends. A month later the valet is affixing a new label to his master's trunk.

" I tell you straight out, François, I don't want to stay in Paris another day. You can't breathe here; it's suffocating. I've rented a place at Chatou."

June, 1887. Maupassant has taken a pleasant apartment overlooking the Seine. It evokes so many memories of the gay past when Pinchon, Petit Bleu, Tomahawk and the others sang like madmen while he rowed them up the river. Much water has flowed past Chatou since then.

" We shall be twelve at dinner," he tells François one afternoon, " but there will be only three gentlemen." He smiles pensively and adds: " What is so amusing is that, except for one or two, they are all countesses."

But he has not forgotten his old friends and invites several of them to join him. He gives a splendid dinner and plays the old trick of making them miss their train back to Paris. The next morning he arranges a boating-party. He is in splendid fettle, rubs his hands impatiently and prepares to out-row any other oarsman present. He looks very sun-burned and handsome in his flannel trousers, bathing vest and white cap.

" Don't forget to bring up the water for my shower at seven," he calls out to François. " I want it very cold, as I shall certainly be feeling warm when I get back."

The boats are lined up for the start of the race and Maupassant pulls away at once. He is back at six o'clock and the valet is shocked by the change in him. Maupassant is half-dead with cold and faintness: his body is frozen blue. The valet helps him to undress and gives him a good massage, but for days afterwards Maupassant feels the effects of his day's sport. He lies on the sofa, stroking his cats, and only gets up to fetch them their milk.

But the depression lifted and he was soon in that mood of pleasant excitement which always preceded the appearance of a new book. He was now correcting the proofs of his novel *Mont-Oriol*, the bulk of which he had written at his villa near Antibes. The story itself had first taken shape when he was taking the waters at Chatel-Guyon with his father.

He had been greatly impressed by the glorious natural scenery of Auvergne. Writing to his mother in August 1886, he says:[1]

" I have made so many excursions that I couldn't find half an hour for writing to you. I've seen Châteauneuf, the prettiest bit of Auvergne that I've come across — a deep valley among superb rocks — Pontgibaud, another valley, not so pretty, then the crater of Nachère. . . .

" I'm doing nothing except preparing gently for my novel. It will be a rather short and very simple story set in this great calm country — quite different from *Bel-Ami*. . . .

" As for me, I am hoping to leave here on Tuesday evening so as to be at Etretat on Thursday. I shall have to do a good deal of work. I shall probably go on to Cannes or Nice, if you're at Nice, so as to write without interruption the novel that l've been preparing here. I want to get it done by next summer so as to have the whole of the summer free for getting around. . . .

" Adieu, my dearest mother, I send you a thousand kisses and a good hand-shake for Hervé.

" Your son,

" GUY DE MAUPASSANT."

It was truly magnificent, this glorious plain with its great sweep of yellow fields, woods and meadows. The mountains were studded with craters and the hidden rifts of steep gorges. This country had stirred his imagination

---

[1] Pol Neveux, p. 160.

and he at once saw its possibilities as a background for a
novel. Life at a fashionable watering-place would form the
core of the story, but the romantic interest would unfold
against this glorious panorama.

The plan of the book evolved naturally. He had met
many doctors and often confessed his disillusionment when
their confident prophecies failed so miserably. He continued to run from one consulting-room to the next, hoping
that one of these learned practitioners would hold the key
to his cure. As time passed and his sufferings became worse,
he developed a kind of cynical tolerance for the men who
looked into his eyes and prescribed all kinds of different
treatment. He could not afford to overlook anything that
might help him, but too many hopes had faded to leave him
uncritical of the doctors who pocketed their fees with such
righteous satisfaction.

At Chatel-Guyon he had been cynically amused by the
jealousy and intrigues which prevailed among the medicine-
men. He noticed how some of them battened on the
credulity of their patients, resorting to all manner of tricks
to outwit their competitors. This was obvious material
for social satire, but Maupassant saw that these quacks
were only part of the mechanism of a watering-place.
Fashionable doctors and people of influence must be can-
vassed and a tremendous quantity of advertisement and
poppycock unloaded before the spa can be made to pay.
Stories of miraculous cures must be spread, physicians
bribed or flattered and patients tempted with an attractive
programme of amusements and diversions. All this meant
money, lots of money, and a clever, if not over-scrupulous,
organisation.

Maupassant soon perceived the satirical content of his
idea. He would trace the development of a spa from the
discovery of a " magical " mineral spring to the time when
patients hobble towards it from all corners of the earth.

With that theme as a base he could tilt his pen at the doctors and financiers who stand prepared to receive the eager visitors.

The love-story which he staged against this background is one of his most tender. The hero, Paul Brétigny, conceives a guilty passion for the Jewish financier's wife, but he is a far more sympathetic character than any other in Maupassant's gallery of amorous young men. The writer is himself so intoxicated with the beauty of Auvergne that he cannot restrain Brétigny from expressing his passionate love of Nature. That passion partly redeems him and invokes the reader's sympathy. Throughout this novel we see Maupassant in the wings prompting his hero.

" It seems as if I were open to every impression, and everything flows in and pervades me, making me weep and gnash my teeth. When I look at that hill facing us, that great green fold, that colony of trees scaling the mountain, I feel the whole forest in my eyes; it penetrates me, pervades me, flows in my blood. It seems as if I am eating it and filling my stomach with it – I become myself a forest."

His heroine, Christine Andermatt, is a hysterical woman who at first finds joy and finally disillusion in an illicit love-affair. She realises, like so many of Maupassant's own victims, that " this man was one of the race of lovers, and not of the race of fathers." In this novel, however, the reader sees Maupassant in a gentle, almost sentimental, mood.

That the writer was himself conscious of this changed attitude, we learn from a letter to Madame Leconte de Nouy:[1]

" I often laugh at the very sentimental and tender thoughts that I'm working out, after so much seeking ! . . . When one's imagination takes a turn, it usually goes on that way; sometimes when I'm walking about on Cap

[1] Cited in *En Regardant Passer la Vie*, p. 102.

d'Antibes – a solitary headland like a Breton moor – preparing a lyrical passage in the moonlight, I begin to think that this type of story is not so silly as one might think."

That was a remarkable admission for the author of " Maison Tellier," but there was nothing during his visit to Auvergne to suggest that Maupassant had at last become sentimental over women. Gustave had brought his palette and brushes and was trying to paint, while his son amused himself with two light-hearted young ladies. He shared a cottage with these women, and the relationship was not at all sentimental or tender.

This novel, *Mont-Oriol*, gave him far more trouble than any other book. Having created for the first time a pair of sympathetic lovers, he found it difficult to adjust himself to the new manner. Again and again he ran his pen through passages which did not please him. This was particularly the case with the romantic love-scenes in the book. Still not satisfied, he returned to Auvergne early in 1886, anxiously determined to verify the setting.

He worked hard during the next few months both in Antibes and Paris. Apart from the normal morning's work, he now accustomed himself to write between four in the afternoon and seven o'clock. That meant eight hours daily at his desk – a good average for any writer, but an excellent day's work for a man in his condition. He had not again produced the 1,500 pages of printed material which represented his output for 1885, but the amount of work written in 1886 still exhibits a remarkable industry. We know that in the year when he wrote *Mont-Oriol*, *Le Horla* and much miscellaneous journalism, he was suffering agonies from migraine, insomnia and occasional hallucinations.

A letter which he wrote at this time to Madame Leconte de Nouy shows how he forced himself to work at *Mont-Oriol*.

"Yacht *Bel-Ami*,
"*November 1886*.

"MY DEAR FRIEND,

"I'm also living in absolute solitude. I work and sail, that's my whole life. I see nobody, not a soul, night and day. I'm resting in a bath of peace and silence, a bath of farewell. I've no idea when I shall get back to Paris. I do hope to be able to work all through the winter, so as to be free for the summer. What about you? Will you not be coming to Villefranche? I should come and see you in my yacht without asking you to join me in a cruise, because I know you wouldn't like that. . . . If you have a minute to spare, do write to me and forgive me for replying so briefly; I can't see much more, my eyes are so strained. I kiss your hands and feet.

"MAUPASSANT."

Maupassant's state of mind was revealed in *Le Horla*, in which he showed how the victim of incurable disease veers from a buoyancy of spirit to complete dejection. Like the narrator in that book, Maupassant knew periods of respite when life was a dancing thing. He was like a man who has eaten a meal or gratified his lust and fondly imagines that he will never know hunger and lechery again.

"Home again. I am cured," he says in *Le Horla*. "Amid the jostling of the crowd, I thought ironically of my terrors, of my hallucinations of a week ago when I had believed, yes, believed that an invisible being dwelt in my body."

Such moments became rarer, and few weeks now passed without some terrible reminder that the invisible being was still tormenting him. We are no longer surprised to hear the author's cry of despair in *Mont-Oriol* soon after a superb burst of lyrical passion. One can see Maupassant taking up his pen after a night of pain and chill fear. Nobody knows, except François, that the great lover and athlete bolts his bedroom door at night and cowers under his blankets, afraid to put out the candle. He will lie sleepless for hours, rearing up in bed every few minutes, hearing sounds behind the door, in the cupboard or under his bed. There is not a soul in the world who will understand all this. Or would they understand only too well? And what can they do? François brews camomile tea and the oculist changes his prescription ordering yet another pair of spectacles.

After a sleepless night, Maupassant invites a doctor to luncheon and tries to pump him. Charcot's lectures on hypnotism are the talk of Paris and the writer asks many questions about hallucinations and the phenomena of nervous disease. Such questions are expected from a Naturalist writer like Guy de Maupassant, and his guest is flattered by the compliment. " I am collecting data for my new book, *Le Horla*," he explains when the doctor protests at this endless stream of inquiries. " I am interested in insanity." He dare not explain that his own symptoms have been artfully packed into all his questions. They would say behind his back that he was mad.

He was alone, alone save for his fears and despair. There were times when he was seized with a terrible desire to confide in someone, but he dismissed the idea before it drove him to some indiscretion. A criminal weighed down by his guilty secret could give himself up and relieve his oppressed conscience. For him there was no such release except in some miraculous cure. He could laugh and whore and bury his hands in gold, but always he felt that sensation of overwhelming solitude.

" All human beings go along, side by side, through events of life, without anything really uniting two beings together," he writes in *Mont-Oriol*. He goes on to speak of " the futile effort, ceaseless since the beginning of the world, the unwearying effort of men to break through the shell in which their soul struggles, for ever imprisoned, for ever solitary – an effort of arms, of lips, of trembling flesh, an effort of love that exhausts itself in kisses and ends only by giving life to another desolate being ! "

The novel was finished before the end of that year, 1886, and appeared, serially, in the *Gil Blas*. Havard, the publisher, was beside himself with delight. He had read the manuscript at a sitting and seemed greatly impressed by the author's new manner.

" I say that this novel is a sublime and imperishable masterpiece," he tells the writer. " It is Maupassant in all the expansion and fullness of his genius and marvellous talent. In this book you strike, with incredible power, a new note, a note which I had discovered in you ages ago."

When the book appeared in the spring of 1887, the critics – headed by Brunetière – all acclaimed the work as a masterpiece. The touches of character were as sure as ever, but there was a balance and rhythm in construction which finally won over those critics who were still sitting on the fence. *Bel-Ami* had proved that this author could move his desk from the brothels to the *salon* without losing his gifts in transit. The new novel showed him to be equally at home with actors, doctors, peasants and financiers. One could disagree with his conclusions – that did not concern him greatly – but even his detractors had to admit the depth and power of his writing. " As a picture of reality," Brunetière rightly observed, " it is truer than reality itself."

The critics had been kind, yet *Mont-Oriol* did not sell nearly as well as *Bel-Ami*. The public seemed to prefer the cynical Maupassant of " Boule de Suif." Havard had expected the new " accents of tenderness " to reach the ears of readers who had previously declined to support Maupassant, but *Mont-Oriol* seemed to have displeased his regular supporters without making much headway with the opposition. The book was not a publishing failure – Maupassant was too well-established for that — but the sale of twenty-five editions in the first few months was a disappointment after *La Maison Tellier* or *Bel-Ami*.

Sales always interested Maupassant, but there were other anxieties. *Mont-Oriol* was not the only volume which appeared under his name in 1887. He had also written a collection of stories which showed all his old power of observation but told some of his readers that all was not well with the author. Everyone knew that Maupassant was interested in the fantastic and supernatural, but his story *Le Horla* gave birth to an uneasy suspicion that he was himself unbalanced. Doctors who had studied nervous disease all their lives were astonished by the writer's remarkable insight into the mind of a lunatic. According to François, Maupassant was himself aware of the probable effect of the book upon his readers.

" To-day I sent off the manuscript of *Le Horla* to Paris," he told the valet. " Within a week every newspaper will announce that I am mad." The French Press was, however, too wary and far too well informed of the writer's litigious nature to come out with any such statement. But people gossiped in spite of the fact that the story had been based on an anecdote related to Maupassant by a friend. According to Goncourt, the anecdote came from Georges de Porto-Riche, who, when told of the rumours, remarked: " Well, if that story is by a lunatic, I must be mad ! "[1]

Wherever the story originated, it is certain that Maupassant was sometimes the victim of that type of hallucination described in *Le Horla*. It will be remembered that the story is written in the form of a diary compiled by a man who is haunted by an invisible spirit of evil. Maupassant was always morbidly fascinated by his own symptoms, and in *Le Horla* he paints a remarkably vivid picture of his

---

[1] M. Dumesnil suggests that Hennique first supplied Maupassant with the story. This is the more likely theory.

nervous disorder.   The anecdote was supplied by another,
but Maupassant undoubtedly wrote this story with his own
flesh.   In *Le Horla*, for the first time, he betrayed his real
physical fears.

"All day and every day I suffer this frightful sense of
threatened danger, this apprehension of coming ill or
approaching death, this presentiment which is doubtless
the warning signal of a lurking disease germinating in blood
and my flesh."

Maupassant had good reason to suspect that his brain had
begun to founder.   Doctor Sollier has reported an incident
which shows that the author had turned the camera upon
himself before he wrote *Le Horla*.   Maupassant was sitting
in his cabin on the *Bel-Ami* when he heard the door open.
He sprang up impatiently and was astonished to see his
"double" enter the room and sit down opposite him.   His
body and mind were weary and oppressed and he began to
take down the passage which the newcomer dictated to
him.   As soon as the man stopped talking, Maupassant
was seized with a strange uneasiness.   He jerked himself
to his feet and staggered to the chair where his visitor had
sat.   It was empty !

It is this type of hallucination which haunts the pages of
Le Horla.

"I am going mad.   My carafe was emptied again last
night – or, rather, I emptied it.

"But is it I ?   Who can it be ?   Who ?   Oh, my God !
Who will save me ?"

An ordinary sufferer would probably have become
completely insane within a very short time.   But Maupassant
had made a close study of hypnotism and knew enough
about this science to realise how much still remained hidden
from the neurologists.   Sometimes he imagined that his
hallucinations might be due to an excessive use of drugs.
Under the influence of ether he had seen strange visions

which he described in many of his stories.[1] That did not prove that he was mad. These strange forms terrified him but he was always rescued by the force of his own logic.

" I should certainly have thought myself mad, absolutely mad, if I were not conscious, if I were not perfectly aware of my state of mind, if I did not get to the bottom of it and analyse it so completely," writes the diarist in *Le Horla*. " I must be, in fact, no worse than a sane man troubled with hallucinations. There must be some unknown disturbance in my brain, one of those disturbances that modern physiologists are trying to observe and elucidate."

When logic failed, there were hordes of fashionable doctors who felt his pulse and recommended bromide or douches. He could draw upon his publisher and editors for the money to buy the drug he craved more than any other — travel. And new scenes always poured blood into his heart, intoxicating him with a fresh eagerness for life.

With *Mont-Oriol* and *Le Horla* off his hands, he hurries across the Mediterranean into Algeria. Everything is exotic, novel, interesting. He seems to be himself again, sleeps better, stores notes for future books, visits hospitals, brothels, palaces. He covers thirty-seven pages of foolscap in one day and seems quite fresh after his work.

" This will give you a headache," murmurs François half-reproachfully.

" Not at all," smiles Maupassant. " It's not fatiguing. These travel sketches just drop out of me quite easily — my memory could supply enough for two pens like mine."

On the return journey everyone had been seasick except Maupassant and the crew. Hardly had he reached Marseilles before he was at the helm of the *Bel-Ami*, steering her through a very rough sea.

After a very pleasant cruise along the Côte d'Azur, he hurried back to Paris. The same old round of dinners,

[1] Cf. " Lui ? " " La Peur," " Qui Sait," " L'Auberge," etc.

flirtations and business matters soon whirled about him. François describes all this with his usual phlegm, but two or three sentences from his chronicle stand out boldly from the interminable list of dinners:

" M. de Maupassant is suffering from an awful headache which he cannot get rid of. . . . He wants to stay a season at Aix-les-Bains before going on to Etretat."

A day or so later, the writer suddenly announces that he is going to fight a duel. " Let them say what they like about my literary work, but they touch my private life at their own risk. I'm fighting a duel to-morrow, and as I'm the injured party, I've demanded pistols at twenty paces. We'll fight till one of us goes down. You can be sure that, with a good weapon, it won't take me long to touch my opponent's skin.

" This afternoon I went to Gastine-Renette's shooting-gallery. Out of seventeen shots I hit the bull's eye sixteen times, and the attendant remarked: ' You're practising for a duel, monsieur, but it's quite unnecessary. With your skill, and given good weapons, I pity the man facing you.' "

When he returned late that night he seemed to have forgotten all about the duel.

" Oh, it's all fixed," he told François, who had waited up for him. " We're not fighting."

That was not the last of Maupassant's violent fits of temper. Ether and other drugs had conjured up evil apparitions, but a far deadlier force was already at work within him. Soon he would be tilting at a hundred and one hostile shapes, all malignant and all determined to persecute the mighty Maupassant.

PART THREE

CHAPTER I

THE P.L.M. EXPRESS

MAUPASSANT'S illness has attracted the pens of several young writers on the scent of a sensational article. That is in itself a tragedy when one remembers how jealously he guarded his private life from the scrutiny of interviewers and " literary " journalists. Men without the slightest qualification have scavenged among the author's symptoms. Most of them have emerged triumphantly with conclusions without troubling themselves with premises. To the average journalist, the writer's disease is far more interesting than the quality of his work.

The " human document " aspect of Maupassant's career has given rise to much that is illicit, ignorant and inaccurate. Contemporary studies of the famous author were full of distortion, chiefly cynical and abusive. After his death, François and several other honest men did what they could to restore the balance in his favour. People who had known Maupassant ransacked their memories for virtues and emptied bottles of indignant ink over those who had defiled their illustrious friend. By carefully dodging the puddles, these well-meaning scribes dragged into the light " official " portraits in which Maupassant wore the sickly smile of misunderstood genius.

Moral indignation is not the best basis for honest biography, and the modern writer on Maupassant finds himself embedded in an extraordinary conflict of testimony. Thanks to Maynial, Lumbroso, Sherard and a few others who have approached the subject in a scholarly spirit, it is now possible to focus the problem with some sense of proportion. Unfortunately, much confusion still remains

concerning the writer's disease, particularly in regard to his
work.   Certain authors have either evaded the issue or
confined themselves to other aspects of the subject with
which they were more qualified to deal.   Others have
separated the " literary " and " medical " portions with a
sort of insolent scientificness.

There have been many attempts at posthumous diagnosis
in connection with Guy de Maupassant.   Some writers date
his insanity from the time when he wrote *Le Horla*, while
a few, more daring, suggest that he was insane throughout
his literary career but subject to lucid intervals !   As his
personality grows vaguer every year the tendency to theorise
upon him becomes more apparent.   Psycho-analysis has
even strayed into the domain of literary criticism, and it seems
to have become possible to plot a graph recording the ebb
and flow of Maupassant's insanity !

In this state of affairs a good deal of nonsense has naturally spread itself over the subject.   So much attention has
been paid to psychological diagnosis that readers may be
pardoned for approaching Maupassant's work with the
earnest sympathy and vigilance of attendants at a lunatic
asylum !   Yet there is little evidence of insanity in Maupassant's novels and stories.   Those who can rid their minds
of guesswork and empiricism will be surprised at the
remarkable unity and clarity of his writings.   Alienists in
search of zigzag thought and other pathological signs will
also be disappointed.   Maupassant's work is always
coherent and beautifully balanced.   Even stories like *Le
Horla*, *Qui Sait* and *Sur l'Eau*, in which he displayed all the
refinements of self-observation, show the steady hand of a
balanced mind.

M. Maynial has rightly remarked upon the significance
of 1884 in the writer's spiritual development.   In that
year appeared his travel sketches, *Au Soleil*, in which he
first announced his disillusionment.   " Travel is only a

kind of door leading from reality," he says, a sentiment which he repeated in many other places. In that book he makes us profoundly aware of his personal misery, but it would be unprofitable and misleading to track down his melancholia through the long sequence of books which followed. There is no *physical* significance in the publication of that work. We know that in 1884 he was greatly troubled by eye-strain and headaches, but the pessimism of *Au Soleil* cannot be linked too firmly with these personal sufferings. No creative writer can be wholly insensitive to his physical condition, but in Maupassant's case his pessimism was reinforced, and not induced, by disease.

Maupassant's writing life began in the shadow of the war of 1870. Like most of the younger writers of the time, his work shows the scars of that defeat. Loti, Bourget, Huysmans and Maupassant were all, in their own way, subjected to this determining influence, and their work is blunted by disenchantment and depression. Nothing seemed to satisfy the needs and aspirations of the young men who took to their pens after the disastrous war. The prevalent feeling was that of pessimism and the vanity of all human effort. It was an era of sneers and folded arms.

France was still shell-shocked, and the results show all through the Literature of the Third Republic. It is not enough to say that realism grew into Naturalism. The early realists had reacted against the poetry of romanticism, but the horror of war definitely played its part in the evolution of the younger members of the new School. Weaned on Taine, the Goncourts and Zola, they had donned their first long trousers with the sound of Prussian guns still in their ears. When these boys reached manhood they were ready for a display of irony and " *je m'en fichisme.*"

It is impossible to separate the new writers from their period, but with Maupassant one is at once arrested by his extraordinary reserve. He cannot be easily considered apart from his work. Great prose is based on logic, not on mere sensation, and Maupassant can never be accused of parading himself before his reader. The success of his writing is largely due to his ability to analyse experience without the aid of sentimental writing. He was undoubtedly allusive in his books, but he had a knack of unloading his misery dramatically and was never guilty of clogging the machinery with introspective matter.

Those who seek progressive signs of insanity in his work will be confronted with blind alleys at every turn. How can the earnest psycho-analyst reconcile the despair of *Le Horla* with the much more cheerful tone of *Pierre et Jean* which succeeded it by a few months ? There is nothing in the writer's psychological condition to account for such a change. He was, in fact, suffering more acutely than ever before.

The relationship between Maupassant's life and his work cannot be established by plotting graphs or dancing round this chapter or that paragraph. He had an equal capacity for introspection and external observation, and knew how to discipline his art. To estimate him in terms of the content of his stories is to belittle him as an artist.

The only safe approach to Maupassant is by way of the fundamental philosophy which he expounds throughout his writings. Looking back over the body of his work, one is astonished at the uniformity of his outlook. With most writers it is not difficult to divide their work into clearly defined stages, but Maupassant refuses to fit into the traditional biographical mould. One can date his transition from the painter of harlots and peasants to the Society photographer, but it is foolish to go further.

Disease certainly played its part in the development of his view of life. It would, however, be idle to speculate on how the writer's early philosophy would have reacted to a healthy physique.   Many youthful pessimists have out-grown an unwholesome mood of despair, but, in his case, illness made him anæsthetic to the mellowing influences of wealth and applause.

The stories in which he snapshots his own symptoms do not belong to any one period of his career.   He was always morbidly interested in disease and some of his early tales reek of the sick-room.   But it is in his philosophy that we really see the distorted comment of a stricken mind.   That reshuffling of ideals which comes in the lives of most normal men is completely lacking here.   Reading and a wider culture might have leavened his half-baked views, but the condition of his eyes prevented that.   He needed his sight for writing rather than reading.   And his illness threatened him at all times, driving him restlessly from one artificial paradise to the next.

The clammy hand of disease rests on all Maupassant's conclusions about life and death.   He emancipated himself from literary conventions but failed completely to snap the apron-strings which bound him to an adolescent outlook. He never redeemed his debt to Schopenhauer.   As a boy he had doted upon the German's perverse philosophy, and disease linked the two minds more firmly.   " Involuntarily I compared the childish sarcasm, the religious sarcasm of Voltaire with the irresistible irony of the German philos-opher whose influence is henceforth ineffaceable," he says in " Beside a Dead Man."   " Let us protest and let us be angry, let us be indignant or let us be enthusiastic. Schopenhauer has marked humanity with the seal of his disdain and disenchantment."   Maupassant followed suit and left on record more fifth-rate philosophy than any other first-class writer.   It is redeemed only by its sincerity.

Maupassant's pessimism is founded on a denial of God. He sees the Deity as " a sly and cynical executioner " who is completely indifferent to human suffering.   It is not the writer's mind but his diseased flesh which cries out whenever he alludes to the Almighty.

"You may be sure that God has not put anything on this earth that is clean, pretty, elegant or accessory to our ideal, but the human brain has done it," he says in "L'Inutile Beauté." "God only created coarse beings, full of the germs of disease, and who, after a few years of bestial enjoyment, grow old and weak, with all the ugliness and impotence of human decrepitude. He only seems to have made them in order that they may reproduce their species in a repulsive manner, and then die like ephemeral insects. . . . .

"Do you know how I picture God myself? As an enormous creative organ, unknown to us, who scatters millions of worlds into space, just as one single fish would deposit its spawn in the sea. He creates, because it is His function as God to do so, but He does not know what He is doing, and is stupidly prolific in His work, and is ignorant of the combinations of all kinds which are produced by His scattered germs. Human thought is a lucky, little, local passing accident, totally unforeseen, which is condemned to disappear with this earth, and to recommence perhaps here or elsewhere, the same or different, with fresh combinations of eternally new beginnings."

These lines were published in 1890 when the writer's disease was far advanced, but this passage should not be interpreted as conclusive evidence of mental aberration. Throughout his writings Maupassant repeats this view of an implacable Destiny. In *Bel-Ami* (1885), as in so many of his books, he returns again and again to his fear of death. The subject obsesses him. He regards all religion as a sham and refuses to acknowledge any faith in a hereafter. Like his hero Duroy, he knew "the terror of that boundless and inevitable annihilation that destroys our wretched fleeting lives. He already bowed his head before its menace. He thought of the flies who live a few hours, the beasts who live a few days, the men who live a few years, the worlds which live a few centuries. What was the difference between one and the other? A few more dawns, that was all."

Maupassant never lost this sense of isolation and futility. Much has been made of an incident which occurred in November, 1889. The writer had been entertaining his friends in his new flat, and the conversation drifted into spiritual matters. The company included several doctors, who took their stand against God and religion. The host had listened carefully for some time, but suddenly he remarked: " If I were dangerously ill, and if the people attending me brought in a priest, I should receive him in order to please them." Knowing Maupassant's dislike of priests, his friends were much surprised and tried to corner him, but he refused to say more and, picking a rose from the bowl on the table, began to strip its petals one by one.

To cite this incident as evidence of a revival of faith would be absurd. Maupassant was already in the grip of general paralysis, and anything might account for such an apparent volte-face. Fear? Annoyance at the doctors' dogmatism? Perhaps it would be safe to dismiss the episode as a pose. Maupassant was hardly the man to air his convictions at a dinner-table, and the rose-picking touch is altogether too De Musset !

His atheism has a corollary in his contempt for humanity. He sees " the futility of all human effort, the impotence of the spirit and the weakness of the flesh." Theoretically, he despises all humanity and refuses to respect masters more than slaves, but it is the mob, collective humanity, that he really hates and fears. " I cannot go to a theatre or any public function without struggling against the spirit of the mob, which tries to penetrate me," he declares in *Sur l'Eau*.

This hatred of the mob was, of course, the logical outcome of his passion for solitude.

" How often have I declared that the intellect grows and becomes exalted as soon as one lives alone; how it shrinks and becomes degraded as soon as one mixes with humanity ! " (*Sur l'Eau*).

This distaste is only redeemed by pity in the face of the common enemy – death. But it is the pity of a philosopher who surveys humanity from a distance. There is nothing warm or intimate in the feeling. He sees men and women at the mercy of a callous Destiny and cannot help pooling his own misery with that of other sufferers. But it is not so much sympathy for his fellow-creatures as hatred of God, Fate or Destiny which makes him raise his voice in defence of suffering humanity.

Maupassant reserved his real sympathy for animals. Who can forget his description of the dead donkey in *Mont-Oriol* ? " The skeleton showed through the worn hair on his sides, and his head seemed enormous. The poor head, with closed eyes, was lying so tranquilly on the bed of broken stone, that it seemed surprised and happy at the new rest. The long ears hung down like rags. Two open wounds on his knees told how often he had fallen, even that very day before he had sunk down for the last time. Another wound on his side showed the place where his master, for years and years, had prodded him with an iron spike fastened to the end of a stick, to hasten his slow gait. . . . Blows ! Blows ! Too heavy loads, overpoweringly hot suns ! And for food, only a little straw, a little hay, some branches of leaves, and the tempting sight of the green meadows all along the hard way."

Parallel to his independence of spirit is his revolt against dogma. He never scoffs at honest faith but cannot stomach a fanatical ritualism. Superstition he abhors, and, with it, jingoism. As far back as " Boule de Suif " he had declared himself a pacifist:

" . . . A glorious army massacring those trying to

defend themselves, making others prisoners, pillaging in the name of the sword and thanking God to the sound of the cannon, all are alike frightful scourges which upset all belief in eternal justice, all the confidence that we are taught to show in the protection of heaven and the reason of man."

Maupassant deplored jingoism as " the egg of wars " but he never overlooked the responsibility of stupid and corrupt politicians. This subject, like practically all others, inevitably brought him back to the stupid masses.

" The mob is an imbecile herd, as stupid in its patience as it is savage when roused," he declares in *Le Horla*. " You say to it: ' Enjoy yourself,' and it enjoys itself. You say to it: ' Go and fight your neighbour.' It goes to fight. You say: ' Vote for the Emperor.' It votes for the Emperor. Then you say: ' Vote for the Republic,' and it votes for the Republic."

Maupassant had his pet topics to which he was always returning. One can scarcely open any one of his books without coming across some reference to his longing for solitude or his fear of death. So frequently do these topics occur that it becomes useless to pin the label of autobiography upon any particular paragraph.

To my mind one is ill-advised to date the author's insanity from any individual piece of work. He had been depressed and irritable since the early stages of his disease, but the first serious suggestion of incipient madness can be safely dated from early in 1888. On January 7 the Literary Supplement of *Le Figaro* had printed his famous preface to *Pierre et Jean*, which Ollendorff was about to publish. To accommodate this lengthy essay, the editor had made several cuts and Maupassant was up in arms at once. Instead of accepting an apology, he filed suit against the paper and claimed 5,000 francs damages. This squib

fizzled out, like so many others, but it has a terrible significance in the light of what followed.

Without overlooking his Norman fondness for litigation,
one cannot help regarding this episode as the first symptom
of persecution mania. Maupassant had good cause for
complaint, but in normal circumstances he would have
insisted upon an apology and gone no further. Two years
later he again complained of being victimised. This time it
was the famous publisher Charpentier who had offended
him by reproducing his portrait in an illustrated edition
of *Les Soirées de Médan*. Maupassant had a horror of being
photographed, and objected vigorously to this new trespass
upon his privacy:

" I have made a definite rule to forbid the publication of
my portrait whenever possible. The exceptions have always
been done behind my back. Our works belong to the
public, not our faces."[1]

In the present instance the portrait had been executed
from a photograph lent by one of Maupassant's friends.
He now demanded that all the copies of the book should be
withdrawn, and new ones substituted in which his portrait
did not appear !

" If you do not agree," he declares, " I shall take legal
proceedings at once."[2] He went so far as to put the matter
in the hands of his attorney, but the affair petered out.

Those who complained of the writer's bad temper were
hardly aware of what he was suffering. With every bout of
migraine he became terrified of what the future might
hold in store, and towards the end of 1888 he received a
blow from which he never fully recovered. His brother
Hervé suddenly became insane ! The cause of the trouble
was alleged to have been sunstroke, but there is a remarkable
lack of data on this point. Monsieur and Madame de
Maupassant persisted with this version, and one need not

[1] From a letter published by A. Lumbroso.   [2] Ibid.

pry too closely into the precise nature of the unfortunate man's condition. It is, however, a remarkable coincidence that these two men, both athletic and robust, ended their lives under the same tragic conditions.

This tragedy completely unnerved Guy de Maupassant. Hervé was married and living happily at Antibes, thanks to the writer's generosity, when he had a sudden attack of fever. The doctors decided that it was necessary to recommend a mental home and Guy undertook the melancholy task of installing his brother. It required great tact and diplomacy, since Hervé was completely unaware of his destination. According to M. Maurice de Waleffe,[1] the invalid imagined that he was being taken to a private country house for convalescence.

While the brothers were chatting, a doctor signalled to Guy, who edged towards the door. Hervé tried to follow, but two attendants restrained him. The writer never forgot his brother's frenzied shriek as he ran from the house.

" Guy, you wretch ! You have had me shut up ! You're the crazy one, I tell you ! You're the family lunatic ! "

The end was not far distant. Guy did everything possible, but there was little he could do except pay his brother's medical expenses and provide for his little niece. The two brothers met for the last time when Hervé was on his death-bed. It was a harrowing scene and one which stamped itself with terrible force on the writer's mind.

" My Guy, my Guy ! " Hervé had cried as they embraced. He had called to him like that years ago when they were boys at " Les Verguies." " Come out and play in the garden, Guy." Maupassant bent over the wasted form, not trusting himself to speak. As he wiped the tears from Hervé's eyes, the dying man took his hand and kissed it.

Hervé's death terrified him. It seemed such a sinister warning of what might befall an apparently robust man.

[1] Cited by M. Georges Normandy, *La Fin de Maupassant*, p. 105.

His brother had doubtless been insane when they first walked into the asylum together, but that shriek would haunt him for ever.

"You're the crazy one, I tell you ! You're the family lunatic ! "

A year later he is still brooding on his brother's death. From the Riviera he hurries to Lyons, to the little cemetery where Hervé lies sleeping. François tries to put in a word of comfort but his master stands for hours staring at the tomb. He does not weep but his face is convulsed and his hands tremble violently. The valet leads him from the cemetery and he slumps into his seat in the carriage. Suddenly he rouses himself to point out a house surrounded by trees.

"There, over there," he stammers, "that's it, that's the house where my poor brother died."

Back at the hotel, François brews some tea, but Maupassant strides up and down the room, talking of nothing but Hervé. Again and again he calls to mind that terrible scene by the death-bed.

"Oh, my poor brother, my poor brother," he groans, "how sincere was his friendship ! How young he was to go like that ! "

That night he did not go out, and the following day they returned to Paris.

It had been a restless year for Maupassant. He had found it increasingly difficult to settle down to regular work. He could no longer boast that his ink was unaffected by change of climate. Wherever he went there was some cause for complaint. The apartment was noisy, the weather impossible, too hot, too cold, too wet, too dry – no excuse was lacking for a change of scene. Physically he was going to pieces, but he never grumbled at his suffering. It was the loss of his day's work that seemed to worry him most. *He must write* – the thought beat into his mind, driving him to work when most other men would have collapsed with a groan. That pile of foolscap on his desk meant the yacht, gaiety, beautiful women, the best doctors. Each book was the renewal of the beautiful drugs which made life tolerable.

Historically, the publication of *Pierre et Jean*, with its declaratory preface, was of great significance. Maupassant was no slave of literary fashion, but he could not blind himself to the reaction against Naturalism. He had already hailed the symbolists but soon realised that symbolism was but one form of the revolt against scientific realism. Sensing the latent taste for romantic fiction, Brunetière had entered the pulpit with a new article (" The Bankruptcy of Naturalism ") tucked under his arm. That was in 1887, only a year before *Pierre et Jean*, but there were many other signs of the times. Wherever he turned, Maupassant saw the débris of the Zola school. Poets like Verlaine and Mallarmé had attacked on one side, but the novelists led the real counter-offensive against the pseudo-science which had held the field for the last decade. As early as 1881 Anatole France had brought out *Le Crime de Sylvestre Bonnard*, and writers like Loti and Marcel Prévost were already finding a public for their work. Finally, from Russia had come a mighty wave of mysticism and neo-Christianity in the form of translations of Tolstoy and Dostoievsky.

Confronted by these invaders, Maupassant had decided to write a psychological novel. He had never been a pure Zolaist and rightly concluded that he could transfer or adapt his usual method to the new style. " Through psychology Maupassant escaped from realism," says M. René Lalou,[1] but that is an overstatement. There was no " escape " in the new cycle inaugurated by *Pierre et Jean* – that remarkable study of jealousy and suspicion. Maupassant

[1] *Contemporary French Literature*, p. 41.

now focused his camera upon the human soul, but he was still the sober Naturalist with a reverence for documentation and architecture.   There is a clear line of demarcation between the psychological novel of Maupassant and that of his friend Paul Bourget.   Both respect clarity, but Bourget's didacticism and his urge towards aristocratic snobbishness are completely absent from *Pierre et Jean* and its successors.

It is misleading to attribute Maupassant's new manner to pathological causes.   That fallacy has arisen from the obvious symptoms of strain in his last novels.   There were no signs of a failing intellect in the new novel, *Fort Comme la Mort*, but the observant reader could detect a certain painfulness of thought.   The book is a masterpiece of psychological investigation, but this is not the Maupassant of " Boule de Suif."   The old vigour and vitality have been replaced by subtlety and a kind of diseased clairvoyance.   The style is no longer sound in wind and limb; it oozes with restlessness and decay.   Instead of keen-sightedness we have the morbid vision of a thinker who has turned his subject inside out again and again.   There is the faint smell of the dissecting-table which lingers after each board had been scrubbed clean.   As in all his work, he displays brilliant portraiture, but here is re-statement and an unusual intensification.

Maupassant had found great difficulty in writing this book.   The theme itself is simple enough.   A painter, Olivier Bertin, conceives a fatal passion for the daughter of his former mistress.   The novelist dramatises this situation with remarkable skill, portraying every nuance of emotion felt, consciously or subconsciously, by the protagonists.   But he does much more.   The three central characters love and dream and suffer – no writer has yet surpassed Maupassant in his treatment of this problem – but there is a shadow which rises and falls over the backcloth.   Sometimes it is one of the women who glides into the shadow, but usually it is the hero. This fourth character, who is not officially included in the cast, is the author. He plays no part, but his tortured whisper floats across the stage. A crack in the scenery lets it in, this little voice, pleading, hopeful, persistent.

We have heard Maupassant complain of the emptiness of life in many of his stories, but here, for the first time, we are made aware of something like artistic despair. In a few tragic words he tells us that the days of rich productiveness are over:

" What is it ? Is it fatigue of the eye or of the brain, exhaustion of the artistic faculty or of the optic nerve ? Who knows ? . . . Once, and not so very long ago, the number of new subjects seemed to be unlimited, and I had such a variety of ways of expressing them that it was difficult to make my choice. Suddenly the world of half-glimpsed subjects has become depopulated, my investigation is impotent and barren. Folk that pass have no significance for me any longer; I no longer find in each human being that character and savour which once I loved to discern and depict."

Fort Comme la Mort is a testament of disillusion. Maupassant had never been uncritical of the rich worldlings with whom he seemed friendly, but there was now something savage in his contempt. His despair has run amok, lunging dementedly at foibles which he had already stripped in so many books.

" The intelligence of fashionable people, even the brightest, is without value, foundation or weight. . . . There is no depth, ardour or sincerity among them. They live on the outside of everything. They are outside of the beauty of the world and the beauty of art of which they chatter without having really discovered it, or even believing it, for they do not know the intoxication of tasting the joys of life and of the intellect."

But social satire is not the dominant note in this book. Every page is heavy with the fatigue of decadence. Here is the despair and disenchantment of a slowly dying man, tired, *blasé* and surfeited. All the author's misgivings seem to pass in dumb show before us.

" I ask myself whether I am not ill. I have such a distaste for everything I used to take pleasure in doing or did with indifferent resignation. . . . Mind, eye and hand are all empty ! . . .

" I am at the age when a bachelor's life becomes intolerable, because there is nothing new for me under the sun. An unmarried man should be young, curious, eager. When one is no longer all that, it becomes dangerous to remain free. . . . For an old bachelor like me, liberty is an empty thing, empty everywhere; it is the path to death, with nothing in it to prevent one from seeing the end. It is the incessant question: ' What shall I do ? Whom can I go to see, so that I shall not be alone ? ' And I go from one friend to another, from one handshake to the next, begging for a little friendship. I gather up crumbs but they do not make a loaf."

This was the bleak confession of a man of thirty-eight. His loneliness as a bachelor seemed to obsess him at this time, but he never permitted himself to confide these pangs to any of his aristocratic friends. He had played the rôle of a cynical Don Juan far too strenuously to risk ridicule. Nobody should accuse him of middle-aged sentimentalism !

Only to François, his valet, did he unbosom himself on this subject. While they were climbing a mountain near Chamonix, Maupassant suddenly declared that he had been at that very place some years previously. He told François that at that time he was very much in love with a young woman whom he wished to marry. " She was very intelligent, broadminded, generous and most cultured. Life would have been very pleasant with her and she would have been a help to me in my work. But Fate . . . ! " According to Maupassant, the budding romance had been nipped by a woman who came between them.

One cannot eliminate the possibility of such a catastrophe, but it is well to remember that there is no other reference to this particular incident. Knowing how Maupassant liked to pose and how well he could sustain a given rôle, one must accept this story with caution. It was at this time that the writer was beginning to suffer from hallucinations. One evening he informed François that back in Etretat he had been attacked by a vicious dog. This was the first time that François or anyone else had heard of this savage encounter. According to Maupassant, he had been set upon by a huge dog who leapt at his throat. Taken by surprise he had been thrown to the ground and bitten by the animal. He had only saved himself by bringing a stone between the dog's teeth. He returned to his villa with his clothes in ribbons, but enormously relieved at his lucky escape. The following day he was surprised to see the same dog curled up on his front-door mat ! The animal seemed most contrite and licked the writer's bruised hands.

A few days later, Maupassant announced that his villa was infested with spiders. " Last night I couldn't sleep. I tried every bed in turn, but the spiders were everywhere." That evening the writer and his valet began to hunt down the vermin. François held a lantern while his master hid behind a black cloth and serenaded the spiders with a series of whistles. In spite of all these elaborate preparations the total bag was two spiders which Maupassant threw to the goldfish.

He seemed to have shaken off all sense of proportion. His disordered imagination was feeling its way ever more obviously towards that dim region in which fiction mocks at fact. Things that had occurred, but were vaguely remembered, suddenly became very real to him. Crossing

the Seine with François, he made this remarkable statement:
" They've refused to give me my life-saving medal,
although I've pulled out thirteen bodies from this river;
two were still alive.   I suppose I'll have to wait for another
opportunity to get the medal I want so much.   As far as I'm
concerned it's worth all the Legion of Honour decorations."

On the way back to Paris, Maupassant waved a hand out
of the carriage window, excited at recognising Médan.
" Zola is probably at home.   The windows of his study are
open."

So much had happened since the long summer evenings
when he had sat in that study listening to Flaubert, Turgenev, Cézanne and the others.   How many happy hours
he had spent lounging at Médan with a line at rest in
the river !   He had thought of life in terms of office and
liberty.   Everything had been so simple and certain.
Rejecting the facts, his memory selected photographs of
those early days. when he was still a robust young clerk
airing his Muse in Flaubert's study.   What fun it was to
bait a line with a bottle of wine beside you and, if you were
lucky, a pretty girl with a ripe full mouth !   It all seemed
so remote and unreal now that his day was divided into
douches, pills and massage, yet only ten years separated
him from that world of sweet dreams.

Physically he was now in a deplorable condition.   He was
tortured by insomnia, and his mouth and cheeks had sunken
as if he had lost all his teeth.   He hurried from oculist to
doctor, restless, inquisitive, clinging to hope.   The famous
specialist, Dr. Grubby of Paris, had recommended a
fattening diet which Maupassant at once adopted without
question.   He was to eat potatoes, eggs, fish, poultry and
butcher's meat.   Wine was forbidden him, but he was told
to drink a minimum of two litres of milk daily.

But his condition does not improve and he is constantly
shifting his quarters.   The specialist shakes his head and

counsels patience, while the oculist informs him that his eyes will improve when he is in better health. Wherever he goes he takes with him a library of medical works which he studies with painful intensity. He cannot stay in Paris, and leaves after a flying visit to his doctors and publisher. It is the South which now calls him all the time. In Paris, he shivers in his furs when everybody else is discarding over-coats.

"I've had to abandon the Bouchard treatment which put my nerves into an awful state and affected my sight," he tells his mother. "I don't know where to turn."

Diet sheets and *wagons-lits*. The nights are racked with insomnia and François no longer retires at a normal hour. Between eleven at night and two a.m. he is usually sum-moned three or four times to his master's bedroom. Some-times it is camomile tea or a cupping-glass that is needed, but more often than not Maupassant is simply terrified of being left alone in the dark. The valet sits by the bedside until his master's eyes have closed.

Maupassant was at this time engaged upon *Notre Cœur*, which *La Revue des Deux Mondes* undertook to serialise. Like *Fort Comme la Mort*, the new novel did not write itself too easily, and in both books there is the same tendency towards over-subtlety and introspection. The appreciative clarity and exactitude of the early books have gone, never to return. Instead of sharp revealing dialogue we have long and intricate discussions. The hero's fatal passion is focused from a dozen angles, but the picture lacks the terrific force and tension which the world associated with the name of Guy de Maupassant. His mind's eye was already over-full of shadows.

As with all his work, Maupassant showed remarkable interest in the box-office side of *Notre Cœur*. Writing to his mother in July 1890, he says: "I shall send you a pile of criticisms of *Notre Cœur* as soon as I've thanked the

various journalists. Let me have them back. The publication [of the serial] in the *Revue* has not done the sales any
good. The big Paris booksellers tell me that 60 per cent
of my regular public have read it in the *Revue* and won't
buy the book. Another point is this – the sensation (which
was enormous) came when the novel appeared in *La Revue
des Deux Mondes*; everybody finished discussing it before
the book came out. In spite of all this, the book is selling,
though slowly, and I think it should have a bigger sale than
Fort Comme la Mort which has reached 32,000 copies. In
principle, of course, the appearance of *Notre Cœur* in the
Revue will do me a lot of good. The special public of that
periodical knows my work and will buy me later on. I've
gained new readers like that.

" I am not yet installed at Rue Boccador; they're still
moving my furniture there every day. It will be a pretty
and comfortable apartment. I won't be in properly until
Saturday, but I spend my days there."[1]

He was moving from his apartment in the Avenue
Victor-Hugo, where, after a residence of five days, he complained of the noise. The basement was occupied by a
baker whose machinery seems to have been the cause of the
disturbance.

" It is quite impossible to sleep or even to work in all this
din," Maupassant wrote to the landlord. In a few days he
followed with another and far more violent epistle.

" I must leave your house immediately, on doctor's
orders. I shall have to go away and recuperate in the South
as a result of the very serious disturbance caused by a
fortnight of insomnia due to the baker's night-work."

This letter, as M. Maynial rightly observed, betrays a
certain painfulness of expression and even spelling mistakes.
To the psychiatrist it affords additional evidence of the
writer's growing paranoia. Finding the flat impossible, he

[1] Pol Neveux, pp. 171–2.

had fled to Cannes, leaving his valet to hunt for a more suitable apartment. This was the place in the Rue Boccador, Maupassant's last *pied-à-terre* in Paris.

The new apartment was sumptuously furnished and must have made a severe inroad into the writer's resources. The furniture was mostly in the Louis XVI style, and a fashionable tapestry-maker had been called in to supervise the interior decoration. In this apartment Maupassant was constantly visited by a mysterious young woman whose presence François greatly deplored. The valet seems to have had a fixed idea that this visitor was the principal cause of Maupassant's downfall. If we are to credit hints dropped by doctors and rumours which had circulated since 1885, François did " the lady in grey " an injustice. Maupassant pursued women while he had strength to stand on his legs, but it was rather in the spirit of a gambler who cannot drag himself from the tables although he does not possess another sou. The " fatal woman " used to sweep into the apartment and mention the writer's name, with scarcely a glance at the valet. Maupassant never breathed a syllable about her, and François contents himself with a vague pen-picture.

" She is not a cocotte, although she uses too much scent. . . . She is a member of the smart upper class."

With *Notre Cœur* off his hands, Maupassant had more time for dalliance. He seemed to have lost all taste for writing the short stories and articles which had been such a reliable source of income. The old passion for the theatre had now returned with irresistible force. One is tempted to suggest that Maupassant turned back to the stage realising that his stock of ideas was running low. With his friend, Jacques Normand, he settled down to write a play based on his short story, " L'Enfant." It was a good dramatic theme – maternal instinct helps a young bride to conquer her prejudices and adopt the fruit of her husband's misconduct. The play, *Musotte*, saw the light early in 1891 and enjoyed a fair success, but Koning, who put it on at the Gymnase theatre, was not enthusiastic.

Maupassant refused to be discouraged.

" Plays ? " he wrote to his friend and collaborator. " I'll do as many as I want to. Just think that apart from my novels, *Une Vie*, *Fort Comme la Mort*, *Notre Cœur*, etc., which all have the germ of a play, every one of them, I've published more than two hundred short stories, all, or nearly all, of which provide a dramatic subject, either for tragedy or comedy." Poor Maupassant ! He could never reconcile himself to the curious standards of the theatre. Accustomed to being wooed and flattered by publishers, he was rather lost in this new world in which the author was expected to take a very humble back seat. Was it possible that the playwright, the creator, could rank so far behind the producer, director and, of course, the leading lady ? He hated intrigue and petty squabbles, and dramatic success seemed to depend upon the thickness of one's skin.

Maupassant did not achieve the stage triumph he had anticipated with the production of *Musotte*. Sometimes, when the subject floated over his dinner-table, he would make some scathing comment on the caprices of leading ladies, but nobody was deceived. I intend no disrespect in suggesting that a theatre manager had only to raise his little finger and Maupassant would have rushed headlong to his desk.

How the famous author would have reacted to dramatic success it is impossible to say. Sustained work had become difficult, and for the last two years of his active life he was constantly moving. Having given up his regular contributions to the newspapers, he now decided to work on a novel, *L'Ame Etrangère*. With a plot ready he could travel and write as he pleased. Journalism, on the other hand, was a constant worry, particularly in his state of health.

Early in July 1889, Maupassant joined the fashionable

crowd at Aix-les-Bains.   He was in good spirits, as always
when he set foot in a new place.

" I'm not here to write," he announced gaily, " but just
taking a few notes for *L'Ame Etrangère*." He soon made the
acquaintance of a Russian princess, and assured himself, no
doubt, that his interest was purely literary.   The lady did in
fact appear in the unfinished manuscript, and Maupassant
was particularly interested in what François had learned
from Her Highness's footmen.   It seemed that the great
lady was attended by two lovers, who both slept in her
bedroom.

" Their little beds are placed one on each side of Her
Highness's," explained François.

While Maupassant was trying to ingratiate himself with
this remarkable woman, his valet spent his leisure in
gambling with the Russian footmen.   It seems to have been
his only vice. Curiously enough, it was one which his master
did not share. To a man like Maupassant, always so eager
for excitement and refuge from his own thoughts, play for
high stakes should have been a great temptation.   The
writer, however, had no taste for such things.   One night, a
few weeks before this trip to Aix-les-Bains, he returned from
a party laden with his winnings.   Taking out a handful of
gold, he threw the coins on the table with a grimace of
disgust.

" I shall take it round to the charity bureau," he
remarked.   " I don't know why these Society people force
me to play."

Owing to the heat — or was it, perhaps, the two Russian
young men with the princess ? — Maupassant decided to
go on to Cannes. When he arrived at the station he was
delighted and flattered by the presence of the *chef de gare*,
who welcomed him with a great show of deference.   He was
no less pleased to see Bernard and Raymond, the crew of
the *Bel-Ami*, who had come to greet him.

The yacht rode at anchor awaiting his pleasure. The air was warm and light, the sky an idle rolling expanse of quivering blue. As he looked dreamily out to sea, the world seemed tender and exquisite. For a few days he had not known the agony of headaches and rheumatism. Skirting the bay on his first walk, his mind discovered fresh hope at every step.

The little white houses among the pine forests winked back at the sun. The waves moved on padded feet like waiters. In that flower-scented stillness he forgot the dread of a new attack and his whole being was filled with the hope of recovery. His old habit of observation he now exploited in fighting off the menace of disease. He knew that his spells of giddiness and depression were partly due to overwork, and that was, in itself, a comfort. Now that he had determined to limit his output, a marvellous panorama of health and ease stretched before him.

After luncheon, Maupassant goes aboard his beloved yacht. Bernard and Raymond leap to sudden life like marionettes. The *Bel-Ami* is sluggish and depressed until the captain takes the helm. He chats familiarly and nautically with the sailors, an excited schoolboy with his first mechanical toy.

The yacht glides along the coast, and Maupassant only gives up the helm to snatch a cup of tea from François. The *Bel-Ami* sails back to Cannes with the calm majesty of a swan on a lake. As the captain springs ashore there is a murmur of approval from a fellow-yachtsman who congratulates Maupassant on the splendid appearance of his cutter. The writer listens with a smile.

" I've had a marvellous day."

Next day Maupassant goes to his mother's villa at Nice. They greet each other affectionately, but the writer is more interested in Hervé's little daughter, now four years old. Simone is trundling a tiny wheelbarrow when her uncle calls her. He loves children, and this little maiden with the golden curls has a special place in his heart.

During luncheon Maupassant asks his mother a hundred questions about her health and comfort. Her eyes have been troublesome but she can now sleep without taking chloral. Both are pre-occupied with their symptoms and their correspondence is full of questions about health and illness. When her son is with her, Madame de Maupassant becomes a new woman. She discusses all his work with him and has obviously not lost her early taste for matters literary.[1]

Knowing how lonely she was, living by herself on the Riviera, Maupassant was particularly considerate and generous. He had freed her from all financial worry, but that did not lessen his duty to protect her from the loneliness of old age. He did everything possible to share his literary life with her, and all his letters are sprinkled with references to sales and reviews.

Pol Neveux quotes one letter which admirably illustrates Guy's concern for his mother's comfort:

" If you would like me to send you some books, let me know; I will select the least stupid among those sent to me. I know you read very little, but perhaps you could glance at a few pages. It worries me so much to think of you so lonely, tormented and ill. I am always looking out for something that would cheer you a little, but unfortunately it is not easy to find.

" Adieu, my dearest mother, I embrace you with all my heart.

" Your son,
" GUY."

A few days after this luncheon at Nice, Maupassant calls on his father, who is also living on the Côte d'Azur,

---

[1] It is of interest to learn that Madame de Maupassant did not approve of her son's ending to *Fort Comme la Mort*. The hero's death at the end seemed artificial to her. One is inclined to agree.

at St. Maxime. The writer is enjoying himself enormously on the *Bel-Ami*. They drop anchor at Agay, before going on to St. Raphael. It is warm but very pleasant, and Maupassant looks healthily sunburned. In the evenings the captain's cabin is hazy with smoke and reminiscence. Prompted by Maupassant, the sailors tell stories of their youth; and knowing his tastes, Bernard talks about his skirmishes in the lists of love while Maupassant roars with laughter. François draws upon his old stock of reminiscence, but the writer is too well-bred to brag of his own amorous exploits in this company. He recalls some of his schoolboy pranks and is particularly proud of having been expelled from the seminary at Yvetot.

The *Bel-Ami* narrowly escapes disaster on the rocks at St. Maxime owing to Maupassant's eagerness to see his father. The latter had been waving a handkerchief for some time, hoping to warn them of the danger. The sailors were terribly relieved at their narrow escape but the writer remained cool.

" Well," he drawled, " we could always have got ashore in our small boat."

They cruised on and Maupassant continually expressed his delight in the scenery. But the shadows soon began to close in. On August 22 he again visited his mother at Nice, but the town no longer appeals to him.

" It stinks too much of commerce," he declares. He still has his meals aboard the *Bel-Ami*, but sleeps in an hotel, saying that Raymond's snoring disturbs him. His eyes are red and watery and he is greatly relieved to find a good medicinal bathing establishment at Cannes. Suddenly he grows tired of the Riviera, pushes on to Lyons where he visits Hervé's tomb, an incident to which we have already referred.

Hardly is Maupassant back in his Paris before he receives a call from " the woman in grey." That night the writer is tortured by insomnia and François runs backwards and forwards, brewing tea and mixing numerous potions. At three a.m. Maupassant falls into a heavy drugged sleep and the unfortunate valet watches him all night.

A few hours later François hands his master an imposing envelope. It is a letter from the Queen of Italy inviting him to pay the Court an informal visit. The writer is flattered and honoured at this opportunity of seeing Royalty in shirt-sleeves, but his comment is rather curious.

" I hope these people have followed progress and overcome their prejudices against daily baths."

He roared with laughter as he made this remark. Was it a joke ? If so, it was not in the best of taste. There is a curious streak of coarseness in some of Maupassant's alleged jokes at this period. When the ceremony inaugurating the Flaubert memorial tablet was being arranged, Zola asked what he should wear.

" Everybody knows that one doesn't dress before six in the evening," laughed Maupassant. It says much for Zola's forbearance that he did not take offence at the younger man's rudeness, but no doubt he realised that a sick man is not always master of his tongue.

A month after his return from the South he went down to Rouen for the Flaubert ceremony.

" Maupassant was unrecognisable," declares M. Pol Neveux. " Those who, like me, met and saw him, thin and shivering, on that rainy Sunday in November when the monument to Flaubert was inaugurated, found it difficult to remember him. All my life I shall see that face, emaciated by suffering, those big eyes at bay, in which kindled his protest against a malignant Fate."

Goncourt's sharp eye also noted that physical deterioration, but he could summon no charity for the man who had dared to criticise his work.

" He won't make old bones," he writes in his *Journal*.

Needless to say, Goncourt did not betray his feelings in
Sm

public. He sat at table with Maupassant and Zola and made pleasant conversation, but he noted with bitterness how friendly and attentive Zola showed himself to the younger man.

Maupassant forced himself to be talkative, but his thoughts were elsewhere. For a long time he gazed fixedly at the memorial tablet to his dead master before turning sorrowfully away. He was alone. It was cold and raining, and he was alone. In a few hours he would lie down again, knowing that sleep had mocked his pillow so often.

As the train passed over the Seine he pointed his finger at the fog-laden river.

" I owe what I am to-day to my rowing down there in the mornings," he exclaimed suddenly. Goncourt smiled thinly and made a mental note for another paragraph in his *Journal.* He had no sympathy for the man who sat opposite him with his wasted face buried in his fur collar. A few months previously Maupassant had been the victim of a remarkable display of savagery. It was at a dinner-party and one of the guests deliberately steered the conversation towards the subject of eye disease. Not satisfied with Maupassant's growing discomfiture, this man went on to talk about cases in which optical disease had proved fatal. Goncourt tells us that the " jester " in question was " a gentleman of letters, wounded by something written by Maupassant." It needs but little imagination to guess the identity of the worthy gentleman in question.

Maupassant returned from Rouen with a heavy heart. Rouen had brought back so many memories of Flaubert and such a dismal reminder of his helplessness and isolation.

" I don't know why," he tells François on his return from the ceremony, " but it's becoming more and more unpleasant to talk to people I don't esteem."

But there were men who had something warmer than ink in their veins. One night, at Cannes, he buttonholed the famous Dr. G—— and began to ply him with his symptoms. He told him of his strength as a young man and asked for some explanation of his present suffering. The doctor tried hard to be matter-of-fact and professional, but the tears ran down his cheeks as he shook hands with the unhappy writer. Fortunately for Maupassant, not all his doctors betrayed their feelings so obviously. It was to these men that he now clung with desperate hopefulness. Reason told him that he was doomed, but his mind ached with a desire to believe in their lies.

CHAPTER II

NEW YEAR'S DAY, 1892

EARLY in 1891, Maupassant again boarded the *Bel-Ami* in search of health and sunshine. In Paris he had complained of the cold, and sat huddled over the fire in his study. Hoping to fly from his gloom, he accepted several invitations to dinner-parties, but the brilliant lights dazzled him and he rarely stayed long. He would pace from one end of his apartment to the other, gnawed by an endless torment. He dared not read because that made his brain reel and brought on the headaches. When he tired of his restless pacing he would go to the kitchen and chat with François.

" You know I've sometimes said I only wrote because I needed money. That's not quite true; there are some things I like writing about," he observed from the kitchen door.

The yacht awaited him at Nice, ready for a cruise to Spain and North Africa, but he was sluggish and listless. He went ashore at Cannes and called on the woman who had followed him from Paris. For a few days, he cruised half-heartedly and tried to do a little writing. Having put aside *L'Ame Etrangère*, he was now working on an idea for a new novel, *L'Angélus*, but it was not easy to write on a diet of pain and insomnia.

" It is so warm at the moment under the sun which fills my windows ! " he writes. " Why am I not part of all this happiness and well-being ? Some dogs that howl well express my condition. It's a sad protest addressed to nobody and nothing, which expresses nothing and hurls into the night a cry of imprisoned agony which I would like to utter. If I could moan like these dogs I should sometimes, often, go out upon a great plain or into the depth of a wood, and I should howl like that in the shadows for hours on end. I think that would soothe me."[1]

One need only read that letter to note the involved constructions and erratic style to which Maupassant had been reduced.

He returned to Paris and lived very abstemiously. To his great joy he put on weight and wrote much more hopefully to his mother:

" I want to feel the effect of early spring in the South: I want to walk about and cruise and finish my novel by May. I've done very little so far, but it will be short and then I'll have a rest. I know you are having grand weather at the moment down there. It's quite fair in Paris, but we can't yet feel the awakening of the earth.

" If our play [Musotte] goes fairly well, it may give me a little financial relief because things are none too good that way – I've really written nothing since last May.

" When I've done L'Angélus I shall settle down to some nice easy work on my play Yvette."[2]

He now decided to hasten the " cure " by taking further treatment at Luchon. En route he visited Arles, Tarascon and Nîmes, showing the liveliest interest in everything. He was now tremendously confident of the success of L'Angélus, of which he had only written a few pages.

" It will be the crowning point of my career," he declared.

For three days all went well at Luchon. He made excursions to the local beauty places but soon complained of the smell of sulphur and hurried on to Divonne, near the Swiss border.

" You have done enough work to kill ten ordinary men,"

Dr. Magitot had told him. " Twenty-seven books in ten years; that savage toil has devoured your body. To-day your body is taking its revenge and disabling your mental faculties. You must have a long and complete rest, my dear sir. I'm advising you as I would advise my own son. . . . Do not return to Nice; it is a most enervating place. . . . Your boat is a delightful toy but it is no sanctuary for a man as tired in body and mind as yourself. Use it, by all means, but don't live on it. I would recommend a very quiet life in a very healthy place, thinking about nothing, doing nothing – above all, no drugs of any kind. Only cold water."

Maupassant could not see the implications of that prescription but the doctor, like so many others, had already detected the truth in his patient's eyes. A specialist who had met the writer on the Paris-Cannes express declared, in private, that the illness was already far advanced.[1] Helpless in the face of a disease which was then considered incurable, the doctors could only offer him comfort and sympathy. Maupassant, for his part, would not easily have given up his implicit confidence in the possibility of a cure. One need look no further than *Sur l'Eau* to suggest in what spirit Maupassant would have received a gloomy physician.

" Our maladies come from microbes ? Very well, but where do the microbes come from ? And the maladies of those invisible germs themselves ? And where do the planets come from ? We know nothing, see nothing, can do nothing, divine nothing, imagine nothing – we are shut up, imprisoned in ourselves." To such a man everything is possible, for his optimism has its deepest roots in pessimism.

At Divonne, Maupassant began to doctor himself with

---

[1] One cannot justly condemn the doctors who pocketed their fees and prescribed drugs which they knew to be useless. It is only in comparatively recent times that cases of G.P.I. have been successfully treated by infecting the patient with malaria.

unabashed cheerfulness. He put up at a farmhouse kept by a physician's widow and had his shower-bath twice daily. To his great annoyance the doctors refused to give him the Charcot douche, a very cold shower which would have staggered a horse. But Maupassant fondly imagined that he was strong enough to sustain it and considered himself persecuted by medical stupidity. He was already well launched on the tide of *folie de grandeur*.

" The waters have fattened me up and my muscles are enormous," he now assured everyone.

He had decided to leave Divonne, where he was sleeping badly, when he received a letter from Taine advising him to try the waters at Champel. The famous historian had invited Maupassant and Dr. Cazalis to luncheon at his country house on Lake Annecy, and the sufferer eagerly accepted the older man's advice. Taine was really taking a rest cure, but Maupassant at once decided that their complaints were absolutely alike. The historian had been cured at Champel in six weeks; why should he not be as fortunate?

For a while his hopes seemed to be justified. He took plenty of exercise on his tricycle, ate with a better appetite and began to put on weight. He was now attended by Dr. Cazalis, who had accompanied him from Divonne and continued to make reassuring statements. Intoxicated with the success of his treatment, Maupassant soon began to exploit his new access of " health." He went on long rides, but the effort proved too great, and one day he fell from his machine in a dead faint. Bruised and terrified, he dragged himself to a shed and rested there for some time. When he got back the doctor bandaged his ribs, but he was still in pain and slept badly. He was cheered, however, by the unexpected appearance of " Madame X," who was passing through *en route* for Switzerland. To François's great disgust, she stayed for a week. . . .

At Champel, Maupassant met an old friend – the poet

Auguste Dorchain, who was suffering from a nervous disorder. To appease his patient, Dr. Cazalis assured him that his trouble was much like Dorchain's. He could expect equally good results at Champel. Dorchain good-naturedly connived at the fable and told the unfortunate novelist that one slept better at Champel than anywhere else.

Maupassant visited the poet practically every day. On one occasion he suddenly appeared with a towel stuffed with papers. Unrolling the towel, he picked up the contents with something like reverence.

" Here are the first fifty pages of my novel, *L'Angélus*," he exclaimed. " For a year I've been unable to do any more. If this book is not finished in three months, I'll kill myself ! "

After dinner, Maupassant read his fifty pages, bursting into tears at the end. " And we also wept," says Dorchain,[1] " seeing what genius, tenderness and pity still remained in that soul which would never again express itself and flow into other souls. In his tone, in his words, in his tears, there was something, almost religious, which went beyond mere horror of life and fear of annihilation."

It is easy to understand the poet's emotion, for in this novel Maupassant had set out to plumb the depths of human sadness and despair. The fragment expresses all his metaphysical doubts in the person of a boy, born crippled on Christmas Eve. His mother is driven out of her château by the Prussians, and gives birth to the child in a stable. He grows up a deformed martyr, suffering the torture of seeing the girl he loves married to his handsome brother.

The theme gave Maupassant an outlet for his own revolt against the cruelty of Fate. The last page he ever wrote is nothing but a piece of shrill blasphemy. " Eternal murderer who only seems to relish the pleasure of creation so as to gratify his insatiable passion for killing again and

[1] Cited by Pol Neveux in his Preface to " Boule de Suif."

recommencing his massacres. Eternal manufacturer of corpses and purveyor of cemeteries. . . ."[1] It is significant that the fragment breaks off in the middle of a sentence (" The sheep which . . ."). Maupassant had driven himself to work at this story, but the effort had become superhuman. The whole manuscript speaks eloquently of the author's frenzied struggle for lucid expression. It is crowded with erasions and spelling mistakes.

Dorchain and his wife had wept at the pathetic recital of *L'Angélus*, but the shadows were now closing in from every side. He spends a few hours at Geneva and comes back teeming with exhilaration.

" There was such a sweet little woman," he whispers to Dorchain. " I was brilliant ! No doubt about it now, I'm quite cured."

He is very excited, brags of the wonderful welcome which the Baron de Rothschild had given him and rattles on for hours in a boastful strain. He shouts at the waiters and orders the most ridiculous dishes. Alarmed for their reputation, the local doctors refuse to give him the Charcot douche. That irritates him; he knows he is strong enough to take the treatment. He is proud and vainglorious, displaying his array of perfumes and drugs to Dorchain with all the vanity of an art collector. Suddenly he departs for Paris.

For a few weeks he seems in better health, but the old bouts of pain and insomnia soon return.

" I'm very upset," he writes to his mother. " I want to reply to your letter and I've dozens of things to say, but they've forbidden me to write a line. Any use of my eyes makes me ill all day. I must rest them completely. I think my trip to Nice did them a lot of harm. They've been better since I got back here, but this awful weather has

---

[1] This fragment was published in *La Revue de Paris* after the writer's death. It is included in the Louis Conard edition of posthumous works.

resulted in a relapse. . . . "[1] He has laid aside *L'Angélus*
and now decides to concentrate upon a study of Turgenev
which has been in his mind for some time. While he
excites himself with the new schemes, he is surrounded by
doctors who watch anxiously and try to calm him. François
alone seems hopeful. Astonished but delighted by his
master's resolve not to see " the fatal woman " again, he
prepares light dishes and prays for a return to the days of
health and Literature.

Maupassant is soon afflicted with intense irritability,
orders his valet to remove all the scent-bottles and grows
weary of the presence of physicians. He broods on a
dozen fancied ills and is remarkably incensed with theatrical
producers. " They're not worth the trouble one takes for
them," he declares. Koning, the manager of the Gymnase,
particularly exasperates him.

" You've got a success with one of my worst stories
[*L'Enfant*]," he writes indignantly. " Well, you are missing
120 successes – in other words, a fortune, years of fortune
that are escaping you. Well, so much the worse for you ! "

Poor Havard, the publisher, also comes in for his share of
abuse at this time. Maupassant is informed by an English
bookseller that for three months Havard has not had any
available copies of *La Maison Tellier* in stock. He at once
communicates with his lawyer, who takes drastic steps
against the unfortunate publisher. Maupassant goes so far
as to threaten him with an action if 500 copies of the
book are not available within twenty-four hours. Not caring
to quarrel with a man who is obviously demented, Havard
at once prints the requisite number of copies.

A month later, Maupassant was again brandishing a writ.
This time he had a much more reasonable ground for
complaint. An American newspaper had calmly taken his
story, " Le Testament," and elaborated it into a long novel

[1] Cited by Pol Neveux, p. 182.

which they commenced to serialise under his name !
Maupassant was furious, and instructed his lawyer to
prosecute, but the legal expenses were heavy. The whole
affair lapsed, but the scarcely legible letters which he
addressed to his lawyer show how quickly the end was
approaching.

" I'm so ill," he writes, " that I'm very much afraid that
I shall be dead in a few days as a result of the treatment that
I'm now forced to take."[1]

But a man of his vitality could not give up without a
hard struggle.

" Do you think I'm heading for insanity ? " he asks one
of his doctors. " If that's the case, I must prevent it.
Between madness and death there is no choice. I've already
decided." Yet there are moments when he halts suddenly
and is beguiled by phantom hopes. He must be patient, not
lose heart, try to follow the instructions of his doctors. To
his mother he shows a brave spirit, urging her not to worry
about his condition.

" The improvement I told you about continues," he
writes from Paris. " I'm not quite well yet, but I'm
getting fatter. Now I must get rid of my neuralgia and
insomnia. . . . The weather was good yesterday and the day
before, but to-day it's misty and very warm. I go for a walk
every day in the Bois de Boulogne, certain parts of which are
very quiet and pretty. I am not allowed to walk too much,
but my eyes are a little better. You can see that by this
letter, which is longer than I had imagined. To my mind all
this points to a revival of good health."

In his heart he knew it was hollow and untrue, but a
white-haired, half-blind woman urged him to fight his
despair. Her husband was only a few miles away but he
was worse than dead. Hervé had gone, and there was
nothing and nobody save little Simone and himself. He had

[1] Cited by M. Lumbroso.

provided generously for them in his will, but nothing would ever console his mother; he knew that.

The temptation to kill himself came and went. " I think of suicide with gratitude," he remarked to the author, Hugues Le Roux. " It's an open door to escape by when one is over-weary." But in November 1891 he again sets out for Cannes, after giving François the most detailed instructions for packing and sending his books. He is eager to leave and does not seem to notice that the doorkeeper's wife is in tears.

He is now living at the Chalet de l'Isère, which gives a beautiful view over the sea. He walks up and down the Croisette under the palms, gazing at the distant Esterel. The fashionable crowd surges about him but he is glassy-eyed, sees nothing. Gamblers, snobs, invalids have begun to arrive for the winter season, and their small-talk would repay the attention of a social critic. Maupassant gives them scarcely a glance. He does not notice the noblemen who bow to him from the sunny terraces of their hotels; he turns his back upon the pretty little actress who is tired of Paris and has come here to offer herself to the highest bidder. He has no more use for sin.

His pale face is drawn and sorrowful, and there is something listless in his glance which warns acquaintances not to accost him. There is a sudden flash of familiarity about a yacht tied to the quay, and he recognises his *Bel-Ami*. Bernard – or is it Raymond ? – is scrubbing the deck, but Maupassant does not go on board. Instead, he walks sorrowfully back to his chalet, a film of tears veiling his eyes.

François anxiously awaits him, but Maupassant has no heart for the chatter with which the faithful fellow tries to rally him. He complains that his food is too salty, but, apart from that, there is no sign of the usual surliness. What François takes for improvement is, however, nothing but stupor or despair. He still has his baths and showers and visits the doctor, but it is purely mechanical to do these things, like dressing or eating. His earthly hopes have congealed, and a book of prayers suddenly makes its appearance by his bedside.

For a few days he tries to raise his soul from the abyss. He goes for a trip on the *Bel-Ami*, lunches two or three times with his mother, and does all he can to reassure her. People have begun to talk. He makes an appointment for six o'clock and arrives four hours too early. " I haven't a consecutive thought," he tells a friend. " I forget words and names; my hallucinations and suffering are destroying me."

Maupassant had always been at pains to conceal his private life from the vulgar attentions of snobs and gossips. The latter now came into their own. Rumour, thickly sauced, was ladled out and stuffed into the belly of Paris. Women, who never read a book in years, now buried their noses in his last novels and hunted out proofs of the author's insanity. A year or two previously these earnest students would have given their souls for a chance to rub shoulders with the celebrated writer. They now dug up his corpse and crawled over it like worms that bide their time for the final orgy.

Maupassant is soon considered worthy of the front page, where he can read the announcement that he has lost his sanity and will shortly enter an asylum. He does not issue a writ for libel, nor does he demand an apology from the newspaper. Instead, he sends his notary his will, but quickly changes his mind and instructs him to arrange matters with the notary at Cannes.

He seemed to have lost all urge to fight. Judging from the erratic notes which he wrote to his friends at this time, it is obvious that he has come to the limit of self-delusion.

" For days on end I feel lost, finished, blind; my brain is

exhausted yet still living. . . . I cannot write, I can no longer see; it's the disaster of my life."[1]

Those who knew what he was suffering tried to pooh-pooh the newspaper placards.

" Why worry ? " they urged him. " We know these headlines are lies."

" Yes," he replied tonelessly. " I'm not mad yet, but I will be."

His mind was failing, and we do not know what he was thinking as his fingers clutched those terrible newspapers. He had cause to throw a backward glance at the crowd of sycophants and voluptuaries whom he had entertained so lavishly in the past. They now showed no eagerness to claim friendship with the man whose great brain was already rotting and decomposing. Only those who respected the artist for his brilliant work offered their loyalty and sympathy. Some may have been wounded by a thoughtless word or some foolish act of snobbishness, but these things were no longer significant. What mattered now was the imminent blow to Literature. At the age of forty-one, Maupassant was laying aside the pen that had fulfilled much but promised so much more.

His friends went to the South to cheer him, but they came away with the sad conviction that the great writer was almost ready to leap across the gap. He dines with Henri Roujon on his yacht and scarcely touches the food. They talk of many things, but Maupassant always returns to the subject of microbes. He can see them everywhere, millions and billions of them, a great malignant army parading through his blood. As he puts his friend on the road to Beaulieu, he inhales the evening air. The moon sprawls over a soft luxurious sky.

" I won't have it for long," he says sadly. " I don't want to suffer too much."

[1] Pol Neveux, Preface, p. 90.

J.-M. de Hérédia, the Cuban-born poet, also records Maupassant's significant words of farewell as they parted on the road to Monte Carlo.

" *Adieu – au revoir –* no, *adieu.* I've made up my mind. I entered the literary world like a meteor; I'll leave it like a thunderclap ! "

The next few days brought terror and despair. He had already decided to commit suicide, but the image of his mother appeared before him and her hand seized his wrist. Meanwhile, Dr. Daremberg watched anxiously, testing his memory with questions, and doing what little he could to ease the suffering.

Christmas Eve, 1891. He had promised to have supper with his mother at Nice, but at the last minute telegraphed to say that he was supping on the Island of St. Marguerite with two ladies. What took place on that excursion may never be divulged. There have been several different accounts, but it is best to state the undisputed facts. The two sisters, one married and the other a widow, left for Paris by the first train on Christmas morning. They would offer no explanation to Madame de Maupassant, with whom they had stayed, and never broke their silence. One can only surmise that they had been terribly shocked by some act of misconduct on the writer's part. They simply abandoned all social relations with Madame de Maupassant, not even sending a note of condolence after her son's death.

On Christmas Day he went aboard the *Bel-Ami,* but the weather was unfavourable and he soon returned to the chalet. He seemed to be in a very good humour and chatted to the sailors who were spending the night under his roof. We know that he was taking ether at this time, which may, perhaps, account for his spells of cheerfulness. In a sudden outburst of confidence he tells them that he is going to write a new story, and outlines the plot.

The following day he goes out for a walk, but soon returns in an agony of fear. He has seen a ghost near the graveyard ! One by one the lamps of sanity are blown out, exhaling clouds of phantoms. He coughs at luncheon, and remarks that he has just swallowed a piece of sole which has entered his lungs and may kill him. That afternoon he decides to go for a sail on his yacht and the sailors notice how he staggers.

It was his last trip on the *Bel-Ami*. On the 28th he lunches with his mother at her villa, but is unusually taciturn. He had recovered his feverish gaiety by the following morning when Dr. Daremberg called to see him. He is in his bath, laughs, jokes, does what he can to deceive the doctor. The days of pumping his acquaintances are long since past. The childish helplessness has gone, replaced by a smiling idiotic calm which saturates his fears like a sponge.

New Year's Day, 1892. Maupassant is up at 7 a.m., eager to start for Nice. He must see his mother as he has promised ! He tries to shave himself but a cloud hangs over his eyes. As the razor trembles in his hand, the faint rhythm of his mother's voice flows back into his memory: he must keep his promise. At last he gives up and tells François that it is impossible for him to go to Nice. The faithful valet forces him to eat a little breakfast and the meal seems to revive him. The windows are thrown open and the warm gentle air flows into the room.

The postman rings, sending a little thrill of excitement through the house. New Year greetings ! Maupassant glances at the pile of messages.

" Good wishes," he murmurs. " They're all the same."

Bernard and Raymond, the two sailors, greet him a little sheepishly, but there is warmth and sincerity in their wishes for the New Year. At ten o'clock he rouses himself and decides to leave for Nice.

" We must go," he tells François, " otherwise my mother will think I'm ill."

From the carriage window he stares out at the sparkling sea.

" Look through the newspapers and tell me if there's anything interesting," he murmurs, but his eyes never leave the curving bay.

He salutes his mother with affection and seems delighted to spend New Year's Day with the family.   They sit down to table – Madame de Maupassant, Guy, Hervé's widow, little Simone, and his aunt, Madame d'Harnois, whom he had always confided in and loved since his childhood.   François says that they left at four o'clock and returned to the chalet for dinner, but, according to Madame de Maupassant, her son dined with her and insisted on going back to Cannes before the meal was over.   She had noticed that he was rambling in his talk and begged him to stay the night.   He refused, in spite of her hysterical pleading, and jumped into his carriage.

That night he complained of violent pains in the back. François brought him camomile tea and tried to calm him, but Maupassant did not close his eyes until after midnight. Hardly had the valet retired before he was awakened by a ring at the garden door.   It was a man with a telegram.

" It comes from the Orient," he remarked, but François was in no mood for gossip.   It was late and he decided not to awaken his master.   What happened in the next two hours can be easily imagined.   Maupassant must have started up from his sleep, oppressed by that feverish weakness which he knew so well.   In that dreadful moment his soul shuddered, and all the unresting instincts of the last few months gathered into one final impulse.   He obeyed mechanically, and slowly, trembling, walked to his desk and took out the revolver.   He pressed the trigger, but François had thoughtfully removed all the cartridges.

Tм

At about a quarter to two the valet heard a noise and rushed into his master's bedroom. To his horror, he saw Maupassant standing in the middle of the room with the blood pouring from a gash in his throat.

"Look what I've done, François. I've cut my throat. It's madness." He had used a metal paper-knife.

The distracted valet called Raymond and, with his assistance, overpowered the wounded man and forced him to rest. The cut was not very deep and the doctor quickly stitched it. According to François, Maupassant had been strangely calm and seemed grateful for what was being done for him, but the sailor insists that he was very violent and had to be put in a strait-jacket.

Throughout that night, Maupassant lay in a deep exhausted sleep while François and Raymond watched over him. To steady his nerves the sailor gulped at a bottle of rum, but his whole body shook with sobs. They sat for hours watching that bandaged throat, not daring to exchange a word.

At eight o'clock Maupassant roused himself and drank some tea, but seemed completely indifferent to his surroundings. He was floating gently among the grasses and willows on that terrible tideless river. Shadows were moving on the bank, but he took no notice. François picked up the telegram that had arrived during the night. The supreme irony ! It was a New Year's greeting from " the fatal woman."

Doctors were summoned, and an attendant arrived from Dr. Blanche's asylum at Passy. According to M. Lumbroso, Maupassant was led down to the harbour in the hope that the sight of his yacht might jerk him back to sanity.[1] He gazed at his *Bel-Ami* for some time; his lips moved, but he said nothing. As they turned back he looked round and

[1] Neither François nor M. Georges Normandy mentions this incident, but M. Gerard de Lacaze-Duthiers accepts it as fact.

seemed to bid silent farewell to the boat on which he had spent so many happy hours.

It was his last sign of sanity. On the evening of January 4 he sat up in bed and called for his valet.

" François ! Are you ready ? War has been declared." The man tried to calm him, but Maupassant was now in a frenzy. " What ! " he shouted. " You try to hold me back when it is so urgent that we should march together ? "

François had been discreet, and Cannes first heard the sad news from the Paris newspapers on January 4 ! A million sharp teeth at once snapped at the titbit, demanding more and more. This was front-page news ! This was the moment that all the editors and reporters had waited for so long. The man who had staved off interviewers all his life was now a lump of stupid flesh in a strait-jacket. Pictures ! Headlines ! More news !

The editors were forced to be patient, for François had removed the doorbell at the villa and those who thumped for admission were turned away. But anyone who had had the slightest connection with the victim was cross-examined and pestered for information.

On January 6 Maupassant left the chalet, attended by François and the attendant. They had reserved a sleeping-car on the express, and the writer returned to Paris for the last time. As the train toiled through France, poor François was so stupefied by fatigue and sorrow that he omitted to shut the door tightly and nearly fell from the train. The patient recognised nobody at the station, and his sleepy eyes seemed to stare through the crowd. He was quickly driven to Dr. Blanche's asylum at Passy, and the gates closed behind him.

A great brain had foundered. For eighteen months the most famous specialists in Paris would stand by, helpless, praying for the swift release of this poor doomed creature.

CHAPTER III

PASSY

PARIS sat back to enjoy this very interesting drama. No, not Paris — the man-in-the-street had his own cares — but that little crowd of worldlings, neurotic, sensual and utterly merciless. How well he knew them, the man who now sat in a strait-waistcoat at Passy !

" They were experts in that sport of brilliant French chatter, amicably satirical, trivial, brilliant but flippant, a certain shibboleth which gives a particular and greatly envied reputation to those whose tongues have become supple in this sort of malicious small talk," he had written in *Fort Comme la Mort*.

While the doctors set about their hopeless task, popular curiosity sponged up the most remarkable details. It was even considered important to know that the author had made his last journey in carriage No. 42 ! Every hour found the gates of the asylum stormed by a hungry crowd, eager for the latest news. Information of the most personal nature was demanded, and several amateur physicians offered their services. The invalid's parents were not long left in peace. Soon they were also besieged by requests for permission to visit the asylum.

The sensation-hunters were not alone in their vulgar curiosity. M. de Goncourt was at some pains to secure up-to-date information, which he gallantly conveyed to the Faubourg Saint-Honoré. He did not see fit to visit his unhappy fellow-author, but chose this as a fitting time to attack Maupassant on literary grounds.

" He is a very remarkable, a very charming writer of

short stories, but a stylist, a great writer, no, no ! " he says in his *Journal* on January 9, 1892.

How he must have licked his lips as he penned another remark just one year later !

" Dr. Blanche gives me to understand that Maupassant is on the way to becoming animalised."

It was in Princess Mathilde's *salon* that the writer's illness was most thoroughly discussed. The elegant snobs sipped their tea thoughtfully and tried to disown the stricken writer. The precise nature of his illness was known, and those who had entertained him socially took good care to dissociate themselves from scandal. This was best achieved by disparaging him whenever his name was mentioned, and, more convincingly, by taking a very high moral stand. It was the punishment of sin, stuttered old ladies who had forgotten their own past. And the beautiful wantons shuddered delicately, fingering their jewelled crucifixes with an air of shocked innocence.

Meanwhile, Dr. Blanche and his assistants did everything possible to make the patient comfortable. He was given a very pleasant room overlooking the park, and two servants were deputed to attend to his needs. There seemed good reason to hope that a partial cure was possible. Maupassant was docile, took his meals obediently and maintained his physical strength. But he was still sleeping badly and soon strayed into a maze of hallucination. All the terrible symptoms of persecution mania were now in evidence. It seemed to him that one of the doctors had stolen his wine and was trying to kill him, because he, Maupassant, had defeated him in a fight for the love of two women. And Ollendorff, the publisher, had stolen half the manuscript of *L'Angélus*.

Religion played a great part in his hallucinations. Sometimes he would order the servant to open the door and " let the devil out." After a sleepless night he would often ask

for a priest.   Malignant faces filled the room while strange
voices beset him, thrusting upwards from his sleep.   He
would get up, run to the opposite wall and strain to hear
their message.   Timidly, but with strange persistence, he
would shape little prayers to this God against whom he had
so often blasphemed.

For a few joyful moments he would talk with Flaubert
and Hervé, the two men he had loved most on this earth.
They had passed into his soul, these beloved images, and
no evil could befall him while he communed with them.

" But their voices are very weak and come from afar,"
he told the attendants.

Dr. Blanche had now given up all hope of a cure, and
François, who visited his master daily, was soon forced
to the same conclusion.   Poor Madame de Maupassant was
too ill to come to Paris, but he had undertaken to keep
her informed of her son's condition.   It was difficult to be
reassuring.   One evening in April, Maupassant had accused
him of having slandered him in heaven and ordered him to
go.   On the following day he welcomed him in the most
friendly manner.

" François, when shall we be going back to the Rue
Boccador ? "

He would never again see that luxurious apartment, but
the half-formed dreams of his last sane years now gazed
down at him in horrible caricature.   He would stride up
and down his room, conscious of glorious strength and
power.

" From the top of the Eiffel Tower God has proclaimed
that Maupassant is the son of God and of Jesus Christ ! "[1]
At times he would be more powerful than God and boast
of limitless wealth.   Ollendorff, M. Albert Cahan, Dr.
Grancher and numerous other friends visited him, but he
would never say much in their presence.   He was far

[1] Cited by M. Georges Normandy, p. 184.

too busy solving the problems which swarmed in his brain.

" My stomach is artificial. That means I must have 1,200 eggs every half-hour."

" François, give Arnaud 1,000 francs for my mother."

" I've been robbed of 600,000 francs."

Sometimes he would call for foolscap and pace up and down impatiently until it was brought. But the famous writer had given up his pen to a host of grinning devils whose feet pattered over the paper tracing a crazed pattern of fantasy.

The nights had become longer and sleepless. He would suddenly start up in alarm and turn to the wall.

" Hervé ! Hervé ! " It is always to his brother that he addresses his wild confidences. When the grandiose mood seizes him, he orders beautiful meals for his family who want to come in, but cannot find the door. Often his lips whisper of glorious enterprises which he and Hervé will undertake together. For several hours this terrible monologue would continue while the attendant sat in the shadows writing down passages which might interest the doctors. This was the fate of the man who had spent so much of his life in taking notes on his fellow-creatures ! After a night of wild excitement he would sink back into his bed, completely benumbed and spent.

When he became violent, the strait-jacket had to be put on, but there were many moments of comparative calm when he played billiards or sat peacefully in the beautiful garden. He had grown terribly thin and his movements were unsteady, but his friends would rejoice to see him taking an interest in the trees and plants. Anything was preferable to those terror-stricken monologues.

These walks in the garden were often characterised by a pathetic mournfulness which harrowed the feelings of his visitors. On one occasion he broke off a branch which he handed to the attendant.

" Plant that here," he murmured with a sigh. " Next year we shall find it sprouting with little Maupassants ! "

One needed strength to visit the Maison Blanche, and many of the writer's friends found it too painful. From all parts of the world came gifts, recipes, advice, but nobody could rescue Maupassant from the octopus which gripped his brain. Those who had known him in health will never forget the dull, unseeing look with which he now greeted them. Sick at heart, his friend Madame Leconte du Nouy sent him a bunch of grapes. He refused them with a mocking laugh.

" They're made of copper ! "

The weary months passed in delirium. His dry anæmic lips whispered little jingles of verse, pathetic pieces which brought tears to the eyes of his attendant. As he became weaker the fits of violence were short, but it was growing more and more difficult to control him. He developed a mania for undressing himself at frequent intervals and was particularly uncontrollable at meals. Terrified that he was being poisoned, he often refused to touch his food.

This hideous decay continued for over eighteen months. One can pass over the details of his suffering: he had already anticipated everything in *Le Horla* when he wrote:

" Under the affliction of certain maladies, all the resources of one's physical being seem crushed, all one's energy exhausted, one's muscles relaxed, one's bones grown as soft as flesh and one's flesh turned to water."

One final touch of irony. On March 6, 1893, his play *La Paix du Ménage* was first produced at the Comédie Française. While the audience chuckled over the delightfully *risqué* situations, the author himself was in the grip of general paralysis. He had aged by twenty years in those terrible months; his eyes were bloodshot-red and his cheeks sunken and ravaged. When the fits of epilepsy passed he would sit peacefully on his bed stroking his chin with a thin, trembling hand.

The end was horrible. On the 6th of July, 1893, the muscles of which he had been so proud were racked for the last time by the enemy that had pursued him for so many years. Like a wounded animal that has grown weary of the chase, he sank into eternal sleep.

U

EPILOGUE

MAUPASSANT was buried in the Montparnasse cemetery three days after his death. He was given full literary honours. Almost every author and artist in Paris attended the funeral, but it was fitting that Emile Zola should pay the last tribute by the open grave. He had known Maupassant from the early humble days, and he was one of the few whose friendship had survived the temptations of fame and jealousy. A lesser man would long since have turned away, but Zola had risen above the little sulks and jealousies. Maupassant's work had given him a new vision of literary genius and it was to this superb artist that he now offered his reverent tribute.

" Let him rest in his good sleep, so dearly bought, trusting in the triumphant health of the work he leaves behind ! It will live, it will make him live. . . . His ancestors were Rabelais, Montaigne, Molière, La Fontaine. . . . He was one of the most fortunate and most unfortunate men on this earth. . . . In time, those who only know him through his work will love him for the eternal love-song that he has sung to life."

After a lapse of nearly half a century it is possible to assess the weight of Zola's prophecy. Time has dealt more kindly with Maupassant's work than with that of his great admirer. Zola's heavy style and grandiose effects were suited to the mightiness of his themes, but there has been a great acceleration of life which is reflected in Literature. The spirit of the motion picture and modern journalism has invaded us all, bringing with it a revolt against the massive Homeric violence of Zola's reporting.

Zola's piano has only the loud pedal. On the artistic plane his work cannot stand comparison with Maupassant's. Not one of his novels is technically foolproof, and the attempts at subtle psychology are childish beside those of Maupassant or Bourget. His great success during his lifetime was partly due to an enormous topicality which gained him the applause of readers who could not admire his methods. His work, seen as a whole, was great sculpture, but it was not the work of a great sculptor.

Unlike Zola, Maupassant killed no dragons and moved no dynasties; and his books have all the virtues of that failure. In remaining deaf to social and political problems, his art stands above yesterday, to-day and to-morrow. He never suppressed the truth as he saw it, and his claim to fame rests entirely upon the skill with which he conveyed that vision. The secret of his success is an uncanny sureness in selection. He is no mere word-juggler, and the anthologist will seek in vain for purple patches. In disengaging the essential episode and projecting it with perfect sobriety, he displayed a self-discipline which has rarely been equalled and never surpassed.

The full value of his craftsmanship can only be focused in relation to his philosophy. Nearly all great art is didactic, and for that reason alone Maupassant's fame is unique. With no system, no real ideas and no deep philosophic purpose, he achieved greatness by sheer photographic force.

Maupassant is a poor dialectician. As debater and philosopher he lags far behind the story-teller. Not only is his philosophy narrow and childish, but its expression completely lacks the hard brilliancy of his usual narrative style. For his stories he was always equipped with thumbnail notes which had been polished and re-polished before they were finally pressed down upon the foolscap. When he began to argue or preach he was at once over-powered by his ego. He failed as a thinker because his thought represents not art but mood. It is a mistake to call him a pessimist; his standpoint was that of a crude optimist who rebels childishly against Fate. Nor is his cynicism the product of a mind which has carefully weighed human values and found them wanting. He thinks humanity unlovable mainly because he is morbidly aware of his own imperfections. Partly through illness, partly through weakness of character, he never gave himself a holiday from introspection. What ailed him spiritually was really a kind of baffled idealism. In all his arguments there is the same tone of petulance, the tone of a writer who never permitted himself the leisure to select and give coherence to his ideas.

During his lifetime his novels enjoyed huge sales, but there has been a strong reaction in favour of the short stories. In all his work there is a shrewd sense of undertones, but the novels expose both his greatness and his limitations. Too often we are aware that he has been tempted to enlarge a " conte." Equipped with a vest-pocket camera, he could take wonderful snapshots. But his horizon was always limited by the particular situation which he was discussing. He could write a brilliant sketch about a soldier but was quite unable to cope with an army in motion. His novels all lack the urgent onsweep of really great fiction.

To-day Maupassant enjoys an international reputation for his " contes." No writer has produced more tales of outstanding quality and appeal. Even when his setting is typically French he somehow disengages what is universal from his landscapes. He reveals an even more remarkable talent for composition in his studies of character. His peasants are not merely peasants, but peasantry. That is equally true of his journalists, harlots and Society folk. But Maupassant refuses to date for a reason altogether apart from his technical genius. He is, as Zola said, the great singer of love, and by tuning his lyre to a universal theme he has gained an audience which renews itself in every generation.

His work does not find its place on every bookshelf. There is an Anglo-Saxon tendency to dismiss his books as the work of a lunatic and pornographer. To my mind this is often due to a dismal Puritanism which condemns without benefit of clergy. It is the logical conclusion of a sublime illogicality, the firm stand taken by those who conclude that a dissipated writer is incapable of producing great Literature. I recognise the futility of trying to convince minds which approach great Literature with the morbid certainty of being shocked.

To pornographic Literature Maupassant made no contribution. If he shocks, he does so as an honest critic of conventional morality. There is neither the self-consciousness nor the extravagance of the pornographer in his work. He indicts our illusions but he is too great an artist to let himself down in print.

Insane he was towards the end of his career, but in his madness he never treads down his mighty art. He made many mistakes in his life, but they were not the mistakes of an incompetent craftsman. For these lapses he paid abundantly enough to satisfy the most rigid moralist. He wrote brilliantly and died miserably; one should look no further.

To this man success came suddenly, a glorious, dazzling success which drove him to many acts of folly. Often he lapsed into vulgarity, but it was a young man's vulgarity, a super-heated consciousness of strength and glory. To-day we can no longer deny him an honourable place in the aristocracy of letters.

BIBLIOGRAPHY

(Works in English are in italics)

BIOGRAPHICAL WORKS

Maynial: " La Vie et l'Œuvre de Guy de Maupassant " (Paris, " Mercure de France ").

Dumesnil: " Guy de Maupassant " (Armand Colin).

Lacaze-Duthiers: " Guy de Maupassant, son œuvre."

Georges Normandy: " La Fin de Maupassant " (Albin Michel).

R. H. Sherard: " The Life, Work and Evil Fate of Guy de Maupassant " (T. Werner Laurie Ltd.).

Dumesnil: " La Publication des Soirées de Médan " (Société Française d'Editions Littéraires et Techniques).

MEMOIRS

The spate of reminiscence is embarrassingly large. Pride of place must go to the indispensable " Souvenirs sur Guy de Maupassant " by his valet, François Tassart (Paris, Plon).

Other important works are:

Lumbroso: " Souvenirs sur Maupassant " (Rome, Bocca).

Madame du Nouy and Henri Amic: " En regardant passer la vie " (Ollendorff).

Hugues Le Roux: " Portraits de Cire " (Lecène et Oudin).

Voivenel and Lagriffe: " Sous le Signe de la P.G."

Frank Harris: " Contemporary Portraits."

Charles Lapierre: " Souvenirs intimes " (" Journal des Débats," 1893).

" Journal des Goncourt," 1887–96.

CORRESPONDENCE

Pol Neveux: " Boule de Suif, Préface, Correspondance "
(Conard).

Pierre Borel: " Lettres Inédites de Maupassant à Flaubert " (Paris, Les Portiques).

Flaubert: " Correspondance."

Marie Bashkirtseff: " Further Memoirs " (Grant Richards).

*" Marie Bashkirtseff's Letters." Edited by Mary J. Serrano
(Cassell).*

Madame du Nouy: " Amitié Amoureuse " (Calmann-
Lévy).

Kaminsky: " Yvan Tourgueneff d'après Sa Correspondance
avec ses amis français."

A USEFUL MISCELLANY

This list is designed for readers with a serious interest in
Maupassant's literary background.

Barbusse: " Zola " (English edition, Dent).

Lalou: " Contemporary French Literature " (Jonathan Cape).

Yarmolinsky: " Turgenev " (Hodder & Stoughton).

Deffoux and Zavie: " Le Groupe de Médan " (Payot).

Brunetière: " Le Roman Naturaliste."

Dr. M. Pillet: " Le Mal de Maupassant."

Dubosc: " Trios Normands " (Rouen, Defontaine).

J. Lemaître: " Contemporaries."

Dumesnil and Descharmes: " Autour de Flaubert "
(" Mercure de France," 2 volumes).

Normandy: " La Vie anecdotique " (Rasmussen).

Dumesnil: " La Jeunesse de Maupassant."

ARTICLES AND ESSAYS

Abel Hermant: " Essais critiques " (Paris, Grasset).

Lemaître: " Portraits Littéraires " (" Revue Bleue," June 29, 1889).

Brandes: " Portraits Littéraires " (" Revue Bleue," September 12, 1891).

" *The French Decadence* " (" *Quarterly Review*," *1892*, *pp. 479–505*).

P. Alexis: " Le Journal," July 8, 1893.

H. Céard: " La Tôque et Prunier " (L'Evénement, August 22, 1896).

" *Love Letters of Maupassant* " (" *Fortnightly Review*," *1897*, *pp. 571–82*).

M. De Waleffe: " Un hommage à Guy de Maupassant " (" Le Journal," September 3, 1925).

Madame X: " Guy de Maupassant Intime " (" Grande Revue," October 25, 1912).

COLLECTED WORKS

Several French publishers have brought out collected editions. Ollendorff, Flammarion and Conard have been responsible for excellent productions, and the last-named has an edition which includes correspondence and verse.

One must also note Marjorie Laurie's capable translations (published by T. Werner Laurie). The American publisher Knopf is responsible for another edition of collected works (translated by Ernest Boyd).

The Blue Ribbon Books (at five shillings each) form an excellent introduction for English readers. Maupassant's works are in two volumes – novels and short stories.

Finally, the Everyman Library publishes a useful selection of Maupassant's short stories (Introduction by Gerald Gould, excellently translated by Marjorie Laurie).

INDEX